MANAGING
IDEAS
FOR
PROFIT
The Creative Gap

MANAGING
IDEAS
FOR
PROFIT
The Creative Gap

Simon Majaro

McGRAW-HILL BOOK COMPANY

London · New York · St Louis · San Francisco · Auckland · Bogotá · Caracas
Hamburg · Lisbon · Madrid · Mexico · Milan · Montreal · New Delhi · Panama · Paris
San Juan · São Paulo · Singapore · Sydney · Tokyo · Toronto

Published by
McGRAW-HILL Book Company Europe
Shoppenhangers Road · Maidenhead · Berkshire · England
Telephone: 0628-23432
Fax: 0628-770224

British Library Cataloguing in Publication Data
Majaro, Simon
  Managing ideas for profit: the creative gap.
  I. Title
  658.4063
  ISBN 0-07-707598-6

Library of Congress Cataloging-in-Publication Data
Majaro, Simon.
  Managing ideas for profit : the creative gap / Simon Majaro.
  p.   cm. — (Marketing for professionals)
  Includes bibliographical references and index.
  ISBN 0-07-707598-6 (paperback)
  1. Creative ability in business — Management.   I. Title.
  II. Title: Creative gap.   III. Series.
HD53.M35   1992
658.4 — dc20
                                                             91-40443
                                                                  CIP

1 2 3 4 5   CUP   9 5 4 3 2

Printed and bound in Great Britain at the University Press, Cambridge

Simon Majaro

Simon Majaro is one of the foremost names in management today. Currently Professor of Marketing at the Cranfield School of Management, he is also Managing Director of an international management consultancy and Director of Strategic Management Learning.

With extensive qualifications and a wide range of top level experience, his management expertise is regularly sought by major international companies such as ICI, Heineken and Phillips. Previously Managing Director of EEC Unilever company and Head of the marketing department at IMI — the Geneva based Business School — he is constantly involved in lecture tours to business schools and training centres worldwide.

Author of 'International Marketing — A Strategic Approach to World Markets' and 'Marketing in Perspective', Simon Majaro is also co-author of 'Strategy Search — A Guide to Marketing for Chief Executives and Directors'.

To my grandson Benjamin, whose coincident arrival stimulated inspiration and made perspiration more bearable.

Preface

'Creativity' and 'Innovation' are two words popular with modern managers. They form part of the current jargon often heard in the corridors of the corporate environment. The notion that creative and/or innovative organisations are more likely to attain excellence than those which are devoid of these two ingredients is universally accepted. However, in practice, not many organisations know how to develop or stimulate a so-called 'Creative Mode' in their midst. One often meets senior managers who encourage their subordinates and other members of the firm to 'become more creative' or to 'encourage others to become more innovative'. However, the gap between good intentions and reality appears almost unbridgeable unless a few basic conditions exist in the organisation.

My interest in the whole subject developed during my years in industry. I had a boss who was recognised by all as an extremely creative gentleman. The success of the company seemed to be eloquent proof of this. He used to chide me constantly for not being sufficiently creative in solving problems or developing new marketable ideas. I was determined to meet the challenge and prove him wrong by galvanising myself towards generating and submitting what I considered were 'good ideas'. Unfortunately I soon discovered that they were not 'good ideas'. With very few exceptions, my boss proceeded relentlessly to demolish all these ideas. On the one hand I was exhorted to try to become more creative; on the other, my ideas were always found lacking. I found the situation frustrating and somewhat dichotomous. I was prepared to assume that it either represented a quirk on the part of my busy and impatient boss or a personal shortcoming on my part. Nevertheless, I made a genuine attempt to gain an intellectual insight into the creative process and establish whether or not I was destined to lead an uncreative existence in the business world.

Years later, in my capacity as management consultant, I was once invited by a client to 'audit' the managerial quality of a company that he was about to acquire. 'Make sure that the company is both creative and innovative. . .' was part of my terms of reference. I agreed to undertake this additional task without checking with the client precisely what he had meant by the two words – 'Creativity' and 'Innovation'. He assumed that I knew to what he referred and I felt that as an experienced management consultant I should not ask for an explanation of what sounded like a straightforward and sensible instruction. It was only when I commenced the 'auditing' assignment that I discovered that I was in trouble – I simply did not know how to proceed with such a task. I came to realise that in the absence of clear definitions of 'Creativity' and 'Innovation' it is difficult to evaluate the true performance of a firm in these areas. I decided to close a gap in my education by pursuing a systematic study of the literature on the subject. I read many books – some were fascinating but not very practical; others somewhat incomprehensible through the excessive use of jargon from the behavioural sciences. I also undertook research on this subject among companies and among managers, who participated in the many courses that I ran in a number of Business Schools and management development establishments. Furthermore, I had some opportunity of researching the level of creativity and innovation on an international basis by observing and analysing the behaviour of managers of different nationalities. To the extent that one is allowed to generalise, I have come to the conclusion that managers in some countries are more creative and/or innovative than in others. Rare is the nation that is excellent in both. This is a field in which I am pursuing my research and hope one day to summarise my findings in a separate treatise.

I gradually gained an insight into the mysteries of creativity and its vital role in promoting innovation. As a consultant and educator, I found myself assisting companies in establishing programmes designed to enhance creative management at all levels. This helped many companies to introduce integrated systems for stimulating and holding onto good ideas, and helped others in setting up 'Creativity Circles' and 'Think Tanks'. I have also participated in many *ad hoc* creativity sessions aimed at solving specific problems or innovating in well-defined areas such as product development or the search for strategies.

All this work has led me to the realisation that a serious gap exists among the vast majority of firms between the process of idea generation and implementation. Whilst many organisations understand the need for creativity, only a small proportion have succeeded in translating theory into practice.

This book represents the outcome of years of work, research and reflection on that vital subject. My main aim has been to compile a book on creativity which is readable, practical and useful. I have endeavoured to remove some of the mystique associated with this subject. If any readers of this book manage to apply, successfully and profitably, some of the ideas and recommendations developed therein, I would feel that my efforts have been worthwhile.

When planning this book I tried very hard to assemble material which could be of help to small and large organisations alike. Indeed, I hope that even very small organisations such as minor legal firms, retail establishments or medical practices can derive some benefit from studying the content of this book. Nevertheless I do recognise that the larger the firm the greater the challenge it has to face in seeking to enhance its creative climate and output.

I wish to thank all those who provided me, directly and indirectly, with ideas and material for this book. They include the many students who attended my seminars and workshops over the years and the many managers I had the pleasure of leading towards greater awareness of the need for creativity. Each event and each assignment gave me new insights into this fascinating subject. To all of them I wish to express a collective 'Thank you'. To list them all by name would be a pretty demanding, albeit pleasurable, task. Nevertheless I wish to name two individuals who deserve especial mention: my associate Sheila Hall spent many precious hours reading the manuscript and making most valuable and helpful suggestions; Roger Pilgrim ploughed through all the material and offered very constructive criticism especially in relation to the 'auditing checklists' at the end of the book. To both of them I express my deepest gratitude.

Simon Majaro

Contents

1 The role of creativity in successful organisations

The world was created in seven days. Six days were of creative work and one of well-deserved rest. The 'Creation' brought into existence the world we live in and all its creatures. The exact date of this event is a matter of considerable debate which we can leave to theologians, historians, philosophers and anthropologists.

The word 'creativity' comes from the same root as 'creation'. Yet when I last had occasion to look up 'creativity' in the Shorter Oxford English Dictionary (1975 revised edition) I was surprised to discover that the word was not there. I could find 'create', 'creation', 'creative', 'creatively' and 'creator', but not 'creativity'. Is the term so unimportant or so new that it did not deserve a mention in that edition of one of the most illustrious English dictionaries?

What does 'creativity' mean?

I first started investigating the etymological meaning of the word when, in my role as a management consultant, I was asked by clients to undertake a 'management audit' of a company which they were about to acquire. The brief given to me was:

'To evaluate the level of creativity that exists in this company. Our enthusiasm for this acquisition will depend, to a large extent, on the quality of creativity that its management is able to demonstrate. We consider creativity as the main asset of a successful company . . .'

I accepted this enlightened, albeit vague, request without demur. However, I soon discovered that not only did I not know how to evaluate and measure creativity, but also that I did not even know exactly what the word encompassed in a managerial and organisational context. Measuring an attribute that one does not fully understand is not an easy task.

As an experienced management consultant, I knew how to measure companies' general performance, efficiency and productivity. I had been trained in undertaking the auditing of product

1

quality and market position. I also knew how to evaluate the track records of individual managers. However, gauging the quality of a firm's creativity in unequivocal terms did not come naturally to me. Many questions for which I had no ready answer began to occur to me, for example, 'What exactly does creativity mean?'; 'Is creativity an essential, or even important ingredient for success?'; 'Can creativity be stimulated and enhanced?'; 'Is organisational creativity a function of the number of creative individuals in it?'; 'Do individuals in a firm become more creative when the organisation tolerates and encourages creativity?'; 'If creativity is important for success, who is responsible for developing this vital ingredient in the firm?'; 'Is creativity a genetic trait or can most people become creative?'.

My interest in the whole subject commenced at that point in my consultancy career when the aforementioned brief confronted me with these problems. The project fired my imagination, and I decided to devote time to trying to understand the workings of the creative process and its true role in the life of successful organisations. I read a large number of books and treatises on the subject, ranging from books dealing with functions of the human brain and mystical views of human creativity to self-help books on how to become creative. I carried out research projects into the creative process in a number of companies and in a number of countries. I observed the demeanour of many managers at work in situations demanding a creative input. The more I investigated the subject, the more enthralled I became by the intricacies of the subject-matter. These must be mastered in order to understand fully the nature of creativity in general, and the role it can play in a successful organisation in particular.

Influences on creativity

Many aspects of medical and behavioural sciences and the arts affect creativity. For example, understanding how the mind works entails some knowledge of the functioning of the brain—after all, it is the human brain that provides organisations with creative ideas. Therefore, an insight, however superficial, into the physiology of the brain can be valuable.

Grappling with organisational creativity requires an appreciation of the main principles of group behaviour and an understanding of the barriers that group dynamics can place upon the proper functioning of the creative process. Organisational creativity cannot live alone. As we shall see later, it can only thrive in a corporate environment in which ideas can be generated and communicated in a continuous way. Clearly, this demands some stimulus from above, and this can only be achieved when senior management, including those responsible for the personnel and management development functions, are able to direct the appropriate motivational stimuli that help people to exercise their hidden creative talent. It is not sufficient just to exhort members of an organisation to be creative. In other words, the lessons that psychologists, sociologists and other behavioural scientists have taught us can enrich our ability to stimulate and enhance creativity in the firm.

Last, but not least, empathy towards the visual arts is also vitally important in helping us to relate to creativity in design and graphic artefacts. We all recognise that design has become one of the major ingredients in successful marketing and communication. A manager who understands the rudiments of pictorial representation, the basics of shape, colour and form and also possesses some knowledge of the history of art is more likely to appreciate creative design. Moreover, such a person can normally extract much more value from the services of design organisations or consultants. Most professional advisers, such as designers, consultants and advertising agencies, appreciate clients who understand, in detail, the nature and scope of the professional service which they, the clients, are 'buying', and invariably this results in a far better quality of service.

All in all, very few subjects entail such a fascinating variety of complex topics. Unfortunately, because of this complexity many managers simply shun the whole subject. They might make glib remarks about the need to become more creative and innovative, but they refuse to become too deeply enmeshed in the relentless development work which the nurturing of creativity calls for.

The missing ingredients

Ask a manager to define the words 'creativity' and 'innovation' and you will be surprised by the degree of bafflement that this simple request engenders. I have collected as many as eighty different definitions for both terms. It is difficult to see how creativity and innovation can be effectively managed in an organisation if the meaning of the terms is not understood. Can one be 'honest' if one does not understand the meaning of the word 'honesty'? Can one be 'productive' if the word does not carry any meaningful connotation? Can companies be 'customer-orientated' if they do not know who their customers are? But the odd thing is that many people can be honest, productive and customer-orientated without being able to *define* the meaning of the words. Nevertheless, those who understand fully the meaning and implications of concepts and words can behave 'knowingly', thus removing the element of chance from the attainment of excellence.

Anna Freud said that 'Creative minds always have been known to survive any kind of bad training'. She referred in the main to the training of creative individuals. The implication is that creative people retain this quality in spite of the constraints placed by their teachers or trainers upon their creative ability. Two major corollaries seem to emerge from Freud's statement: (*a*) if an organisation is lucky enough to have acquired creative individuals, not even their trainers can diminish their creative prowess; and (*b*) there is little point in training a person to become *more* creative, inasmuch as this innate quality cannot be increased or diminished.

Creative entrepreneurs will applaud this conclusion. Successful businessmen will no doubt feel that their own success proves that creative people are born rather than made. However, if this hypothesis is correct there is little point in proceeding with this book. Success, according to this school of thought, will remain the prerogative of those who were born with a creative mind. I do not subscribe to such a pessimistic viewpoint. Whilst I agree that some people are more creative than others, I also believe that many have trained themselves to respond to external stimuli in such a way as to behave in a creative fashion. We know that some families have produced a large number of so-called creative geniuses: the Mozart family, the Bach family, the Huxleys, the Freuds. To what extent the creativity of individual members of those families was the happy result of the right cocktail of genes as opposed to the stimulation they all derived from their respective environments is difficult for us to judge. I believe that it is a combination of both. It is impossible for us to take a person and inject new genes into him. It is not impossible for us to develop cultural, educational and psychological environments in which the individual's creative abilities can thrive. Clearly the individual who is lucky enough to have inherited creative abilities from his parents and has enjoyed an environment in which creativity can be stimulated and encouraged, will probably attain a high level of creative output.

The same questions occur with respect to creativity in the business environment. Is a firm's innovativeness the function and the result of their creative managers or is it the culture and environment of the organisation which provides the stimulus for creative output? The short answer is that it is the symbiosis between 'creative organisations' and 'creative people' that produces innovation.

Firms cannot be innovative without having managers capable of generating creative ideas. At the same time managers cannot practise their creativity in organisations that stifle and constrain the creative process. The main difference between talented individuals and talented companies is that it is difficult to graft creative genes (if such things exist) onto individuals but it is possible with some effort to make firms more creative. The annals of business history are filled with examples of companies that have suddenly emerged from a period of uncreative sterility into an era of fertile innovation resulting from the arrival of a new and more creative management. It is the interplay between individual creativity and environmental creativity which is the powerhouse of innovation in any organisation. However, it is also important to remember that management can have an impact upon the creative environment and vice versa.

Much has been written about what constitutes an excellent company. '*In Search of Excellence*' (Waterman and Peters, 1982) was the forerunner of a series of books seeking to list the ingredients for success. Most of the lessons presented to the reader are based on the careful observation of successful companies at work. Clearly, if one can identify the characteristic practices of successfully managed organisations, one can derive valuable clues as to how to improve the performance of less excellent companies. Many good ideas emerged from these studies and, if applied judiciously, they may help companies to improve their overall performance. Nevertheless, firms that thought that they had found an elixir for excellence have, on the whole, been disappointed.

Without attempting to contradict or challenge the formulae propounded in the published studies I venture to put forward the notion that no company or organisation can hope to achieve a high level of success without having developed the dual forces of 'creativity' and 'innovation'. Without creativity (internally generated or acquired) one cannot have innovation, and without innovation an organisation cannot be or remain successful.

This is a suitable moment for defining our terms. The definition given here to the two words is a practical one. It may not conform to the officially recognised etymological definition, nor to everybody's perception as to what either term means. However, the aim is to agree on a terminology which is capable of being understood by all, thus facilitating its incorporation in the daily life of an organisation. One invariably finds that the more complex and esoteric concepts that one tries to introduce into firms are soon abandoned for the simple reason that members of the organisation find them too difficult to comprehend. Let us not fall into this trap.

'CREATIVITY' IS THE THINKING PROCESS THAT HELPS US TO GENERATE IDEAS.

'INNOVATION' IS THE PRACTICAL APPLICATION OF SUCH IDEAS TOWARDS MEETING THE ORGANISATION'S OBJECTIVES IN A MORE EFFECTIVE WAY.

These are very simple and basic definitions. Yet they call for some elaboration and reflection.

'Innovation' is the essence of corporate success. Without innovation a firm simply continues to do what it has been doing in the past—a clear formula for stagnation, decay and ultimate death. In order to attain innovation a firm needs creative ideas. Without ideas it is impossible to innovate. In other words, success depends on the dual relationship between ideas and the conversion of the selected ideas into practical innovations. Innovations only occur when the implemented ideas meet some clear objective such as performing a task in a more productive way ('better', 'cheaper' or 'more aesthetically'). Innovations must be useful, practical and achieve results. On the other hand 'creative' ideas can be unusual, even eccentric or bizarre. The development of innovation requires these two ingredients. They are so inter-dependent that a firm cannot hope to be innovative without a significant creative input. At the same time, creativity does not necessarily make a firm an innovative one insofar as an idea is only the raw material for innovation, and does not inevitably bring it about. Between ideas and innovation there must be a systematic screening and development mechanism aimed at converting raw ideas into tangible and valuable innovations.

Figure 1 illustrates this relationship in a diagrammatic form.

I firmly believe that no company or organisation can be truly excellent without the dual existence of creativity and innovation. In fact I would go as far as suggesting that if anybody is on the acquisition trail, companies which are found to be short on creativity and innovation are not worth purchasing unless the aim of the acquisition is to lay one's hands on specific assets.

Firms can be creative and innovative without realising it. Others are convinced that they are creative but, in practice, are the complete opposite. Yet a third category of firms exists—those who possess strong pockets of creativity in various corners of the organisation. In this regard some companies are able to demonstrate a high level of creativity in specific functional areas and/or departments whilst the rest of the firm suffers from an uncreative and unimaginative management.

It is, however, possible for a company to be innovative even though there is a low level of internal creativity. Firms are often prepared to buy creativity from outside sources in a systematic way.

Figure 1. The relationship between creativity and innovation in a schematic form.

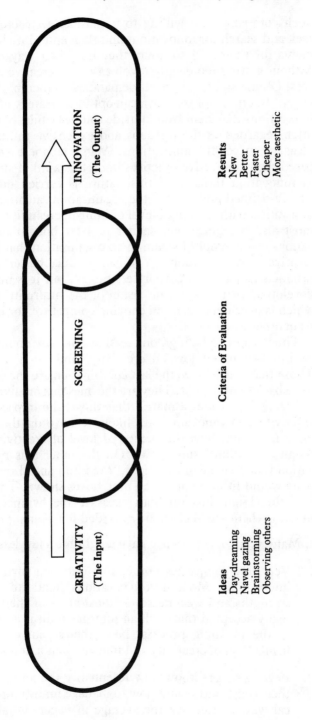

CREATIVITY
(The Input)

SCREENING

INNOVATION
(The Output)

Ideas
Day-dreaming
Navel gazing
Brainstorming
Observing others

Criteria of Evaluation

Results
New
Better
Faster
Cheaper
More aesthetic

Such companies are willing to undertake a structured process of seek and search for innovations and then enter into licence arrangements for them. By so doing they buy their way into innovation without getting too deeply involved in the creative end of the process. Obviously, this in itself demands a modicum of creativity and vision. In other words, a firm can opt for a strategy of implementing innovations that stem from outside sources whilst bypassing what is often regarded as the tortuous and expensive route from creative ideas to successful innovations. Many Japanese companies have based their innovative practices upon this kind of strategy. As long as innovation transfer of this nature is carried out as part of a clearly-defined philosophy, the organisation can attain considerable innovation without a high level of built-in creativity. However, one must also recognise that sooner or later bought or copied innovations can run out of steam in an organisation that has allowed its creative spirit to atrophy. You can produce better and/or cheaper products as part of a corporate strategy, but it is more difficult to develop a creative strategic vision of the future in an organisation which is over-dependent on copying competitors or buying licences from other innovators.

Thus firms can be high on creativity but low on innovation; high on innovation but low on creativity; and 'high' in both camps. Those that can achieve the last combination are the ones that ought to be backed to the hilt. They are the ones that are likely to succeed.

Figure 2 provides a matrix that shows the impact that levels of creativity and innovation are likely to have on the firm's performance. On one axis the perceived level of creativity is shown as 'High', 'Medium' and 'Low'. On the other axis measured innovation is shown again as 'High', 'Medium' and 'Low'. Every company would fit into one of the nine boxes shown. The firms that fit into the 'High' box on both axes are the 'winners'—those who invest in them are likely to be rewarded for their support.

Many years of experience have taught me a few lessons:

1. Very few companies bother to audit their own creativity and innovation. Modern organisations tend to analyse their strengths and weaknesses in most areas of the firm. It is normally accepted that such an internal audit is an essential input to the planning process. Nevertheless, an evaluation of the firm's level of creativity and innovation is a minority practice.

2. Few managers know how to enhance the level of creativity in their organisation and how to manage innovation in a methodical way. I often ask the average manager 'What steps do you

Figure 2. Creativity and innovation excellence matrix.

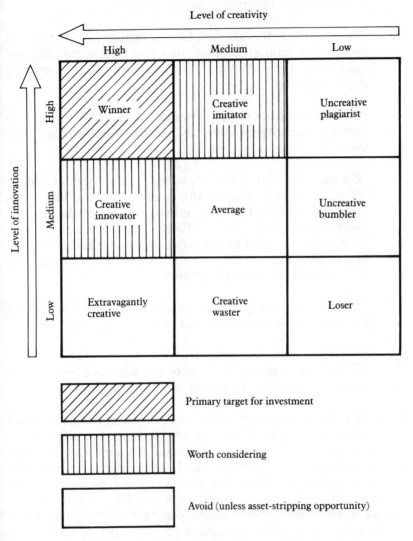

Level of creativity

	High	Medium	Low
High	Winner	Creative imitator	Uncreative plagiarist
Medium	Creative innovator	Average	Uncreative bumbler
Low	Extravagantly creative	Creative waster	Loser

Level of innovation

Primary target for investment

Worth considering

Avoid (unless asset-stripping opportunity)

take to make your organisation more creative or more innovative?' The answers vary from those who honestly reply 'None' to those who waffle on at length.

Periodically one encounters the rare manager who has given the whole subject considerable thought and replies with clearly thought-out statements like:

'We spend a lot of time developing a climate in which ideas can thrive.'

'We have developed a system for motivating our employees to communicate ideas.'

'Every individual in the firm has a statement in his or her job description reminding them that they are responsible for enhancing creativity and innovation in their respective department.'

'We have a Director of Innovation whose responsibility is to develop "Creativity Circles", screen ideas and manage innovation throughout the firm.'

'We run a "Think Tank" designed: (*a*) to solve problems; (*b*) to stimulate creativity throughout the firm, and (*c*) to screen ideas submitted from other members of the organisation. Membership of the "Think Tank" is changed from time to time in order to gain fresh approaches and provide an opportunity to as many as possible to gain an insight into the way the creative process functions.'

'We insist that every manager allocates at least 15 per cent of his time to generating ideas and managing innovation.'

'During personnel appraisal period we ask every member of the staff to tell us what he or she has done towards the enhancement of creativity and innovation in the firm.'

3. Very few companies bother to audit the quality of creativity and innovation of firms which they are planning to acquire. Comprehensive checklists are used during the audit of companies under acquisition investigation. I have seldom seen anything other than a cursory look at the creativity and innovation activities of the companies under investigation. However, on the few occasions when I came across company investigators using thorough questionnaires aiming to assess the creativity and innovation of acquisition prospects I was impressed by the valuable insights that were derived from such an exercise. At the end of the book the reader will find a number of 'audit questionnaires' designed to help in gauging the quality of both creativity and innovation (as defined earlier) at corporate level and also in a number of functional areas.

The inescapable conclusion that I have reached by observing a large number of companies in many parts of the world is that the truly excellent ones are those that have consciously learnt how to harness creative ideas from within the firm and from the external environment and at the same time manage the firm's innovation in a systematic way. This may seem like stating the obvious. Nevertheless, not many managers can place their hand on their heart and say: 'We have taken all the necessary steps to ensure that creativity is fostered and stimulated in our firm and ideas screened in a systematic way in view of identifying those that deserve implementation.' The gulf between promise and fulfilment can be a vast one.

Moreover, excellent companies are those that are able to demonstrate the use of creativity and the achievement of innovations in all parts of the organisation and not only in isolated corners of the firm. If one searches long and hard one can almost always find some creativity in one department or another of most companies. The winners are those who understand the process of innovation and attempt to promulgate it at all levels of the organisation and in all operating units and/or functional areas. In order to achieve such an

Figure 3.   A firm's structure – a conceptual framework.

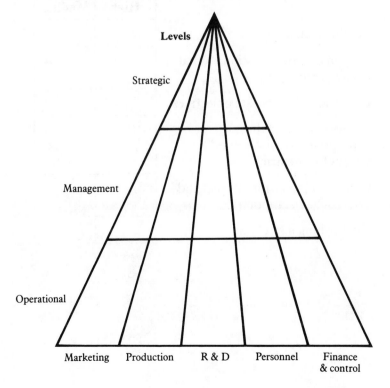

all-embracing level of innovation the process must start from the top, from the chief executive of the firm or from the so-called strategic level of the organisation. In order to foster creativity in an organisation it must be developed in a 'top-down' manner. The commitment, stimulation and encouragement must come from the top. This means that creativity must be seen to be used by top management in relation to strategic issues and decisions with the same steadfast dedication that those at lower levels are expected to apply.

If one accepts the concept that a firm is normally structured as a pyramid consisting of three levels, (*a*) strategic; (*b*) management; and (*c*) operations (see Figure 3 above) it is easy to list a number of areas relating to each level of the organisation which could derive great benefit from the injection of creative thinking.

The strategic level and creativity

Areas that can benefit from creativity

Rate your firm's performance

	High	Medium	Low
Mission statement			
Response to the question: 'What business are we in?'			
Definition of corporate objectives			
Determination of the most appropriate 'shared-values' system for the firm			
Corporate image for internal and external 'consumption'			
Establishing a structure			

Areas for planning/decisions   *Rate your firm's performance*

	High	Medium	Low
Search for strategies			
Developing a sustainable competitive advantage			
Developing creativity in the firm			

These are just a few areas that managers belonging to the strategic level ought to explore from time to time. Readers are simply invited to reflect upon these issues and consider whether their own firm's creativity and innovation in each area deserves a tick in the 'High', 'Medium' or 'Low' boxes. Obviously this is a subjective test for honest people. If a preponderance of ticks appears in the 'Low' boxes, a case for taking drastic steps to improve the situation would be warranted.

The management level and creativity

Areas that can benefit from creativity   *Rate your firm's performance*

MARKETING	High	Medium	Low
Improved intelligence-gathering			
Market research activities			
Departmental/market strategies			
Product development/ improvement			
Improved packaging			
Pricing strategy			
Better and cheaper distribution systems			
Promotional activities (advertising, sales promotion, publicity)			

Areas that can benefit from creativity

Rate your firm's performance

	High	Medium	Low
MARKETING—*contd*			
More productive sales force			
Market testing procedures			
PRODUCTION			
Procurement policy			
Factory logistics and 'Just-in-Time' strategies			
Productivity throughout manufacturing cycle			
General approach to quality control			
Engineering and technology enhancement			
Industrial relations policy throughout plant(s)			
Better factories layout and landscaping			
PERSONNEL/HUMAN RESOURCES Developing more effective motivational policies and practices			
Better and less costly recruitment methods			
Reduction in personnel turnover			
Improved staff communication			
More cost-effective training system			
Better industrial relations			

Areas that can benefit from creativity

Rate your firm's performance

	High	Medium	Low
PERSONAL/HUMAN RESOURCES—*contd* Improved salary/wages structure—cheaper job-evaluation procedure			
RESEARCH AND DEVELOPMENT Better rate of exchange between R & D expenditure and results			
Better screening of projects prior to work authorisation			
More effective assessment of competitive technical capabilities			
Increased number of patentable breakthroughs			
Plan for a more market-led policy in R & D work			
Enhance the image of the firm's R & D establishment so that more qualified graduates wish to join			
Help to turn members of the R & D into better businessmen			
Improve the department's image			
FINANCE AND CONTROL Assemble a better and more meaningful management accounting system			
Present accounts more creatively			
Respond to the managerial control requests faster			

Areas that can benefit from creativity

Rate your firm's performance

FINANCE AND CONTROL—*contd*	High	Medium	Low
Reduce costs of accounts department without reducing its effectiveness			
Better fund management			
Better communication with other departments			
Format and content of statutory Annual Report			
Lowering the audit fees			

The operational level and creativity

Listing all the areas which could benefit from creativity would fill books. Clearly each function of the enterprise includes a large number of operational activities which could be made more effective, better run and at a lower cost. Salesmen can perform their duties in a more innovative way. Similarly computer operators in the accounts department can perform their tasks in a more productive way. Telephone operators can handle the switchboard in a more creative and innovative way, thus saving money for the firm and perhaps responding to callers in a more customer-orientated manner. This also amounts to innovation.

The main purpose of the various checklists given above is to illustrate the importance of creativity to all parts of the organisation. The items provided only represent a minor listing of the areas which could benefit from the combined force of creativity and innovation. The intention is to highlight the fact that creativity can play an important role at the strategic level as well as at lower levels of management. Unfortunately, it is not always recognised that creativity and innovation must be a way of life throughout the firm and not only a sporadic flash of genius in parts of the organisation.

Over the years I have been asked on many occasions to assist companies in developing a climate in which creativity can flourish. Regrettably, on a number of such occasions the work invested by myself and others in seeking to achieve this aim failed inasmuch as top management isolated themselves from the whole assignment. They wanted the whole firm to become creative, but refused to take some of the medicine themselves.

Readers who wish to 'audit' the creativity and innovation quality of their respective organisations will find a number of detailed checklists at the end of the book. These checklists are designed to undertake audits at various levels of the organisation and also in specific functional areas. The aim of these checklists is partly to evaluate the true quality of the creative cycle in the firm but also to make management aware of the elements and conditions that help an organisation become more creative and innovative. The mere process of responding to all the questions posed can have an extremely salutary effect on the management development welfare of the organisation—standing on the scales every morning does not help to lose weight, but it does help a person to realise if he or she is overweight.

The 'funnelling' of ideas

How many ideas does a company need to have in order to attain one innovation? As was emphasised earlier, creative ideas are the raw material and innovations are the ultimate result. One needs many ideas before one can identify the one which deserves to be implemented and commercialised. Ideas can be generated internally or acquired from the external environment but one thing is clear: one needs many ideas before the idea with the winning streak is found. A parallel may be drawn with the process of personnel recruitment. An advertisement for a 'Director of Innovation' is placed in the papers and many candidates apply for the position. They need to be screened; a number of them will be interviewed and finally a smaller number will be interviewed for a second, and possibly a third, time. Finally one person will be offered the job. Of course, it is believed and hoped that the person in question would meet the firm's objectives and job specification. It is as rare to be able to select the winning candidate out of a shortlist as it is to identify an innovation out of a list of ideas.

A number of attempts have been made to establish the decay factor between ideas generated and ideas implemented. Research has shown that the 'rate of exchange' between ideas and innovations varies enormously among industries, companies and even countries. Moreover, many organisations do not monitor the quantity of ideas they analyse in the course of a year, with the result that they are simply unable to respond to the question in point. On the other hand some pharmaceutical companies would assert that they screen thousands of product ideas every year before they discover one worth developing on a commercial basis. Without the former the latter could not happen. In other industries the 'rate of exchange' between ideas and resultant product innovations is relatively small. However, we are only talking here about new products. We saw earlier that innovation can take place in every activity of the organisation and therefore counting the number of innovations in product development is simply the tip of the iceberg.

My own research, based on controlled measurement of the creativity and innovation activities of a representative number of client organisations, has shown that, on average, one needs sixty ideas for one successful innovation. Other researchers have reached somewhat different ratios such as 56:1 and 50:1. Whether one accepts the lower figure or my own, the fact remains that one needs to gather a large number of ideas to obtain the relatively small number of exploitable ones.

It is therefore essential to establish a machinery for generating this stock of ideas.. The larger the number of ideas in the system, the higher the chance that one of them will get through the funnelling process and reach the innovation stage. If one believes the rules of statistics and averages a firm that wishes to attain ten innovations would require six hundred ideas!

For the extraction of precious metals like gold, silver and platinum, many tonnes of ore are required in order to obtain an ounce of precious metal. Similarly, in order to achieve one innovation one requires a mountain of ideas for processing through the funnel. Figure 4 illustrates the steps involved in funnelling ideas from creativity to innovation. It is a sequence of logically interrelated steps comprising:

(*a*) Idea generation. This is essentially a matter of picking up a large quantity of ideas in order to fill up the funnelling system. At this stage one is not interested in their quality. It is simply a matter of topping up the reservoir of ideas which feeds the screening system.

Indeed, among the plethora of ideas assembled there will be a number of 'Intermediate impossibles'. An intermediate impossible is an idea which on the face of it looks totally impractical and one is tempted to reject it out-of-hand because it looks absurd. It is worth remembering that many brilliant innovations have emerged from what appeared at first as absurd ideas.

In subsequent chapters we shall look at a number of tech-

Figure 4.   The idea funnelling process.

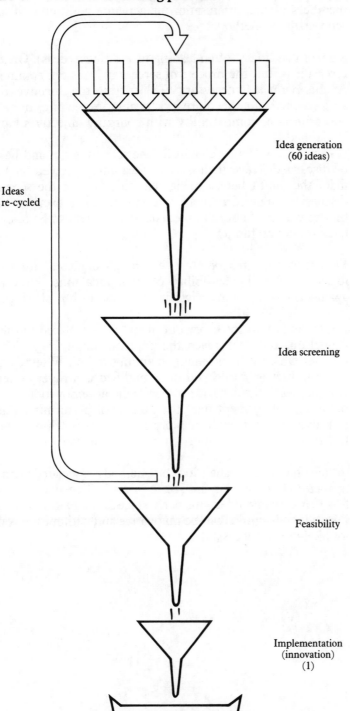

Idea generation
(60 ideas)

Ideas
re-cycled

Idea screening

Feasibility

Implementation
(innovation)
(1)

niques designed to help management to collect ideas from members of the organisation or generate additional ideas by semi-artificial methods.

(b) Screening of ideas (often leading to additional ideas). Once the reservoir is full, the process of screening ideas can commence. At this point it is necessary to shift from the unconventional and eccentric to the more practicable. Screening guidelines and criteria of compatibility with company objectives have to be defined.

    Many ideas will be caught by the screening net and have to be discarded. Nevertheless every idea must be given the benefit of the doubt before being rejected. During the screening discussion some ideas may give rise to other exciting possibilities which, if not of immediate value, ought to be re-cycled back to the top funnel.

(c) Feasibility. At this point a very much depleted number of ideas is left. The feasibility of each idea must be studied against rigorous commercial, financial and technical criteria.

(d) Implementation. In theory out of sixty ideas placed in the top funnel one only will reach the implementation stage. This is the idea which will culminate in an innovation. Whether it is a new product or a sales aid or a modified computer system it will only earn the accolade of becoming an innovation if it can prove to management that it is capable of performing a given task in a better/cheaper or more aesthetic way whilst meeting the firm's objectives and/or criteria of excellence.

In other chapters we shall look at methods associated with the management of innovation in greater detail. The main message which is being promoted at this early stage is the fact that without creativity a firm is unlikely to be innovative and without innovation it is not likely to be successful.

2 The creative organisation

I hope that by now that every reader who works for any organisation, large or small, will wish to see his or her firm become more
creative and ultimately more innovative. With these two ingredients in the corporate system, the prospects for the firm and for the
people who work in it should be much brighter. It is essential also
to remember that creative individuals can only thrive and sublimate
their creativity in creative organisations. In an organisation which
does not allow the process of innovation to function properly, creative individuals are unlikely to exercise and demonstrate their
talent. They either wither away or leave, and both events are
extremely regrettable.

What is a creative organisation? The reader who wishes to assess
the quality of creativity and innovation of his or her firm is invited
to complete one of the audit checklists contained at the back of this
book. The first checklist seeks to audit and assess the creativity of
the corporation as a whole—a useful exercise for chief executives
and top management. The other checklists focus more specifically
on functional areas such as marketing, production, finance, R & D
and personnel. They all represent valuable exercises insofar as the
sheer process of responding to the questions contained in these
checklists makes the participants reflect upon issues of major
importance pertaining to the creative mores and practices of the
firms they work for.

In practice it is very unusual for managers to take stock of their
firm's creativity in a systematic way. Top management of many
companies recognise that it is fashionable to talk about 'creativity'
and 'innovation' and the two words crop up in many press releases
and promotional material at frequent intervals. An increasing
number of companies have developed the habit of incorporating
either word into annual reports, prospectuses and advertising connected with the publishing of annual results and/or corporate iden-
tity campaigns. It would be interesting to know how many of the
firms who use the two interrelated terms have actually stopped to
analyse what they mean and whether they truly reflect what
happens in their organisations.

For a period of around six months I scanned annual reports of many companies and also the advertisements of firms communicating their successes during the previous year. Every time the expressions 'creative', 'creativity', 'innovative', 'innovation' and associated terms were mentioned I made a note of the companies in question and studied their results with particular care. In theory, companies that believe in 'innovation' should be the most successful and profitable ones in their respective sector. Unfortunately, this is not always the case. The reason is probably simple: companies often use the word 'innovation' gratuitously without understanding the true meaning of the term and the organisational implications associated with it. They simply feel that using certain words in their public communication programmes makes them look good in the public eye.

Here is a selected number of statements derived from the advertising copy of a number of well-known companies:

Company A
' "A" is one of the world's largest and most innovative electrical and electronics companies . . . '. Their main motto was 'Innovation, Technology, Quality'.

Company B
'Innovation is our life-blood . . . '.

Company C
An advertisement for the Head of Retail Marketing:
'You have a proven pedigree in a fast moving retail marketing environment. You're innovative, creative, and you are looking for a top management role to match your talent and potential . . .'.

Company D
An advertisement for Product Marketing Management seeking to recruit somebody with 'Flair and Creativity'.

Company E
Wishes to recruit salesmen who have the 'creative flair to operate in a consultative role with personnel professionals . . . '.

Company F
A group promoting its annual report and accounts under the banner:
'With XYZ's innovation and enterprise, no wonder ABC called on us'.

Company G
Once again a corporate image advertisement associated with the publishing of the annual report of a well-known company. One of the main messages provided is:
'Successful new product innovations provide base for future growth . . . '

Company H
'We have attained this position in the market place through a committed policy of innovation and excellence, both in terms of product creation and by harnessing the most advanced technology available in the information services field . . . '.

Japanese companies
Many Japanese companies appear to like the word 'innovation' and incorporate it quite lavishly into their corporate advertising. One encounters statements like:
'Our innovative approach to new products and aggressive new product strategy have thrust us to the fore in world capital markets . . . '.
'Innovation is the secret of our growth . . . '.
'Innovation is our business . . . '.
' . . . Investors turn to us for a conservative yet innovative approach to capital preservation and enhancement . . . '.
' . . . Innovative banking for today's broader financial needs . . . '.

It is a good game: 'Spot the creative innovators'. Every age has its fads and jargon and the incorporation of the clichés of the moment in public utterances is deemed part of an up-to-date communication strategy. It is fun to pick up a newspaper, especially one that enjoys a substantial business readership, and study the content of corporate advertisements. It should not take long to identify and list the popular phrases of the moment. Variations on the theme of 'creativity' and 'innovation' are currently the 'in' words and appear to be hawked around with enthusiasm as part of a firm's corporate communication. Unfortunately, not every organisation that claims to be creative is justified in doing so. Similarly, not every firm that puts the word 'innovation' in its banner or promotional material is entitled to do so. It is not implied here that all those who purport to be creative and/or innovative are making false statements, but it is probably true to say that quite a few of the companies boasting about either of these attributes do not know what the terms mean in practice. My advice to top management is to reflect upon the meaning of the terms before using them indiscriminately. Moreover, it might prove very useful to undertake an organisational creativity and innovation audit before blowing one's trumpet about a claim which may prove tenuous in the extreme.

The main characteristics of a creative organisation

It is fair to assume that every firm would wish to become more creative and innovative. It is hoped that enough has been said so far to convince most readers of the fact that the combined pay-off of these two ingredients is worth investing in. The following are the main prerequisites for the development and maintenance of a dynamic spirit of creativity coupled with an effective system of innovation:

(*a*)   the climate for creative thinking must be right;

(*b*)   an effective system of communicating ideas must exist at all levels; and

(*c*)   procedures for managing innovation must be in place.

It is important to recognise that all three elements must exist in comfortable harmony. The existence of one or two of these without the third would be sufficient to constrain the successful development of innovation in the organisation. These three conditions apply with equal validity to large and small firms; commercial and non-commercial organisations; and to domestic and multinational companies. In order to attain a high level of innovation all three conditions must exist regardless of the nature of the organisation and its size. The main difference lies in the amount of emphasis and procedural support that must be associated with each one of these three elements. Obviously, if a small firm of accountants wishes to improve its general level of innovation it will not need to invest as much time and effort in developing a better system for communicating ideas as a large multinational firm will need to do!

The organisation's climate

Creativity can only survive in organisations in which the climate is empathetic to the whole process. Generally speaking, a firm's climate is one of the most difficult developmental areas to change and invariably requires total commitment and involvement from top management. It is futile simply to issue a command from above: 'On the eighth day thou shalt be more creative'. It calls for an imaginative and multi-faceted programme of work coupled with dedicated persistence from the top of the hierarchy and from those responsible for management development in the organisation.

A firm in which the climate is either hostile or indifferent to ideas is extremely unlikely to be creative. Hostility or indifference to creative ideas can take many forms—some are overt and some are more subtle in their approach. For example, a boss can stifle subordinates' creative thinking by looking bored when an idea is presented. By the same token, it is important to remember that subordinates, too, can discourage their bosses' creativity by appearing bored or disinterested. Asking people to write a report justifying the viability of an idea is another killer of creativity. Refusing to listen to a subordinate's idea owing to pressure of work can act as a dampener of creative enthusiasm, especially if it occurs at regular intervals. Also, suggesting to a person that he or she ought to discuss the idea with a third party is a subtle way of saying 'please leave me alone—I am not interested in your half-baked ideas'.

A boss who maintains a permanent 'closed-door' policy towards members of the organisation coupled with a battle-axe type secretary is also well on the way towards stifling creativity in the firm. In this regard, senior people should always reflect upon the impact that the wrong secretary or personal assistant can have on the environment's creative climate. How many managers can truthfully state that when recruiting a secretary they have considered the effect that the selected person might have on the company's creativity? This remark applies with equal validity to small solicitors' offices and medical practices.

One should also be aware that facial expressions and other non-verbal communication messages can act as a deterrent to people's eagerness to be creative. Further, criticising people on a regular basis for having generated ideas that failed to achieve hoped-for results in the past is a sure way to de-motivate them from putting forward additional ideas.

If one wants to build and develop a climate in which creativity can flourish all these 'don'ts' must be avoided. Yet, in practice, it needs considerable wisdom, self-awareness and self-discipline for a manager to avoid all these pitfalls. For some managers all this sounds like commonsense. Unfortunately many people, both in commercial and non-commercial organisations, drift into a management style which is far from conducive to the fostering of creative ideas around them. It is strongly recommended that every manager should devote some time to analysing and reflecting upon his or her personal contribution to the development of a climate in which creativity can survive.

The existence of the 'right climate' can help a firm to be creative and innovative and the lack of the appropriate climate can have the opposite effect. The Chief Executive of one of the most creative organisations with whom I have had the privilege of working keeps saying: 'I consider that the climate for creativity is right when every person in the firm, senior or junior, talks about creativity and ideas all the time . . . '. He also talks about the 'glow' that creative firms radiate internally and externally at all times. I recognise that such statements may sound like hyperbole. Nevertheless, the existence of an organisational commitment to a behavioural and attitudinal pattern can only be developed when top management is willing to be obsessive about the implementation of such a creed or ethos.

'Superordinate goals' and innovation

In an interesting paper called 'Structure is not Organisation' that appeared in *Business Horizons* in June 1980, from which the quotation below is taken, Waterman, Peters and Phillips (the former two of 'In Search of Excellence' fame) suggested that when seeking to diagnose and solve organisational problems one needs to look beyond structural reorganisation. One must look at a framework that includes a host of related factors. The authors have recognised that major structural shifts are not the only way in which to respond to a changing environment. Excellent companies such as IBM, Hewlett-Packard, GM, Dupont and P & G manage to respond to external pressures without necessarily undertaking an internal change in their respective structure. Yet they appear to be more responsive to change than their competitors. This is achieved through a series of temporary devices aimed at focusing the attention of the entire organisation, for a limited time, on a single priority goal.

'Our assertion is that change is not simply a matter of structure, although structure is important. It is not so simple as the interaction between strategy and structure, although strategy is critical too. Our claim is that effective organisational change is really the relationship between structure, strategy, systems, style, skills, staff and something we call superordinate goals'.

The main thesis of the three authors is that organisational effectiveness stems from the interaction of seven factors, which conveniently all start with the letter 'S'—'Superordinate Goals, Structure, Systems, Style, Staff, Skills and Strategy'. Figure 5 shows the 'Seven S's' and highlights their interconnectedness. The

Figure 5.   The 'Seven S's' framework for effective organisations.

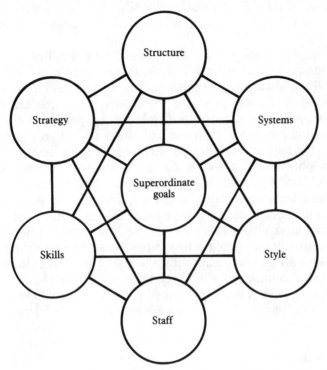

shape of the diagram and the position of the 'S's *inter se* is deliberately non-hierarchical inasmuch as any one of the seven can be the
driving force of change at a given point of time.

The meaning and role of each of the six 'S's' on the outside of the
framework are self-explanatory and their interconnectedness fairly
obvious. It is the seventh 'S'—the 'Superordinate Goals' which war-
rants some additional exploration in the context of this book. By
superordinate goals, the authors mean 'guiding concepts—a set of
values and aspirations, often unwritten, that go beyond the conventional formal statement of corporate objectives'. They are the pos-
tulates upon which the firm's climate and shared values system is
based. The drive for their accomplishment pulls an organisation
together. It provides the intellectual and conceptual locomotive that
pulls the organisational train in a desired direction.

'Superordinate goals' is a fancy name for something that most
companies understand but few manage to attain. The authors go on
to quote examples of companies that have developed superordinate
goals around which the business is built and the organisation seeks

to express itself, for example: 'Customer service and the pursuit of excellence' guides IBM's marketing; 'Progress is our most important product' is GE's slogan, and 'innovative people at all levels in the organisation' is Hewlett-Packard's motto.

I tested the validity of the Waterman, Peters, Phillips framework in a number of consultancy assignments and found it helpful especially in attempting to enhance the creativity and innovation of companies. It is easy to see how each one of the 'Seven S's' can impinge upon the quality of the firm's creative process both favourably and unfavourably. However, it is the organisation's 'superordinate goals' that represent the driving force in this direction. It is an elegant phrase and a sound notion which encompasses a more powerful connotation than the word 'climate' which I used earlier.

If top management truly desire the company to become more creative in order to become more innovative they must incorporate these two interrelated concepts into the firm's superordinate goals. It is almost like adopting a new religion and incorporating it into the firm's culture and organisational ethos. This is what is meant by developing 'a climate in which creative thinking must be right . . . '. This in turn means that every function of the firm and every corner of the organisation must be galvanised towards the attainment of these superordinate goals. It also means that every 'S' in the framework described in Figure 5 must make its full contribution towards the attainment of these 'goals' in a total state of harmony and interconnectedness with each other. The right structure can enhance creativity and innovation whilst the wrong structure can stifle both. Similarly, having the appropriate staff and skills can help both creativity and innovation to thrive. The absence of the right personnel and/or skills can have the opposite effect. Each one of the other 'S's' can have a beneficial or harmful impact on the ability of the firm to innovate.

If one accepts the validity of the 'Seven S's' concept, and if one is willing to adopt it as the framework around which to strive for corporate excellence every function, every operating unit and every department must seek to make its management understand and accept the value of each one of the stated factors. If 'innovation' is part of the firm's stated 'Superordinate Goals' all the other six factors must respond to this challenge in a balanced and interactive way. A 'Structure' and 'Strategy' empathetic to the creative processes must be evolved. Management development and training must undertake a programme of work to improve the 'Skills' and 'Style' of the organisation so as to help the 'Staff' to become more creative and innovative. Clearly the 'Systems' that facilitate innovation, such as systems for communicating ideas, screening and implementing them, must be installed. Moreover, this orchestration of the 'Seven S's' must take place at corporate level as well as in marketing, production, R & D, personnel, etc, if the desire to develop a more creative and innovative firm is more than just a pious hope.

An effective system of communicating ideas

When seeking to evaluate the quality of creativity and innovation in any organisation a valuable acid test is the response one gets from company's personnel to one of the following questions:
'Do you know what to do with an idea when you have one?' and 'do you know who to communicate an idea to?' The contrast in this regard between creative and non-creative organisations can be very eloquent—in the former people know precisely how, when and to whom to transmit their ideas; in the latter ideas often get lost for the simple reason that no system exists in the firm for catching them.

It is unfair to expect a company's personnel to become more creative and generate more ideas if the organisation is unable or unwilling to provide a facilitating communication system. One cannot exhort people to become more creative and at the same time leave them to overcome the hurdles of unreceptive communication procedures. Ideas are like gold dust and if the system is incapable of catching each one of them and evaluating them the organisation is the loser.

The firm's climate and procedures are interrelated. A firm can have a climate which is supportive of creativity yet fail in achieving any worthwhile innovations simply because the communication system is incapable of benefitting from the fruit of the personnel's creativity. On the other hand, in the unlikely event that a firm enjoys an effective communication system, but the climate for creativity is non-existent, little innovation is likely to occur. Innovation must have the combined presence of a climate and effective communication procedures. These two elements must be developed in tandem whatever the effort. At the same time it is important to recognise that the rewards can be truly significant.

An organisation needs ideas, and the more the better. If the theory discussed earlier is right one needs an average of sixty ideas for each successful innovation. Ideas can emerge from every function and from every echelon in the organisation. Moreover, ideas can be generated internally and also gleaned from the external environment in which people or groups of people live or work. Every time a person goes shopping or visiting a park or a zoo he or she is able to pick up ideas. A salesman can identify valuable ideas during sales calls, during contact with customers or during sales conferences. R & D people can come across ideas during technical meetings with members of their profession. Finance and accountancy personnel should be able to do likewise during contacts with bankers, auditors and other members of the profession. It is important to recognise that every individual in the organisation has an opportunity to scoop ideas from the external environment. However, very often this does not happen because (*a*) the motivation to do so (namely the climate) does not exist and (*b*) communicating the idea to anybody in the organisation involves a hassle. I knew a boss of a medium-sized company in the packaging industry who used to say to his subordinates before they departed on a foreign trip: 'I expect you to bring back from your trip to the USA at least three good ideas'. Moreover, when the subordinates returned from their trip he insisted on hearing all about the 'three ideas'. On reflection, it is not difficult to see what a subtle device this was. Travelling members of the organisation had been provided with positive motivation to be vigilant for ideas, and had also been given a channel of communication for transmitting details of ideas observed during their trip. In other words, an effective system for communicating ideas does not have to be sophisticated and complex. The important thing is that individuals know what to do with their ideas and to whom to transmit them.

In small organisations the method of communicating ideas can be informal and simple. Members of the firm can drop into each other's office whenever it is appropriate and report something interesting that they saw or heard or some idea that occurred to them in the middle of the night. It is not difficult to create a climate in which ideas flow in all directions. The essential point is that the people in the firm are willing to listen to each other's ideas and recognise what a valuable input it can be to the firm's future success. A thinking boss can bring such an atmosphere about through example and readiness to listen to ideas and stimulate people around him or her to communicate their ideas irrespective of whether they are earth-shaking or relatively trivial. The creative 'glow' must be accompanied by the willingness to listen, and this is the essence of effective communication.

As the firm grows and the number of functions and/or departments and/or levels of management increase, the informal system of communication starts suffering from the myriad of 'contact points' that emerge in the organisation. The chance that ideas will find an appropriate ear diminish and that in turn means that creativity suffers. If in addition to normal growth the company starts operating in international markets the probability that creative ideas will not flow freely among the various operating companies will increase tenfold. Growing companies must recognise this risk and work extra hard at ensuring that a communication system is established aimed at neutralising this erosion in ideas flow. Steps must be taken in this direction because the communication of ideas on a multi-functional or multi-company or multi-national scale is unlikely to happen by itself.

Figure 6 illustrates the various sources of ideas that surround a typical company. It is often forgotten that ideas can emanate not only from internal parts of the organisation (such as marketing, production, R & D, personnel and finance) but also from external sources such as competitors, customers, marketing institutions and advertising agencies, etc. Moreover, in an open-minded and open-hearted organisation good ideas can transcend functional barriers. There is absolutely no reason why an idea with a winning streak for the marketing area cannot originate from the production department and vice versa. The ability to encourage and exploit everybody's ideas regardless of functional and operational affiliations is one of the secrets of a creative organisation. On the other hand the imposition of artificial barriers whereby the only good ideas are those that are deemed to have emerged from a 'proper source' is a definite way to weaken the creative glow in the firm. This is what is often referred to as the 'not invented here syndrome'. It is an easy pitfall which discourages people from 'importing' ideas either from outside the firm or from different departments and functions. I recently met an insurance company that purported to be creative. Yet every idea for new product development, whatever its source, was killed by the actuaries. The only ideas which were given a positive hearing were those that emanated from other actuaries in the group or even from external actuaries. In other words, the receptivity to ideas was so selective that people ceased to communicate ideas pertaining to new products. Clearly, such a state of affairs is extremely regrettable.

Figure 6 incorporates a number of external sources of ideas that can enrich a firm's creative input. Clearly bodies like financial institutions, channels of distribution, research organisations and academic establishments can all provide valuable ideas at one stage or another. All these ideas are there for the plucking, but the motivation and mechanism to scoop them must be in place before one can hope to benefit from their existence.

The diagram seeks to illustrate the random pattern which normally exists in the flow of ideas from internal and external sources. It is only a matter of happy chance when an idea is caught,

Figure 6. Sources and flow of ideas in firms that have not organise themselves to catch and communicate such ideas.

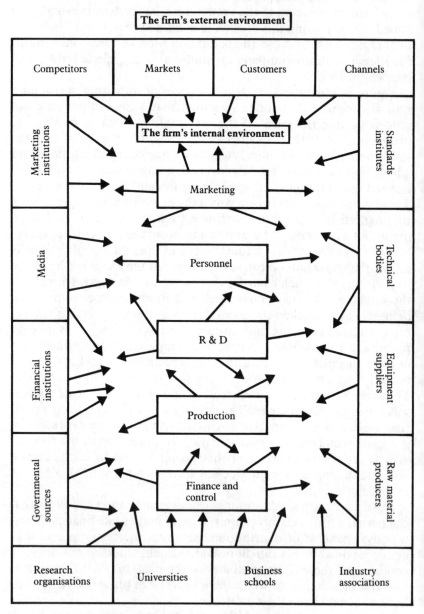

Arrows indicate possible sources and flow of ideas

evaluated and implemented by the firm. The aim of establishing an effective system of communication is to ensure that the waste element is reduced and that a systematic channel of ideas flow catches as many ideas as possible. Ideally, the system should go a step further: it should act as a multidirectional conduit that collects ideas, collates them and redirects them to the parts of the organisation that can derive maximum benefit from them.

Figure 7 provides an alternative model: it represents, in a diagrammatic form, an idea-flow pattern in a firm that has taken steps to establish a mechanism for communicating ideas from sources to a 'focal point' and their redirection to suitable beneficiaries. The purpose of such a system is to ensure that people in the organisation, whatever their job and function, know who to transmit their ideas to and also know from whom to expect to obtain the additional flow of creative raw material. Ideas can shower on an organisation like rain and, like rain, vanish into the ground without leaving a trace. In dry lands the vanishing droplets represent a tragic loss of an opportunity to create life in an arid environment. The wise and diligent inhabitants of such areas take steps to catch the precious liquid and direct it to those who can benefit from it most. The analogy is obvious and extremely relevant to the idea-flow system under dis-

Figure 7. Flow of ideas in an organisation that has established a communication system.

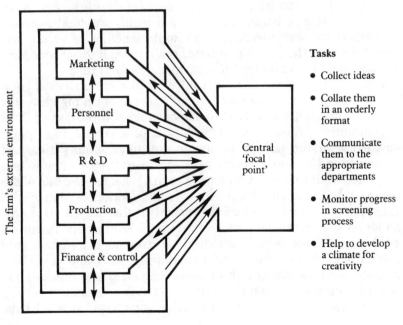

The firm's external environment

Marketing

Personnel

R & D

Production

Finance & control

Central 'focal point'

Tasks

- Collect ideas

- Collate them in an orderly format

- Communicate them to the appropriate departments

- Monitor progress in screening process

- Help to develop a climate for creativity

cussion. The successful implementation of such a communication infrastructure carries the additional benefit that it helps to improve the overall climate for innovation. The person who remains totally impervious to the existence of such a system and refuses to partake in the idea-flow, either as a transmitter or the recipient of ideas, is rare.

Communicating internationally

So far it has been assumed that the firm operates in one country. If the international dimension is added, the problems associated with the flow of ideas can become monumental. Yet the benefits of grappling with such a problem far outweigh the effort. Phillips, IBM and 3M operate in dozens of countries—what is the chance that an idea generated by the marketing personnel in a remote country of their respective organisations will be caught and aired at the organisational centre? If the answer is 'high', that firm has a winning streak on its side. When working with many multinational organisations, I have often been staggered by the fact that problems that plague one part of the organisation have in fact been solved by another part of the firm in another country. It is the inadequacy of the communication system in respect of the flow of ideas and innovation which is the main culprit. What I tell such organisations is that the successful transfer of only one winning innovation from one country to another, resulting from the establishment of an effective system of communication, will justify the total expenditure associated with the design and implementation of such a system. Whatever the cost, the benefits can outweigh the expenditure in both tangible and intangible ways in a very short time.

Figure 8 shows how ideas get diffused in a multinational company which does not possess a system for communicating ideas. On the other hand Figure 9 seeks to demonstrate how the flow of ideas can improve through the establishment of a central focal point charged with the task of receiving, collating, summarising and transmitting ideas on a regular basis to all parts of the organisation that have volunteered to take part in such a scheme. The title of the person who mans the 'focal point' is unimportant—'Manager of Innovation' is used by some companies in this regard. Unfortunately, it is a somewhat pretentious and misleading title inasmuch as the underlying notion is that the person in question is only responsible for collecting and transmitting ideas and is seldom charged with the actual task of converting ideas into innovations. What is important is that the existence of such a catchment service and its exact purpose, role and location are known by all. I have

Figure 8. **The flow of ideas in a multinational firm not organised to catch ideas.**

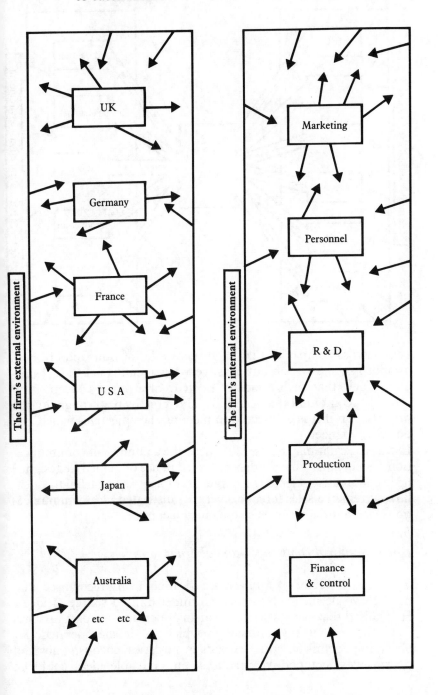

Figure 9.   The flow of ideas in a multinational firm organised to communicate ideas.

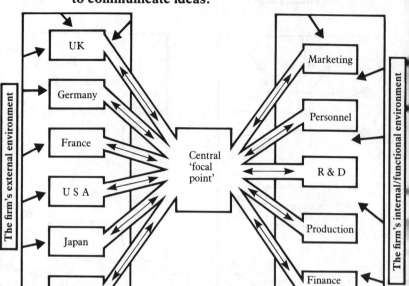

come across companies that have spent a lot of time and effort to establish such a system but, alas, very few members of the organisation knew that such a facility existed. Clearly the concept itself must be communicated carefully and creatively throughout the organisation if it is to succeed in meeting the objectives which it is designed to meet.

In this regard it may be useful to describe a number of communication systems that I have either observed in use or helped to design. I have deliberately selected disparate examples varying from the idea-flow system of a sales force to a very sophisticated idea-communication system utilising an electronic mail facility.

Pharmaceutical company—ethical drugs sales force

The Sales Director of a pharmaceutical company recognised that his eighty salesmen represented an under-utilised source of ideas. He realised that every salesman had an opportunity to pick up ideas from the market environment in which he or she operated. By observing doctors at work, patients in surgeries, chemists, hospital pharmacists, competitive practices, etc, valuable ideas could be gleaned from time to time by every vigilant salesman. Attempts at exhorting members of the sales force to transmit ideas to their superiors somehow fell on deaf ears. A decision was taken to grapple with this problem in a radical and imaginative way.

The following interrelated steps were taken:

(*a*) The job description of each member of the sales team (Regional Managers, Area Managers and Sales Representatives) was changed by the incorporation of an additional item conspicuously positioned: 'You must be alert, at all times, in your sales territory to ideas which may help the firm to improve its overall creativity and effectiveness. You are responsible for assembling such ideas and transmitting them through the designated channel and in the prescribed form. During your performance appraisal session you will be invited to provide a record of the ideas you have submitted during the period under review.'.

(*b*) Every member of the sales team was provided with a very attractive pad consisting of sets of scribbling notelets with the wording 'My Idea' printed in a conspicuous way at the top. Each set consisted of three self-copying notelets in three colours, green, yellow and blue. When one wrote on the top green sheet the text was automatically copied to the second and third notelets. The instructions were that an idea should be scribbled in triplicate: the top two copies (green and yellow) were meant to be passed to the appropriate 'ideas reception centre'. The third, blue, copy was retained in the pad. Every individual was meant to keep the blue copies in the pad and bring them along during the appraisal session. The yellow copy was used for easy feedback from the recipients of the ideas: a short note on the bottom half of the note stating what was happening to each idea and, if rejected, a brief explanation as to why it was decided to do so.

(*c*) A whole page was allocated in the company's 'House Magazine' towards summarising the five 'best ideas' which were picked up by the system during the previous period (two months). The names of the providers of the ideas thus selected were conspicuously shown. Steps were taken to ensure that people considered being on such a list as a desirable accolade.

(*d*) Ideas selected as 'best ideas', whether implemented or not, earned 'dividend points'. The 'dividend programme' entitled people to claim various items from a gift catalogue consisting of such items as pen sets, cameras, briefcases etc. The inspiration for the whole scheme came from the 'dividend programme' of a well-known credit card organisation.

The whole scheme was well-designed and well-integrated. The main result was that everybody in the sales force started recognising the importance that the firm attached to creative ideas and understood clearly the mechanism that had been set up for syphoning ideas.

Fast-moving consumer goods—international marketing

This brief case study describes a very ambitious programme to create an effective idea-flow system to cover the marketing activities of a very large organisation operating in (i) many consumer products and (ii) in most countries outside the Communist bloc. Most of the operating companies round the world, especially the ones in the more industrialised countries, were self-contained, encompassing both marketing and production activities. The result was that the communication among operating units was tenuous in the extreme. Top management in the UK felt that one of the benefits of being an international company was the opportunity to cross-fertilise ideas emanating from the many different environments in which the many subsidiaries were operating. 'Somebody, somewhere in Peru may have the answer to the maiden's prayer—yet nobody in the rest of the world has access to such a winning idea', the Chairman of the company was heard to say. A task force was appointed to review the situation and put forward proposals for the establishment of a mechanism designed to catch ideas and communicate them on a global scale. Top management commitment to the whole concept was total and it was made clear to the task force that resources would be made available for the appropriate solution.

The task force investigated the situation in great depth and submitted a detailed programme of work which was implemented in full. The salient parts of the programme were:

(*a*) A Director of Innovation was appointed with main board status. The main reason for giving that person such a high-faluting title was to communicate to every member of the organisation the importance that the firm was attaching to the role of creativity and innovation for success. The duties of the Director of Innovation were spelt out as follows:

(i) to stimulate a climate throughout the organisation in which ideas can be created and communicated;

(ii) to establish an effective system for communicating ideas from all parts of the world;

(iii) to take steps to ensure that the momentum and enthusiasm for the communication of ideas is maintained at all times;

(iv) to collect ideas submitted from all units and/or functions throughout the world;

(v) to provide an initial screening aimed at avoiding duplication, repetition and well-established ideas;

(vi) to collate and communicate ideas in a bulletin form to all marketing personnel of a certain level of seniority. The theory was that the latter would be responsible for transmitting the relevant portions to lower echelons in their respective organisations;

(vii) to design a system of motivation aimed at encouraging members of the organisation to observe and conceive new ideas. It was made clear throughout the deliberations that 'motivation' in this regard need not be monetary;

(viii) to monitor innovation activities and record success stories with regard to providing feedback to members of the organisation about successful implementations.

(b) A training film about 'Creativity and Innovation' was produced. The main objective of the film was to highlight the importance that top management ascribed to the subject and also to the need to communicate ideas throughout the firm. Furthermore, the film was designed to explain the role of the Director of Innovation and to provide him with 'promotional support'. It was made clear throughout that top management were committed to the whole notion of creativity and were addressing themselves to the need to improve the communication of ideas.

(c) An 'Innovation Award' scheme was set up. The idea was to reward those people whose ideas resulted in valuable innovations with a certificate which they could display in a prominent way. The Director of Innovation was asked to promote the scheme in such a way that the award scheme would earn a prestige value among the company personnel.

The system implemented became very successful. Judging by the number of ideas communicated from all over the world and by the number of successful innovations all the effort was fully justified. The secret of this success stemmed from the fact that (i) a 'concept champion' was appointed, namely, the Director of Innovation, and (ii) the whole programme was fully integrated and 'marketed' in a creative way.

Engineering company

A company manufacturing engines and pumps. A new Chief Executive had undertaken a 'Creativity and Innovation Audit' which concluded that the firm was suffering from a paucity of innovations and was starving for ideas. A decision was taken to rectify the situation by establishing a system for catching ideas from members of the organisation at all levels.

The system designed was called 'The Treasure Chest'. A number of interrelated steps were taken:

(a) The rationale for the whole campaign was summarised in a 'little red book'. The boss felt that a little red book might have some association in people's mind with the famous 'Thoughts of Chairman Mao'. The booklet emphasised the importance of creativity and the role that every member of the organisation could play in this regard.

(b) The concept of the 'Treasure Chest' was marketed like a brand. It was promoted at every opportunity and in every media available for internal communication in the firm.

(c) 'Treasure Chest' boxes were installed in prominent places on the firm's premises. Everybody knew what they were and why they were thus installed.

(d) A huge diagram, in the shape of a histogram, was installed at the entrance of the main plants and offices showing the number of ideas submitted during each month of the year since the scheme came into operation.

(e) A screening committee was established under the chairmanship of the Chief Executive. The committee consisted of two senior people, two representatives of middle management and two members of the workforce. It was agreed that members of the committee would be changed at regular intervals in order (i) to keep everybody fresh and maintain enthusiasm, and

(ii) provide as many people as possible with the opportunity to become familiar with the whole system.

(*f*) Publicity, prizes and congratulatory letters from the boss were given to those who submitted winning ideas.

The system worked well and provided an effective vehicle for communicating ideas. However it was discovered that whenever the monthly histogram started sagging an additional impetus had to be injected by giving the 'creative flywheel' a few more turns . . .

An international bank

A large international bank operating in major money centres decided to use their recently-installed international telecommunication network for collecting ideas from their various affiliates. Members of the organisation were encouraged to use the 'electronic mail' system for transmitting ideas gleaned from their operating environments or from other sources. The main purpose of such a sophisticated request was to ensure that (i) a sense of urgency was injected into the idea generation and transmission activities, and (ii) ideas were funnelled to a clearly-defined focal point.

At the time of writing it is difficult to evaluate the success of the scheme. Members of the organisation are slightly bemused by the whole concept. There is a general feeling that the firm is using a 'sledgehammer to crack a nut'. The idea functions well on the technical level but has probably not been fully exploited owing to the fact that other supportive steps, like the ones described earlier, have not been undertaken. The idea-flow system has been established but the climate itself has not been fully orientated towards a creative process with the result that some lack of commitment is weakening managerial resolve in this regard.

Procedures for managing innovation

It is all very well catching lots of ideas in one's net. By the very nature of the creative process some of the ideas thus caught are probably inappropriate, impractical or too difficult to implement. Others are more relevant in the circumstances but entail costly and lengthy development periods. Yet others are not only attractive but also easy to commercialise. Obviously, these latter ideas are those that should be developed and turned into innovations. These are the ones that enable a firm to perform its tasks in a more efficient way.

This process of selecting the 'stars' from among the multitude can only be achieved if the organisation has taken steps to develop procedures for managing innovation. The funnelling cycle described earlier must be translated into a practical set of procedures which can be applied whenever the 'ideas reservoir' is full. This reservoir is full when an adequate number of ideas has been picked up from the communication system established by the firm. Alternatively, the reservoir can be filled with ideas by semi-artificial methods such as brainstorming or other techniques designed to generate lots of ideas and at speed. Companies that devote an inordinate amount of time on generating and catching ideas without giving enough thought towards the establishment of a mechanism or procedures for screening, evaluating and implementing ideas are bound to be disappointed with the gains which are achieved. The trouble is that very often disappointment in this regard leads to an abdication from the whole process.

The ability to screen and evaluate ideas and pick the best among them for implementation is the secret ingredient which completes the cycle that characterises a creative organisation. The 'Trinity', it will be recalled, consists of the 'climate', the 'communication of ideas' and the 'management of innovation'. They are interrelated and interdependent—each one on its own does not make a company into a creative one. In fact two of the three, on their own, do not make a creative organisation either. All three must exist in comfortable harmony. Clearly, it calls for an imaginative and persistent development work supported by a total commitment from the top. This point cannot be over-emphasised: anybody in authority who wishes his or her firm to become more creative *and* innovative must take steps to ensure that all the three ingredients described are in place.

Figure 10 shows in an algorithmic form the relationship that must exist between the three ingredients of the creative process. It seeks to demonstrate the interdependence between climate development, idea generation and the evaluation and implementation of ideas. The diagram summarises the developmental steps that the firm's management must undertake, in a systematic way, if the organisation is to become more creative and more innovative. The effort in this regard must be relentless and consistent. There is no scope here for short-cuts and intermittent spurts of enthusiasm.

When one is ready to screen ideas it is important to remember that not every idea which appears attractive is necessarily appropriate in the circumstances in which the company finds itself. An idea

Figure 10.   The management of innovation—the full cycle.

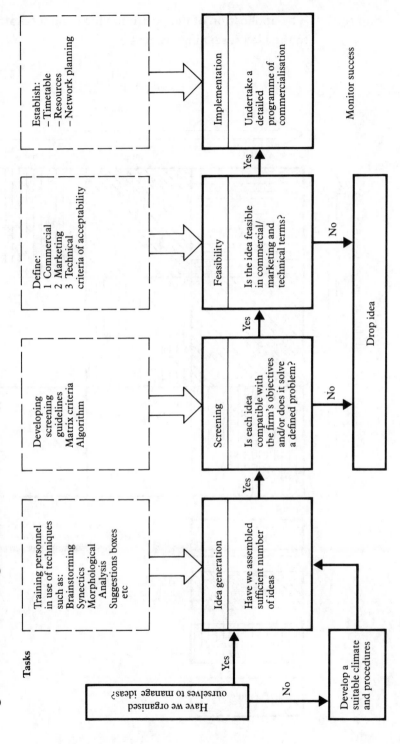

Figure 11. **The application of the portfolio management matrix to the idea screening process.**

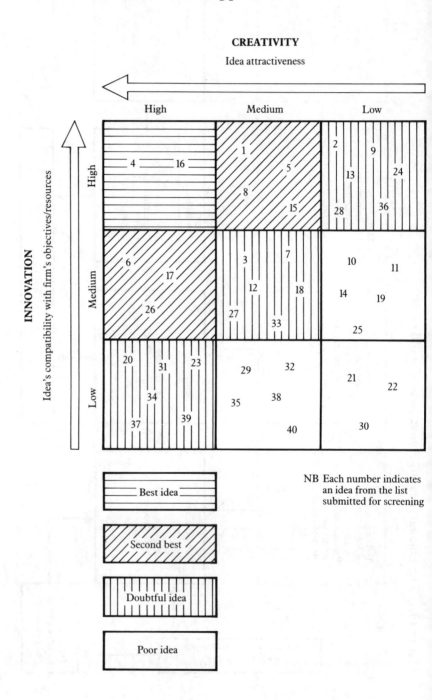

may be superb per se but totally irrelevant to the firm at a given point of time. Similarly, an idea may be very attractive and original but incompatible with the available resources of the firm at the point when the screening is taking place. The best ideas are the ones that are attractive on the one hand but also meet the firm's objectives, on the other.

A useful aid to screening ideas against these two dimensions is described in Figure 11. The matrix shown represents an extrapolation from the very helpful 'portfolio management matrix' or 'dimensional policy matrix' which is often used in strategic analysis or product management. The horizontal axis represents the level of attractiveness that the screening team has decided to ascribe to each idea under evaluation: 'high', 'medium' and 'low'. The horizontal axis represents the compatibility of each idea with the firm's objectives and resources. Once again the team is invited to express its judgement on three levels: 'high', 'medium' and 'low'. Obviously the best ideas are the ones that gain a 'high' on both axes. The 'high/mediums' and 'medium/highs' are still very interesting but represent a secondary choice. As the ideas move downwards towards the right/bottom corner their commercial attractiveness deteriorates.

I have found this concept extremely valuable in my work inasmuch as it encompasses the 'creativity/innovation' game on one matrix. The horizontal axis describes the 'Creativity' content of the whole exercise: the vertical axis represents the 'Innovation' part. The former can be esoteric, eccentric and even day-dreaming in its content. The latter must be realistic, practical and results-orientated. Where the twain meet one gets the absolute best of both worlds.

If one decides to use this matrix two points ought to be borne in mind:

(*a*) It is essential to define the 'criteria of attractiveness' and the 'criteria of compatibility' before embarking on a detailed process of screening and evaluation. Figure 12 contains examples of the kind of criteria which one needs to list in relation to the two dimensions of analysis. The actual criteria would differ from case to case and would need to be adapted to the circumstances of each situation.

(*b*) Whenever the screening is carried out by a group of people it is important that a simple system for collating and averaging the opinions of those present is agreed in advance. Thus one can ascribe numeric values to each axis: '3' for 'high', '2' for

Figure 12.

Criteria of attractiveness	Criteria of compatibility
(Examples only)	**(Examples only)**
– Originality	Compatible with:
– Simplicity	– Company objectives
– User friendly	– Available financial resources
– Easy to implement	– Available human resources
– Elegant	– Corporate image
– Difficult to copy	– Ability to protect (eg patent)
	– Needs to solve problem

'medium' and '1' for 'low'. One asks the participants to express their views in these numbers and compute the average.

The evaluation matrix described in Figure 11 is not very scientific and its reliability cannot be considered as foolproof. Nevertheless, it represents a valuable opportunity to discuss and explore the viability of each idea on the two dimensions that matter: its creative content and its true scope for innovation. Inevitably a considerable amount of subjective judgement is bound to creep into such an evaluation, but the scope for subjectivity is strongly reduced if the process is submitted to the rigours of a 'jury of executive opinion', deliberation and assessment. A group of thinking people can bring an idea closer to an objective evaluation than each independent individual can do on his or her own.

Instead of using a matrix containing semi-emotive terms such as 'high', 'medium' and 'low' one can use a somewhat more quantitative screening procedure as the one described in Figure 13. The merit of such a method is that the evaluating team has a wider choice of scoring points. Choosing a number out of 10 provides a more meaningful judgement zone. If this is done on both axes a simple multiplication can give a total score. Moreover it is easier to

Figure 13.   Screening matrix for ideas.

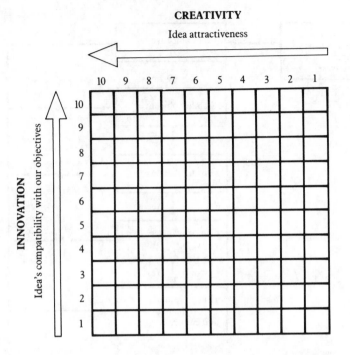

average the scoring of a number of people on such a basis. At this point one can decide that any idea which gains a total score of less than, say, 60 (namely average score on the horizontal axis multiplied by the average score on the vertical axis) should not proceed to the next step. Once again clearly-defined criteria should help the screening team in deciding what is an 'attractive' idea and which one is compatible with the firm's needs, objectives and available resources.

Variations on the theme can be easily conjured by those responsible for developing screening procedures. The format of these procedures can be flexible and can match the needs of specific situations. However, the one thing which is important is the ability to match the attractiveness of each idea with its practicality.

Another valuable tool is described in Figure 14. It represents a screening procedure based on an algorithm which encompasses the various criteria that the screening team has selected for the evaluation system. The algorithm is only shown as an example of the kind of questions against which each idea or the more promising ideas must be screened. Each company, each department and each specific situation would necessitate a separate listing of the appro-

Figure 14.   A screening procedure—an algorithm.

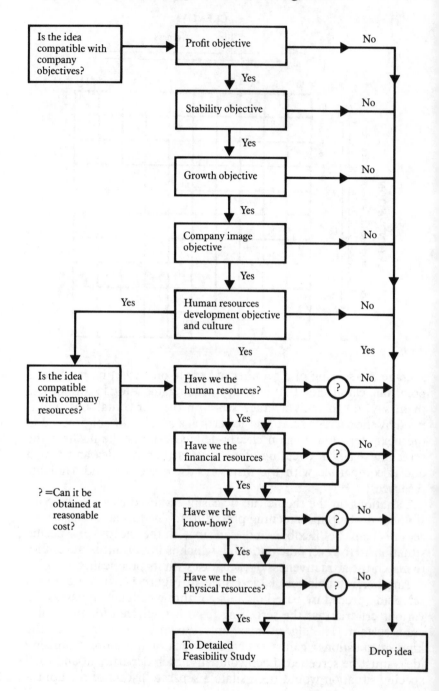

Figure 15. Aid to idea screening.

Criteria of evaluation (Examples only)	A Weight	B 10	9	8	7	6	5	4	3	2	1	0	A x B Score
Idea attractiveness													
Ease of implementation	0.10												
Originality	0.15												
Protectable/sustainable	0.10												
User-friendly	0.10												
Global acceptability	0.05												
Compatibility criteria													
Available finance	0.20												
Provision of solution to specific problem	0.10												
Our image	0.05												
Our ability to protect (eg patent)	0.05												
Our marketing competence	0.10												
	1.00											Total score	

priate evaluation questions. The preparation of the screening algorithm and the identification of the most relevant questions can be lengthy and fairly demanding mentally. Nevertheless, the sheer task of developing such a screening flow-diagram provides the organisation with a valuable tool for understanding and empathising with the process of managing innovation. The management development payoff can be most valuable and therefore the more people in the firm who gain the experience of undertaking such an activity the better.

The algorithm described in Figure 14 below can be used in addition to the screening matrix described in Figure 13 or on its own. With experience and practice the team can work out its own favoured approach.

Another procedure which can help to identify the 'most attractive' and the 'most compatible' ideas is described in Figure 15. Once again it may appear a laborious procedure, but like all these activities the effort is fully justifiable in terms of the prize that can be gained at the end of the process.

3 The creative person

'The history of scientific and technical discovery teaches us that the human race is poor in independent and creative imagination. Even when the external and scientific requirements for the birth of an idea have long been there, it generally needs an external stimulus to make it actually happen; man has, so to speak, to stumble right up against the thing before the idea comes . . .'

Albert Einstein

'Genius is two per cent inspiration and 98 per cent perspiration' was attributed to Thomas Edison.

Nobody would doubt that Thomas Edison was a creative person. In fact, he was probably a genius. Does that mean that in order to spark creative ideas one needs to labour at it ceaselessly? It is very unlikely that Isaac Newton spent 98 per cent of his time working himself to a frazzle in order to discover the law of gravity. Similarly, it is most unlikely that Archimedes of 'Eureka' fame formulated his displacement theories whilst washing off the perspiration of a 98 per cent exhausting working day.

We know that the inventor of the 'cat's eye' road markings stumbled right up against this brilliant discovery when one night he shone his torch at a cat whose eyes reflected back at him. Alexander Fleming discovered penicillin by sheer accident. Neither seemed to have been working frantically at being creative.

What makes a creative person?

The annals of invention and discovery history are full of stories of individuals who came across events or incidents that gave them the inspirational spark that led them towards monumental innovations. What distinguishes all these people from lesser mortals? The easy answer is to say that they are more creative. However, this brings us to the trap of having to define what a creative person is. We have no difficulty in saying that a person is creative when we see the results of his or her actions. If asked to list the names of creative people one automatically thinks of Archimedes, Brunel, Leonardo da Vinci,

51

Picasso, Thomas Edison, Albert Einstein. One seldom thinks in terms of the accountant who invented the double entry system or the actuary who formulated the original life-expectancy actuarial tables. Surely in their respective fields the last two were also extremely creative?

In the world of business and commerce one accepts the notion that creativity is a useful ingredient for success. Nevertheless, great difficulties are experienced when the need arises to recruit 'creative' individuals. It is quite amusing to note how often recruitment advertisements state that 'the company is looking for a creative manager to fill a certain job'. It is never clear whether the advertising companies understand what they are looking for. Do they expect the would-be applicant to undergo a self-screening 'creativity test' before applying or do they provide such a test themselves during the interviewing process?

The term 'creative person' is most difficult to define in a convincing way. The result is that it is difficult to identify a highly creative person in advance of his or her creative production. Over the years we have seen the advent of a large number of psychological tests and psychometric assessment methods that claim to be able to determine whether a person is likely to be creative or not. Unfortunately all these tests are limited in their predictive value insofar as they seek to identify circumstantial 'signs' of likely behaviour rather than judgmental assessment of a track record. The state of creativity occurs rarely, even in creative individuals. People who have experienced 'creative states' would affirm that they are often remarkably spontaneous, even capricious. Inevitably, anything which bears the hallmarks of unpredictability is a difficult quantity to measure and predict.

'Every creative act involves . . . a new innocence of perception, liberated from the cataract of accepted belief . . . ' Arthur Koestler stated in 'The Sleepwalkers'. In other words, a creative person is one who can process in new ways the information at his or her disposal. Maybe this wise statement may provide us with the clue as to the main attributes of a creative person.

A lot has been written about the characteristics of a creative person. The subject has been tackled from a large number of disciplines and viewpoints. The behavioural sciences have been particularly prolific in seeking to define the 'identikit' of a creative individual. In spite of the vast literature on the subject, industry and commerce find the process of identifying and recruiting true creative talent an onerous task. Many misconceptions still persist among talent searchers. The notion that you can tell whether a person is creative by the way he or she dresses still exists among some managers. Although one rebels against such a popular mythology it is not unusual for candidates to be rejected during an interview because they appear physically 'square' and therefore likely to be less creative.

Another mythology is based on the notion that some professions or disciplines are less likely to bring along creativity into an organisation. It is a fairly common belief that accountants, lawyers and actuaries are less creative than artists, designers and musicians. Businessmen accept too readily the idea that individuals who have had a spell in advertising or promotion agencies are by definition shining examples of creative thinking.

I subscribe to the thesis that everybody is capable of being creative. Unfortunately, many people have had their creative talent dulled through an unempathetic environment or upbringing. Children often demonstrate remarkable signs of creativity which are rare among inhibited adults. Parents often demolish their own children's creativity through a misplaced attempt at improving their standards of behaviour and manners. It is not rare for a child to surround itself by the most imaginative and enjoyable make-believe cluster of illusions. A swivel chair represents a beloved pony; a retractable umbrella becomes the child's intercontinental ballistic missile; a thermos flask is a spaceship. 'Simon, you will damage Dad's chair. Dad will wallop you.' 'Why don't you grow up? This is an umbrella, not a missile!' 'God help you if you break this thermos flask!' What a crippling blow to a child's creativity when all these wonderful illusions are shattered through well-meant parental chastisement.

Then come teachers who can lower a child's enthusiasm for creative thinking and action. Verbal and non-verbal signals of displeasure at deviations from acceptable norms of behaviour can inflict untold damage on a child's creativity. A creative adult can often relate his or her excellence in this area to a teacher in the distant past who provided the stimulation and support to his or her idiosyncratic, free-spirit, non-conforming attitudes and excursions at a formative age.

Having been buffeted by parents and teachers the potentially creative individual has another hurdle to overcome: unempathetic barriers at university and/or professional training establishments. Again much of the damage is done unintentionally through an insidious adherence to an institutional code of practice.

Finally the poor individual, who has had his or her creative wings clipped, joins an organisation. The residual creativity that is still there is threatened by the constraints placed upon it by an uncreative environment and possibly by an uncreative peer group.

At the opposite end of the spectrum one encounters people who were brought up in a home in which creative ideas were never stifled or discouraged. They were later fortunate to meet teachers who fostered their imagination and creative stimuli and ultimately studied in establishments that tolerated and nurtured creative excursions. Among individuals like this one can find the true creative personality that organisations so desperately need.

In other words, creativity is probably more a function of a person's upbringing and educational background than a deep-rooted genetic inheritance. Scientists may not entirely agree with this oversimplified statement. Nonetheless most of them will agree that individuals will be wise not to accept too readily the judgement by their peers or bosses that they are not creative. It is easy to perpetuate such a stigma and unfortunately it has been known for the victims of such an assertion to accept their destiny in life as uncreative persons.

Let us start from the notion that we were all born capable of being creative and that we have managed to survive the onslaught upon our potential creativity.

A few simple exercises will put us to the test. They do not represent a scientific assessment methodology nor should they be taken as irrefutable evidence of creative prowess or lack thereof. They are purely an attempt at exploring how far the reader is able to think laterally and look for solutions outside the obvious search area. A few of these exercises are well-established games known to some readers. Clearly where the solution is known there is no point taking credit for having done it successfully.

The figures follow the questions, and answers and explanations are provided at the end of this chapter.

1. The beauty and the beast

What can you see in Figure 16? Do you see the face of a pretty lady or an old hag?

2. The awkward treasure box

Figure 17 describes a box consisting of two halves dovetailed together in an awkward way. Can you visualise a way in which the two halves could be separated without inflicting damage on the structure of the two dovetails?

Figure 16. 'The beauty and the beast'.

Source: Picture Collection, The Branch Libraries, The New York Public Library

Figure 17. The awkward treasure box.

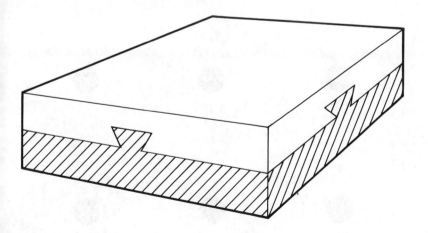

3. The nine-dots puzzle

Try to cover the nine dots shown in Figure 18 with four straight and continuously drawn lines. In other words the lines must be drawn without lifting the pen or pencil off the paper.

4. The nine-dots puzzle—harder version

If you managed to do the previous one try the following: cover all nine dots with *one* straight line. If you can do this one you are a genius!

5. Equidistant trees

Figure 19 shows four trees. Plant them in such a way that they are equidistant from each other at their base (where the trunk touches the ground).

Figure 18.   The nine-dots puzzle.

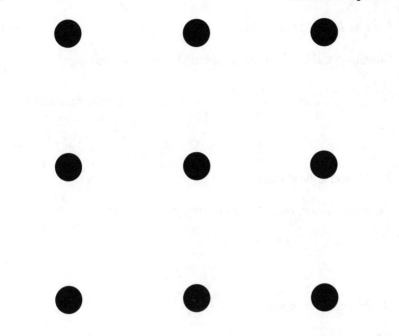

Figure 19.   Equidistant trees.

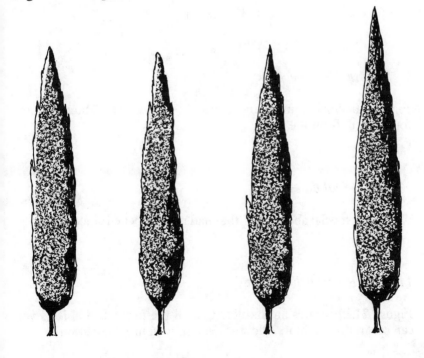

6. *The letters progression*

Continue and explain the following letters progression:

$$\begin{array}{llll} A & E\ F & H\ I\dots\dots\dots\dots\dots\dots \\ B\ C\ D & G & J\dots\dots\dots\dots\dots\dots \end{array}$$

7. *Numeric progression*

Continue and explain the following progression:

$$3\ 1\ 2\ 8\ 3\ 1\ 3\ 0\ \dots\dots\dots\dots\dots$$

8. *Numeric progression (No. 2)*

Continue and explain the following progression (Tip: for over-25's only!):

$$\frac{1}{2}\ 1\ 3\ 6\ 12\ 24\ \cdots\ ?$$

9. *Spot the difference*

Figure 20 shows four figures marked A, B, C, D. Which of these four differs from the rest?

10. *Historical dates*

What was special about 1961 that had not happened since 1881?

11. *The Rorschach inkblot*

Figure 21 illustrates an inkblot. List all the forms and objects you can see in this inkblot. Allow a free rein to your imagination.

Figure 20.   Spot the difference.

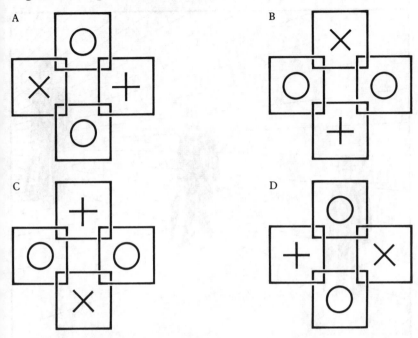

Figure 21.   The Rorschach Inkblot.

Figure 22.   The city gentlemen.

Source: Verlag C J Bucher

12. *The city gentleman*

Figure 22 shows three bowler-hatted city gentleman standing in a row. Which of the three is the tallest?

Use your brain

A brief understanding of how the human brain functions is relevant to a book dealing with the question of creativity. It will go a long way towards giving encouragement to those who feel that they are incapable of being creative.

It is worth recalling that the human brain consists of two halves (or two brains) linked by a complex network of nerve fibres. Seen from above it resembles the two halves of a walnut as shown in Figure 23. From that vantage point we refer to the two halves as the 'left hemisphere' and the 'right hemisphere'. The nervous system is connected to the brain in such a way that functionally the left hemisphere controls the right side of the body and the right hemisphere controls the left side. This means that if an individual suffers a stroke or other injury to the right side of the brain it is the left side of the body that will be most seriously affected and vice versa.

During the last two decades it has been discovered that each side of the brain deals with different types of mental processes:

Left side	*Right side*
Logic	Rhythm
Reasoning	Music
Language	Imagination
Numeracy	Images
Analysis	Colour
Linearity	Shape recognition
Digital	Daydreaming
Abstract	General creativity

At one stage it was thought that geniuses were either 'right-brain' dominant or 'left-brain' dominant. Thus it was assumed that

Figure 23.   The human brain seen from above.

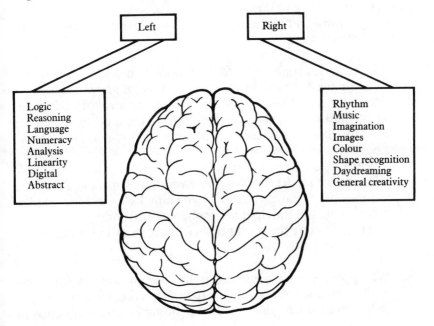

The creative person 62

Picasso fitted into the former and Einstein into the latter categories. It was believed that their respective brains were 'lopsided'. However, more thorough research has taught us that so-called right-brain or left-brain dominant persons are perfectly capable of excelling in activities that are controlled by the 'other side'. Einstein apparently played the violin and painted competently.

The general view among scientists until fairly recently was that in most cases the left hemisphere was the more dominant or major hemisphere. By the same token the right brain was deemed to be the minor one. Scientists realised that language functions were controlled by the left half of the brain inasmuch as whenever a person sustained injury to the left side of the brain loss of speech capability often occurred. Injury of equal severity to the right side of the brain seldom caused loss of speech.

Thanks to the exceptionally interesting work of Roger W Sperry and his team at the California Institute of Technology during the fifties and sixties we learnt that both hemispheres of the brain are capable of complex modes of thinking. The main theme that emerged from this research was that different types of thinking modes were associated with each half of the brain. For educationalists the main practical implication of Sperry's work was that the two mental modes were verbal and non-verbal. The former was controlled by the left hemisphere and the latter by the right. Unfortunately, our educational and scientific systems tended to neglect the non-verbal form of intellect.

Sperry's work and more recent research into this fascinating subject have shown that:

1. The brain is capable of infinitely more complex tasks than has been thought. One can develop the mental areas which were deemed weak. It is too easy to accept one's role in life as an artist, musician or daydreamer ('right-dominant' functions) or a mathematician, statistician or analyst ('left-dominant' functions).

    Thus, according to Betty Edwards in her interesting book *'Drawing on the Right side of the Brain'*, most people should be capable of learning to draw and paint by unlocking hidden artistic talent in the right hemisphere of their brain.

    There is hope for accountants and actuaries to become more creative after all!

2. When people are encouraged to develop the weaker functions of their mental process, rather than detracting from the supposedly strong areas, they produce a strengthening of all areas of

their mind's performance. A computer programmer who seeks to improve his artistic and colour sense will not become a less competent programmer. If the theory is right he or she will in fact develop a fuller mind.

The message therefore is clear: creativity is not the sole prerogative of individuals with a 'right-dominant' mind. Obviously, activities associated with creativity come more naturally to such people. However, others are capable of undergoing the lateral shift from 'left' to 'right' through increased awareness of one's own mind and its workings. There is absolutely no need for any manager to feel that he or she is doomed to an non-creative existence. 'Becoming more creative' is well within the capabilities of most individuals. It needs self-awareness, discipline and a steadfast willingness to concentrate upon the task of improving the part of the brain that was allowed to remain dormant for so long.

The attitude spectrum

It is useful to recall that an effective manager is a person who has acquired through management development and/or self-development three main attributes: (*a*) knowledge; (*b*) skills; and (*c*) attitudes.

Knowledge

The knowledge requirements of a manager are company, level and industry orientated. When an individual changes employment the knowledge requirements of the new job probably change as well. This is particularly true if the new position is at a different level and/or different industry. It is important to remember that invariably a promotion in the firm's hierarchy entails the need to acquire new areas of knowledge without which the new job cannot be pursued effectively. Likewise, moving from one industry to another calls for a good look at the inventory of knowledge that the new job demands.

An individual who wishes to attain performance excellence is well-advised to sit down from time to time and reflect upon the following question: 'What do I need to know in order to perform my tasks in an excellent way?' It is a difficult question to answer insofar as most people are unaware of what they do not know! Nevertheless, a conscientious attempt at thinking about the subject and seeking to list the areas of knowledge that can enrich a person's performance is in itself a most valuable tool in self-development.

Skills

The skills of a manager, on the other hand, are transferable from industry to industry and from company to company. Once acquired, skills represent an integral part of the personal armoury of the manager. The only time individuals should worry about personal skills is when they assume a more senior job which requires a new set of skills. For instance, if a person becomes the chief executive of an organisation, the likelihood is that the public communication skill will become much more important than previously.

The following is a list of the main skills that an effective manager ought to acquire. In the right column the appropriateness of each skill to the creativity and innovation processes are also shown:

Skills	*Appropriateness to the creative manager*
Observing	Can help to identify solution to problems through observing competitors worldwide or picking ideas from the general environment, including nature.
Reflecting	Can help to place problems in their proper perspective with the view of determining priorities.
Fact-finding	Creative solutions to problems often need facts. Clearly an important skill.
Analysing	A useful skill during the evaluation of ideas and their conversion into innovation.
Diagnosing	Helps to distinguish between problems and their symptoms. An essential skill prior to undertaking creative problem-solving exercises.
Formulating solutions	Helpful during problem-solving sessions.

Skills	*Appropriateness to the creative manager*
Deciding	Valuable during the management of innovation.
Communicating	Essential during the process of stimulating a climate for creativity throughout the firm. Useful during idea-generation sessions.
Motivating	How can one get others to become more creative without possessing the skill of motivation?
Delegating	Inviting other members of an organisation to undertake creativity activities calls for the ability to delegate . . .
Organising	Every creativity activity must be organised by somebody.

It thus appears that most of the skills of management can impact upon the creative process at one stage or another. The tragedy is that in many organisations the creative process is considered as a peripheral game that a group of eccentrics undertakes instead of managing the business. In organisations in which the importance of creativity is fully accepted by all, a recognition of the role which each skill can contribute to the overall enhancement of innovation is almost axiomatic. An acceptance that all the managerial skills have to be orchestrated and galvanised if the firm is to become more creative and innovative must exist at all levels.

Attitudes

An organisation's cluster of attitudes is probably the most important and sensitive area in which top management can impact upon the firm's climate and operational ethos. The development of attitudes for the organisation is the basis upon which the firm's style and mode of conduct is structured. Attitudes must be planned and developed as part of a system of 'shared values' and people persuaded to adopt them: they do not just happen. The people at the top of a hierarchy, like the leaders of a nation, are responsible for selecting and formulating attitudes which are (*a*) compatible with the needs of a modern enterprise; (*b*) compatible with the behavioural style of the people in the firm and (*c*) compatible with the personality of the leaders at the top.

It is evident that creative individuals have to exercise their creativity within the framework of an organisation. If the climate of the firm encourages and tolerates creativity the individuals therein stand a better chance of asserting their creative talent. At the same time it is relevant to reflect on whether individual managers who genuinely want to be creative can make a conscious and disciplined effort to ameliorate their personal attitude in this regard.

" 'Improve your personal 'attitude spectrum'."

This expression is normally used in connection with a person's response to other people's ideas. Every person reacts to ideas with a mixture of feelings. Typical responses can be listed:

> 'It is an excellent idea *but* . . . '
> 'It won't work—we have tried it before . . . '
> 'It is bound to be a very expensive solution . . . '
> 'Our parent board will not approve of it . . . '
> 'Most probably it will breach our industry's code of practice . . . '
> 'It will lead to many unforeseen complications . . . '
> 'Competitors will copy it very quickly . . . '

These are the kind of statements that one encounters in response to ideas in a typical environment.

From time to time one is more fortunate: a member of one's audience oozes enthusiasm and reacts to the idea offered in an entirely positive and supportive way. An individual who is capable of approaching other people's ideas in such a constructive and tolerant manner is the sort of person who can enrich an organisation's creativity in a most dramatic way. Moreover, other members of the organisation tend to gravitate towards such a person when they wish to discuss their ideas with somebody. People, of course, prefer to present their ideas to the tolerant type because he or she shows interest, enthusiasm and encouragement. The tolerant types know that every idea, however apparently far-fetched, deserves the full benefit of the doubt.

Every person has a different mixture of responses to the ideas of others. Critical managers will find many faults in the ideas presented to them. Individuals with a greater threshold of tolerance will find some good in the ideas but at the same time will probably dredge up a myriad of obstacles to detract from their attractiveness. As the level of tolerance and positiveness towards other people's ideas increases among individuals, so does the chance that creativity will survive. The extremely tolerant person is the one who can even save the 'intermediate impossible' from peremptory rejection.

Figure 24 describes in a diagrammatic form the 'attitude spectrum' that one encounters among a group of people in an organisation. It shows the varying degrees of positive/negative ratios that individuals normally manifest. It is a difficult ratio to measure in advance, but in most instances can be gleaned from the behaviour of individuals in group creativity sessions. Alternatively, one can assess a person's attitude spectrum by throwing a few semi-cogent ideas at him and listening carefully to the response. The individual with the poor attitude spectrum will spend time demolishing the ideas; the person with the tolerant attitude will seek to develop the

Figure 24.   The attitude spectrum of individuals.

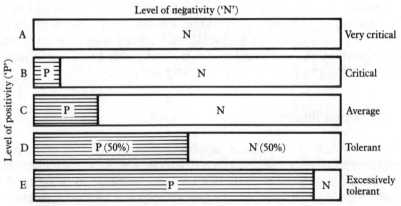

A = Killer of creativity. Needs total change of attitude prior to being asked to participate in creativity sessions. If the 'boss' God help the firm!

B = Unhelpful participant in 'creativity circles'. . . .

C = Average participants. Must be exhorted to improve their personal spectrum attitude.

D = Excellent individuals in 'creativity circles'. Very even-handed in response to ideas.

E = Useful during idea-generation process but weak during ideas evaluation and management of innovation.

same ideas and build upon them. It is a crude test, but it normally works.

Every person is capable of changing his or her attitude spectrum by sheer self-discipline and self-awareness. Improving one's attitude towards other people's ideas does not imply a change either in personality or in character. It simply means that one forces oneself to focus generously, however frustrating it may appear at first, one's intellect, feelings and intuitions upon the worthwhile portions of an idea propounded. Only then one can feel that one has earned the right to express doubts and weaknesses. The notion that a generous support of half-baked ideas makes the recipient appear weak or flabby is totally misplaced. An effective and confident manager can afford to appear soft when ideas, the gold-dust of the creative process, are being aired. The manager who can train himself to modify his attitude spectrum from a narrow and negative one to a tolerant and generous one is more likely to develop a fertile climate for creativity in the organisation. This is particularly relevant to a person who is in authority and capable of formulating and stimulating a set of 'shared values' in the firm.

Spot the creative manager

As we saw earlier, it is not easy to spot creative persons before one has had an opportunity of working with them or observing their creative production. Yet a few tale-tell signals may help such an identification. A creative person is normally able to demonstrate a few, if not all, of the following characteristics.

Conceptual fluency

A creative person is normally capable of generating many ideas at a great speed in response to a given situation. On the other hand, the less creative individual finds it a lot more difficult to bring forth more than a small number of ideas in response to the same challenge.

A number of simple exercises can help to test candidates in this regard:

(*a*) List new and novel uses for paperclips;

(*b*) Explore additional services that an airline can offer its passengers during a flight;

(*c*)   List additional products that could be sold at post offices;

(*d*)   List parts of the anatomy that begin with h;

(*e*)   List ways for combating terrorism.

Carrying such an exercise towards the end of a recruitment campaign when one wants to identify the most creative members of a short-list of candidates can be a most valuable addition to the screening process. The exercise can be undertaken in an open forum with all the candidates on the short-list participating in a workshop-type gathering. If conducted by an experienced tutor the exercise can be not only useful in its screening quality, but also enjoyable for the participants.

Clearly one must be careful not to place excessive reliance on such a crude test. Nevertheless, experience has taught me that where creativity is an important adjunct to a job, testing the conceptual fluency of individuals is of great value to the organisation and should not be ignored.

Mental flexibility

Some people have the ability to shift 'mental gears' at the slightest press of the button. They can discard a line of thought and take a lateral leap towards a loosely related frame of reference. To the casual observer it may come across as conceptual grasshopping. However, the gear change often stems from a fertile mind rather than a capricious and unstructured mental process. The spontaneous change in direction is the result of a creative and flexible mental algorithm.

The following story illustrates an example of an individual who would have failed the 'mental flexibility' test. An insurance salesman came to visit me at my own request. I saw an advertisement describing an insurance policy with interesting tax efficient elements attached to it. The conversation went like this:

Salesman: "Let me first describe to you the excellent tax benefits associated with this new product . .   "

Me: "You do not have to spend time telling me about the tax benefits. I appreciate them perfectly well . . . "

Salesman: "Oh! I understand. Let me first describe to you the excellent tax benefits . . . "

Me: "I told you that I am fully aware of the tax benefits. Tell me about the terms of the policy itself . . . "

Salesman: "Of course. Let me describe to you the excellent tax benefits . . . "

My rudimentary diagnostic skill told me that I was dealing with a person of extremely poor mental flexibility who was incapable of changing gears. He was driving on 'automatic pilot'. He was a 'low' on my second test.

In my opinion, the whole essence of de Bono's concept of 'lateral thinking' revolves around an individual's ability to shift mental gears and change approaches almost spontaneously. The exercises described earlier on page 54 can also help to diagnose people's flexibility.

Another useful exercise: give the participants a short case study describing a problem (e.g. how to reduce queuing in banks during lunchtime) and invite them to list other organisations that have faced analogous problems. The creative person will be able to list many situations in which comparable problems have occurred. Many of the situations thus listed will be from extremely disparate environments but congruence will be evident.

Originality

A creative person is able to demonstrate a higher level of originality than his or her less creative counterparts. Originality in this context means the ability to give unusual answers to questions or atypical responses to specified problems.

In this connection the Rorschach Inkblot is a useful method for evaluating a person's originality. It may be a slightly unorthodox use of the technique inasmuch as its main application is as a diagnostic tool in psychology. Nevertheless, for our purpose here it is a useful device for comparative analysis of individuals' level of original thought. The same blot will be interpreted by different people in a countless number of ways. Yet most people will give a fairly standard and 'popular' list of interpretations. The person who can put forward rare and unusual interpretations of what an inkblot conveys to them should score highly on the originality hit parade.

In response to the inkblot on page 59, the average person will probably list a bat, a butterfly, lungs, human torso, a jacket, a cloud. An original person might add a person in a free fall, a hut with thatched roof, siamese hippopotami. Deriving judgement about a person's originality on the basis of such a test is purely comparative. In other words the person who consistently generates a longer list of unusual perceptions is the one who demonstrates a higher level of original thinking and should earn marks for potential creativity.

Suspension of judgement

Suspending judgement is a lot more difficult than it may sound. Most people find that in response to ideas, especially eccentric or unusual ones, they tend to flood the creator of those ideas with reasons as to why they will not work. A few of the comments thus expressed may be perfectly legitimate, but ideally they should be left for a later stage and only after the possible virtues of each idea have been explored in some depth.

Truly creative persons do not fall into this trap. They intuitively know that the magic of the creative process can be damaged or even destroyed if an idea is 'placed in the dock' too early. They understand that every idea is innocent until the contrary is proved. They also know that not infrequently half-baked ideas, the 'intermediate impossibles', can be the source of dramatic innovations. Consequently, instead of raising obstacles they look for positive angles that can save each idea from premature rejection.

Moreover, people who can suspend judgement are more valuable during idea-generation exercises such as brainstorming. These sessions are aimed at producing as many ideas as possible in a short time. Having members of the group who cannot suspend judgement is the perfect way to mutilate the quality and quantity of the group's output.

Testing people's ability to suspend judgement can be easily achieved by presenting them with a number of fairly sensible, albeit unusual ideas, and asking them to comment upon them. This kind of exercise is particularly helpful in group discussion. The observer can soon identify those who can suspend judgement and those who cannot.

Impulse acceptance

A popular cliche says that the dividing line between a madman and a genius is a fine one. Similarly the dividing line between a creative and an uncreative person, at least superficially, can appear a fine one too. A creative person is normally more willing to entertain and accept a bizzare or unorthodox solution to a problem than a less creative individual. The latter sticks to a more conventional and seemingly respectable pattern of behaviour.

The creative individual is more likely to react impulsively to an idea because it triggers his or her inner imagination and fantasy. Others may not always be able to share such a person's enthusiasm insofar as they are not aware of the inner stimuli that have brought the impulsive behaviour about.

It is rather difficult to establish whether individuals tend to manifest this characteristic except by observing them during creativity sessions. Nonetheless, it is worth trying to identify this trait because a certain amount of 'impulse acceptance' can help to enrich the quality of creative activities in an organisation. At the same time, it is fair to say that few firms could afford to sustain too many individuals who are willing to entertain what appear to be irrational impulses.

Attitude towards authority

This is an important issue, but must be treated with some circumspection as the difference between 'highs' and 'lows' can be marginal in this area.

Highly creative people are more willing to challenge authority than less creative individuals. The latter tend to view authority from above as absolute and would not dream of challenging their superior's right to direct and command. Their allegiance is unequivocal and their view of authority is permanent. To that extent one cannot escape from the conclusion that a large number of Japanese managers fall into this category. They represent a group of individuals who accept authority as 'given' and offer obedience and deference at all times. To that extent it is harder to find creative managers in a Japanese hierarchy.

On the other hand one finds that highly creative people are less willing to accept the invincibility of superiors' wisdom. Whilst they may behave with demonstrable respect towards authority they are not prepared to pay unquestioned allegiance to their bosses. They demand information and expect explanations. In some organisations like the army or the police, which tend to be hierarchical in character, individuals who question the power of authority too often may find that their career path will suffer as a result of such an attitude. In many respects this is regrettable because these are the people who can enhance the creativity of the organisation. He who wants to enhance creativity in the firm must learn that having a few rebels in its midst is a valuable help towards achieving this aim.

It is important to emphasise that the relationship between creativity and an attitude towards authority can be fairly spurious on occasions. Not every person who challenges authority is necessarily creative and not every person who obeys orders blindly is by definition uncreative. What has been described is based on empirical observation and years of experience. It highlights a probabilistic pattern rather than an irrefutable norm. In most cases there is a probability that the creative person will be ready to challenge authority and the less creative person will show continuous allegiance to superior authority.

Gauging a person's attitude towards authority can be done in two ways:

(*a*) careful assessment of past behaviour; and

(*b*) observations of the individual's demeanour and statements in group discussion based on a case study in which a hierarchical conflict between boss and subordinates forms the main issue. The person whose attitude towards authority is a questioning one is more likely to take the side of the subordinates than the person who accepts authority as absolute.

Tolerance

One of the attributes of a creative person is tolerance. A tolerant person is more likely to be creative than the one who has a low threshold of tolerance towards the ideas of colleagues, subordinates or bosses. The paradox is that a person can have an obedient attitude towards authority and yet have a low tolerance towards a boss's ideas. The only difference is that in the case of superiors, the intolerance towards their ideas is not overt but covert. A person can say one thing to his boss but his body language or non-verbal communication can say something else. Moreover, one can obey one's boss diligently and attempt to implement his ideas without being stimulated and enthusiastic about them.

At the other extreme one encounters individuals who accept authority as a matter of expedience rather than a moral obligation, but at the same time manifest considerable tolerance to the ideas of a creative boss.

Tolerance to other people's ideas can be evaluated during a brainstormimg session, and in particular during the subsequent process of screening ideas

In summary, if a company wishes to have a few ultra-creative individuals in its midst it ought to endeavour to ensure that as many of the characteristics listed above are present in at least a few of them.

The following checklist can help to identify the creative whizz-kids either from inside the firm or from the outside. Scoring should be graded from low (0) to high (10).

	0	1	2	3	4	5	6	7	8	9	10
(a) Conceptual fluency											
(b) Mental flexibility											
(c) Originality											
(d) Suspension of judgement											
(e) Impulse acceptance											
(f) Attitude towards authority											
(g) Tolerance											

Obviously, the scoring will be based on the personal judgement of the selectors. However, where the final selection is carried out by a committee each member can be invited to place his or her score on each of the characteristics listed. An average score can subsequently be calculated so as to reach a 'jury of selectors' opinion' score. The maximum score is 70. This is reserved for the Lord, who could create the world in six days. For the rest of us, the following scores should apply:

over 60	A rare species. Almost too good to be true.
50–60	Very creative person. Grab him/her.
41–50	Useful to have around during creativity work.
31–40	An acceptable average.
21–30	Worth working on, but will not invent the wheel.
under 20	Lock them up when creative groups are at work.

Answers and explanatory notes to puzzles

Puzzle   **Implications for the creative**

1 *The beauty and the beast*
   One should be able to see   Those who can see both
   both a beautiful woman   pictures simultaneously
   (looking backwards) and an   demonstrate a strong
   old hag (looking sideways/   observing skill and mental
   downwards). Most people   flexibility.
   can see either the one or the
   other.

2 *The awkward treasure box*
   The arrow in the figure   Developing a solution to this
   below shows a possible   problem calls for lateral
   solution.   thinking and a creative mind.

Figure A.   **Solution to the awkward treasure box.**

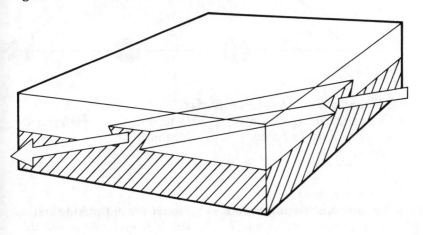

3 *The nine-dots puzzle*
   The figure below provides a   Once again solving this puzzle
   simple answer. Most people   requires lateral thinking and
   who see this puzzle for the   the ability to escape from the
   first time find it difficult   trap of seeking solutions
   inasmuch as they look for a   within the narrowest field of
   solution inside a self-   search.
   imposed square.

Puzzle   **Implications for the creative**

Figure B.   Solution to the nine-dots puzzle.

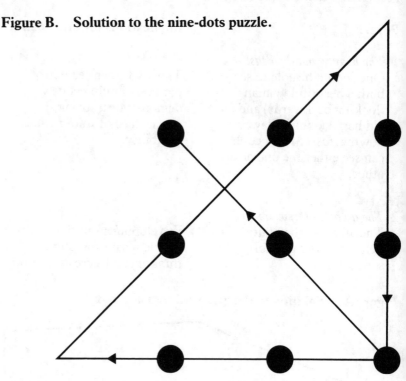

4 *The nine-dots puzzle—harder version*
One can cover all the dots
with one line of a broad
brush.

Lateral thinker, original and
flexible mind.

5 *Equidistant trees*
Planting one tree on the top
of a hill (or in a deep hole)
makes it possible to plant
the other three in a circle,
thus they will be equidistant
from each other. The
problem seems difficult to
solve when one is looking
for a solution in one plane.

Needs lateral thinking and
flexible mind willing and able
to search for solutions outside
the narrow and conventional
frame of reference.

Puzzle	**Implications for the creative**
6 *The letters progression* The letters in the top have straight lines only; those at the bottom have curves. The solution is now obvious.	Good observing skill; flexible and original mind.
7 *Numeric progression* The numbers indicate the number of days in the months. Thus January = 31, February = 28; March = 31 etc.	Anybody who solves this quiz without any prompting demonstrates a creative mind.
8 *Numeric progression (No. 2)* The numbers do not represent an arithmetic, geometric or algebraic progression. The numbers represent the UK coinage before decimalisation. Hence the next number is 30 (half-a-crown).	Same comments as above.
9 *Spot the difference* Figure D is the different one. The linkage is reversed.	Good observing skill—important.
10 *Historical dates* Both 1961 and 1881 read the same if turned upside-down and are read back to front. No other dates between these two years manifest this characteristic. After 1961 the next one is 6009—a long time to wait!	Good lateral thinking.

Puzzle	Implications for the creative
11 *The Rorschach inkblot*	The ability to list many unusual perceptions is a signal of an original and free thinking mind. Good for creativity.
12 *The city gentlemen* They are all of the same height.	Good observing skill (coupled, of course, with an understanding of the rules of perspective—for which no marks are earned!)

Any person who has managed to solve all the exercises without pre-knowledge of the solutions represents a safe pair of hands in any 'Creativity Circle' activities that the firm may decide to mount!

4 Barriers to creativity

As we saw in earlier chapters, creativity and innovation cannot spawn in an organisational environment which is not fully empathetic with the whole notion and process. A firm's top management may ordain 'let us be creative' but it needs a lot more than exhortation from above for something to happen in this regard. Strong emphasis was placed upon the importance of developing an all-embracing climate in which ideas can be generated, communicated, screened and, for a selective few, implemented. Unfortunately, this is easier said than done. One of the most difficult challenges to any organisation is the process of changing a climate or corporate attitudes or, using the expression borrowed earlier, the firm's 'superordinate goals'. It requires an imaginative, consistent, persistent and integrated programme of work aimed at modifying people's personal attitudes and stimulating their enthusiasm. The creative 'glow' must be ignited and kept alight at all times.

In seeking to achieve these aims it is useful to remember that a number of barriers can make the task more difficult. Some of these barriers can be removed; others are an integral part of the firm's history and traditions and therefore can only be circumvented, not removed.

Moreover, a few barriers are simply the result of strategic or structuring steps taken by the firm at some earlier period without paying attention to the impact that they may have on the firm's creativity over the long term. Thus, for instance, one may have good reasons for restructuring the firm's organisation from a decentralised to a centralised pattern. The new structure may prove to be effective and efficient yet, owing to the lengthening of hierarchical lines of communication, far less creative. The people responsible for the design of the new structure may have considered every advantage and disadvantage of the new organisation, with the exception of the impact it may have upon its creativity and innovation. The main message here is that any manager who decides to tinker with the firm's structure must consider very carefully the way the changes envisaged are likely to affect the climate and flow of ideas in the organisation. It is too easy to implement organisational changes without paying heed to this vital issue and inflict long-term damage to the company's ability to innovate.

An appreciation of the existence of barriers and a full understanding of the impact they are likely to have on the firm's ability to innovate are, in themselves, helpful to those responsible for developing a more creative environment in the firm. It is only when one ignores the existence of such barriers to creativity that one is certain to encounter disappointments in seeking to evaluate the benefits of all the work invested in attempting to enhance the firm's creative processes.

The main barriers to creativity are listed and discussed hereunder. The list is not meant to be exhaustive, but is designed to alert the reader to a few major issues to watch when attempting to tackle the question of creativity and innovation in any organisation.

Lack of organisational 'slack'

'Slack' is a fairly emotive word—it smacks of indolence and poor productivity. I have met bosses who regard any employee who sits in his or her office gazing through the window, for however short a time, as parasites. 'What are you doing at the moment?' an old client of mine who believes in the 'management-by-walkabout' concept, keeps asking any of his subordinates who appears to be momentarily daydreaming. 'I am thinking' or 'I am being creative' or 'I am exploring ideas' are the kind of answers that place staff in the proverbial 'dog-house'. I even heard the gentleman in question retort on one occasion: 'Please do all your thinking in your own time!'

The reader may find this attitude reprehensible. However, it is important to remember that it is not as uncommon as you might think. The main difference is that the boss in question expresses his prejudices in an overt fashion. The less insensitive individual communicates the same message in a somewhat more covert manner. Body language and non-verbal signals can communicate the same disapproving message. The fact is that bosses do not like their subordinates to waste their time on non-productive activities. 'Thinking' is deemed in some quarters as a non-productive pastime.

Creativity does require a certain amount of slack in an organisation and the absence thereof can act as a barrier to the successful implementation of the whole process. This can present management with a real problem: if one wants to run a 'tight ship' without any floating spare manpower, one is running the risk of weakening the firm's ability to innovate. Spare manpower or under-utilised resources are anathema to modern management. Nevertheless, firms that have a certain level of slack are in a far better position to generate ideas and identify valuable commercial innovations. Moreover, they are the kind of firms which are well placed, if the need arises, to field a task force to manage and implement a rush of innovative ideas. Companies that have deliberately reduced the available slack in their system can be extremely productive in terms of output per capita, but will probably find that their creative output is fairly limited. This raises two important challenging points:

(*a*) When one undertakes a radical cost-cutting exercise with the view of improving the firm's productivity one must, at the same time, reflect on what impact the reduction in personnel is likely to have on the firm's long-term innovation.

(*b*) During inter-firm competitive analysis one tends to be alarmed by the fact that a competitor has achieved a greater productivity level. This is always a disappointing discovery. However, the shrewd manager should attempt to assemble as much data as possible in order to highlight how far such a lean competitor has left himself sufficient scope and resources to stimulate and manage creativity and innovation issues. It is not unusual for a competitor to improve his short-term performance through a swingeing cut in costs and reduction in manpower, but by doing so emasculate the firm's ability to innovate.

Brave is the manager who recognises this reality and takes steps to ensure that a certain quantum of slack is built into the organisational system which he manages.

In case the reader gets the impression that I am recommending surplus resources in the organisation, I hasten to refute such a conclusion. Whether one likes it or not, every organisation has some slack in its midst. Even 'workaholics' have some slack time in their lives. It all boils down to the effectiveness with which they manage their time. Some people know how to manage their time to such a degree that they always appear to be relaxed and well-organised. Others do not know how to manage their daily routine, with the result that they are in a constant state of flap. The respective output of the two individuals can be similar or, in fact, quite often, the person who manages his or her time well may achieve more than the 'extremely busy' counterpart.

Taking stock as to how company personnel manage their time can be a very valuable exercise. It can pave the way towards the identification of the slack element that the firm requires. If people are taught how to manage their time better and establish a 'pecking order' of priorities they can generate a certain level of spare time for non-operational activities. It is important to appreciate that once some slack is identified one must not be tempted to remove it through additional redundancies. This is a wonderful way to generate an efficiently uncreative organisation. Slack properly channelled and utilised can be a precious commodity in a competitive environment.

In seeking to identify slack among senior levels of management I resort to a simple device: I ask individuals to keep a 'log book' of how they spend their day over a period of, say, one month. The 'log book' need not be detailed but must highlight, in the form of headings, all the activities that each individual undertook during a day's work. It is a useful exercise insofar as (*a*) it makes individuals reflect upon the way they spend their time and (*b*) it helps the external facilitator (myself in this case) to judge whether people spend their days effectively or not. Over a number of years and many assignments I have discovered that this little exercise helps intelligent managers to identify areas of lesser importance which can be delegated to other members of the organisation. In other words it is a device designed to unearth the slack which, I believe, exists in every organisation.

Slack can be formalised by being incorporated in the company's stated corporate philosophy or shared values system. It can be included in the job description of every individual. As part of their desire to encourage members of the organisation to be creative and innovative 3M specify that each individual must devote 15 per cent of his or her time towards the generation of ideas and the management of innovation. At Honda in Japan the firm's message to all employees is conspicuously displayed and, inter alia, it states: 'Respect sound theory, develop fresh ideas and make the most effective use of your time.' The corporate attitude towards the importance of time availability for creativity, in both examples, is made patently clear to everybody around.

'Thinking' and 'doing'

Whilst discussing the question of time and creativity it is perhaps appropriate to mention another point of significance. Every person in an organisation spends time on a plethora of activities. Some of these activities are of a routine nature; others are of an exceptional, ad hoc, deviation from a norm. Moreover, the nature of the tasks vary significantly from level to level. Thus at the strategic level (see Figure 25) the emphasis is, in the main, on THINKING tasks such as: the formulation of mission statements, the search for strategies, the formulation of policies, corporate planning, the management and effective control of resource allocation (in the broad sense). At the other extreme, at the operational level, the day's routine consists, in the main, of DOING activities such as manufacturing, selling, issuing invoices, chasing money etc. In the middle, at the management level, individuals spend their time on a mixture of DOING and THINKING activities. The sad thing is that as people progress through the organisation's hierarchy they do not always recognise the necessity to shift the time allotted from 'doing' to 'thinking' tasks. This is an area in which managers often find difficulties in adjusting their orientation to more senior responsibilities. Operational tasks are practical, positive and usually measurable. Furthermore, they often are more satisfying than the more esoteric tasks which require excessive reflection and intellectual effort. Dealing with a broken-down mill is often more exciting than pondering on whether the firm should have a mill in the future. Buying

Figure 25.   Relationship between 'thinking' and 'doing' activities at various levels of management.

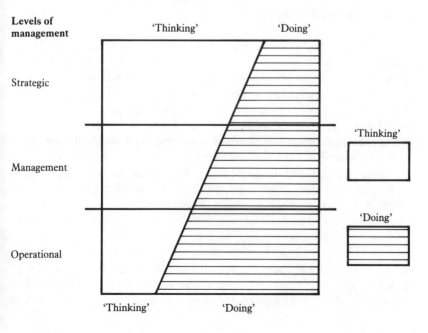

an aircraft is greater fun than contemplating the future direction of an airline.

With this observation in mind it is worth remembering that every manager has a mixture of 'thinking' and 'doing' activities to deal with during his working day. The higher up the organisational ladder one climbs, the greater the proportion of time one needs to allocate to 'thinking' tasks. This is a point which every manager must recognise and accept and deserves greater attention from management development advisers. 'Thinking' at the top is not a redundant activity which can be dispensed with when business is bad. On the contrary, when things are bad every grain of 'thinking' must be harnessed to the full.

Figure 25 attempts to illustrate the point in a diagrammatic form. The relationship between 'thinking' and 'doing' shown in the diagram is purely symbolic. The true ratio may vary from company to company and from industry to industry—it may be 80:20 or 70:30 or even 60:40. What the diagram is trying to convey in an unequivocal way is the fact that 'thinking' is an important part of a manager's job and the more senior he or she become the more they have to think. If 'thinking' is part of the organisation's slack it must be sustained and fostered. The chance of being creative with such slack is much higher than without it.

Bureaucracy

Bureaucracy can be the scourge of creativity and innovation. It can lower the ability of companies to innovate and, indeed, in some countries can act as the dampeners of national creativity.

Companies and nations often introduce a bureaucracy under the misguided notion that it is a way of ensuring administrative and managerial effectiveness and productivity. A bureaucracy starts from the idea that an effective administration must have clear procedures, coupled with the appropriate forms, to handle every conceivable activity and/or eventuality. In a national context, there is some attraction to the concept that the administration of the country's institutions is capable of dealing with every conceivable eventuality in a methodical fashion. It is good to know that a procedure exists for every imaginable or unimaginable event.

Unfortunately, bureaucratic systems often tend to become the end rather than the means of an administrative infrastructure. Most readers can probably recount endless episodes in which they encountered the cold wall of heartless bureaucratic procedures. The

sad truth is that bureaucratic constraints are not the sole prerogative of large organisations or governmental bodies. Small firms can
easily fall into the same trap. I recently had occasion to contact a
very small firm of solicitors who had worked for me on various
assignments. I could not remember the name of the person who had
dealt with me on a number of occasions. The receptionist insisted
that without the 'Reference Code Number' shown on each letter it
would not be possible to trace the name of the person in question.
The firm has two partners and three clerks!

Another episode that sticks in my memory relates to a story that
was reported on television a short while ago. A lady wanted to buy
two bananas in a well-known multiple store. It was a Saturday after-
noon, only a short time before the store was due to close for the
weekend. The store is known for its excellent merchandise and
their normal habit is to get rid of all perishable goods before closing
for the weekend. The lady found two loose bananas on the almost
empty shelf. The store refused to sell her two loose bananas. The
reasons given were: 'we only sell bananas in bunches—we would
not know how to price two loose bananas. We are not allowed to sell
loose items.'. The story was reported on a prestigious television
programme to the firm's enormous embarrassment. No excuse can
justify this gaffe. The only explanation is that the firm has allowed
its bureaucracy to get the better of its personnel's ability and desire
to respond to a customer's special needs in a flexible and creative
manner.

Bureaucracy is the antithesis of flexibility and the latter is an
integral part of being creative. It is strongly recommended that
firms 'audit' their bureaucratic procedures with the view of assess-
ing what impact they have on people's willingness to be creative.
With the best intentions in the world one cannot expect individuals
to generate ideas which fly in the face of procedures that are
accepted as immutable. The only hopeful point to make in this connection is that top management, either in corporate or in governmental environments, can take steps to neutralise the effect of
bureaucracy upon the organisation's ability to become more creative. However, such steps must be clear and positive.

(a) Petty, irrelevant or inexplicable bits of bureaucracy must be
    eliminated;

(b) The overriding role of innovation must be 'promoted' at all
    levels. In other words, specific edicts explaining the kind of
    circumstances in which creative behaviour must override
    administrative rules must be spelt out in unequivocal terms.

(c)   The rationale for procedures must be reviewed at regular intervals. Over the years bureaucratic instruments tend to grow in layers. A keen administrator develops a procedure without removing the previous one and so it goes on. A periodic clean-up can help to make the bureaucracy more manageable and more palatable to those who have to cope with it.

In many companies bureaucracy is a way of life, a corporate ethos. Company personnel come to accept petty rules and regulations as a normal routine and sometimes even enjoy the process of complying with such procedures. In such circumstances it is difficult to see how the introduction of creative activities can succeed. One comes across companies with good intentions who set up 'Creativity Circles' or 'Innovation Groups' or 'Think Tanks' aimed at (a) improving the firm's climate for creativity and (b) generating ideas in response to identified problems or exploring new directions for the firm. Unfortunately, in some cases one discovers that the whole exercise is futile because the participants are shackled by an insatiable urge to 'keep books', 'fill forms', 'maintain diaries', 'circulate memos', etc. The creative 'glow' soon departs from such well-intentioned gatherings.

Bureaucracy can act as a severe barrier to the development of a more creative organisation. If management truly desires to improve the creativity and innovation of the firm it must, at the same time, take steps to 'clip the wings' of the bureaucratic machine.

The structure

It is not always appreciated that the way the company is organised can have a marked impact on the organisation's overall creativity. It would be interesting to ask those managers who indulge in frequent structure changes how much thought they have given to the way the new structures may affect the quality and quantity of creativity in their respective firms. This is a question which is often overlooked by people undertaking organisation development activities.

Some structures are more empathetic to creative activities than others. It is difficult to state categorically what kind of structure is ideal in this regard. After all, when an organisational pattern is established there are many conflicting needs which the structure is seeking to meet. The need to provide an organisational environment in which creativity and innovation can thrive is only one of them, albeit a vitally important one. Nevertheless, my deeply-felt advice to top management is that in no circumstances should they authorise structural changes until (a) the impact of such changes on the firm's ability to innovate has been thoroughly explored and (*b*) steps to mitigate an undesirable impact of such changes on creativity in general have been planned. Inevitably, there are occasions when the commercial realities of the firm dictate a change in structure. The new structure may not be the ideal one for a 'creativity-friendly' climate. In such circumstances it is particularly important that deliberate steps are taken to neutralise the effect that the new structure is likely to have on creativity.

The following example may illustrate the point. Experience has shown that in a multinational company a decentralised structure can normally produce, at least in parts of the organisation, a greater level of creativity. The main reasons are: (*a*) smaller national units are more self-contained and are therefore better able to communicate and respond to ideas; (*b*) the fact that such units are responsible for their own destiny acts as a spur to innovation; and (*c*) the relative independence of decentralised operating units cushions them from the debilitating impact of the bureaucracy of a giant organisation.

Now let us assume that the example relates to a multinational car manufacturer like Ford Motor or General Motors. During the last few years all major car manufacturers have learnt an important and bitter lesson: enormous benefits can be derived from globalising and standardising product policies. The so-called 'world car' is part of every large manufacturer's product strategy. Many significant strategic reasons can be put forward in justification of such a route. Having said all this, it is fairly obvious that in companies that strive to standardise their products on a global scale the propensity is to move the structure towards a more centralised pattern. Major strategic decisions are taken in a central location—at the nerve-centre of the enterprise—whereas operational activities are carried out in national outposts. The exigencies of a competitive world propel the firm towards a centralisation policy especially in relation to strategic planning and decision-making. All this is fine and understandable but, at the same time, it is important to recognise that such moves can weaken the free communication of ideas among national companies or between the outposts and the centre. The motivation to innovate can suffer a severe set-back. Once top management appreciates this risk they can go out of their way to take steps to remedy the situation. Without such corrective measures existing patterns of creativity in the firm can easily atrophy.

Small firms seldom have major organisational problems. The firm can function extremely well without a formal structure. The boss knows precisely what is going on in every function of the enterprise and can respond to the need to guide or take decisions in a pragmatic fashion. In theory this kind of informal relationship among people is ideal for establishing a climate in which creativity can thrive. Provided the boss has the right 'attitude spectrum' towards other people's ideas the company can benefit from a relaxed and informal flow of ideas and the implementation of innovations.

The danger point for small firms occurs when they have grown to the point when top management is tempted to establish the first formal structure. This is the point at which the first seeds of the creativity-destruction process are sown. Whichever style of structure one chooses one must consider the advantages and disadvantages of each in relation to the continued creativity welfare of the firm. Thus if one chooses a product-orientated structure the risk is that communication among the various product groupings will gradually erode to the point that little exchange of ideas will take place among them. If one chooses a functional structure the risk is that the cross-fertilisation of ideas among functions will ebb away. The almost natural conflict that often develops between, say, marketing and production will act as a barrier to creativity. If one opts for a geographical structure there is a pretty good chance that the flow of ideas among the regions will cease once the regional structure is fully operational.

The message to the senior managers of small firms who are about to develop a formal structure is that, when choosing a structure, favour the one that will be supportive and empathetic to the continued creativity and innovation processes of the firm. It is not possible to go beyond such a statement because the ultimate choice of a structure depends on a myriad of factors beyond the scope of this book. However, it is fair to say that when the choice is between two or more equally attractive structures the one that will facilitate the continued 'glow' is the one to go for.

At the other extreme, one can explore the problems associated with the management of innovation in multinational companies. Their structures can have a marked effect on the level of creativity and innovation which they manage to promulgate in their respective firms.

Companies operating on an international scale fall into three main organisational patterns:

(*a*) 'macropyramid' structure;

(*b*) 'umbrella' structure;

(*c*) international conglomerate.

The macropyramid structure (Figure A)

This is an organisation which has opted for a centralised approach to the management of its affairs. It has a well-defined strategic focal point and most important strategic decisions are taken at the centre. Whilst most managerial and operational activities take place in the various countries in which the firm has a base most strategic decisions, corporate plans and major policy matters emanate from the central 'nerve centre', wherever it may be located.

Figure A.   Macropyramid.

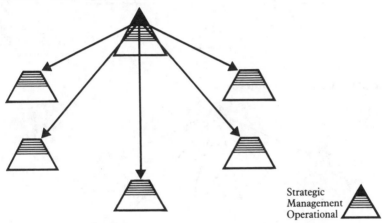

Strategic
Management
Operational

The umbrella structure (Figure B)

This structure is based on the recognition that markets and countries differ and should therefore be approached with a local and semi-autonomous style of management. Whilst some 'nerve centre' still exists, its role and power are often constrained by the freedom of action that the strategic and managerial levels of the subsidiaries abroad enjoy. The 'centre' monitors and controls performance and also provides an 'umbrella' of central service departments which are available to all those units that wish to use them.

The international conglomerate (Figure C)

This is an organisation that encompasses a number of diverse activities with little 'synergy' between them. It often embraces multi-national, multi-market, multi-product and possibly multi-

Figure B.   Umbrella.

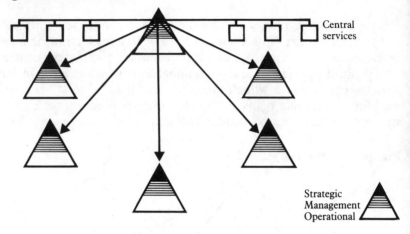

Figure C.   Conglomerate.

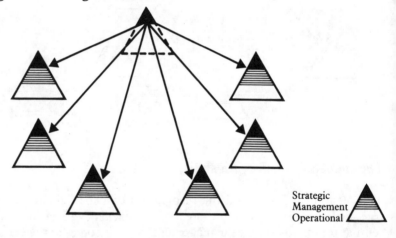

technology operations. The connecting link between the units is very often simply a financial one. All that the 'centre' expects from the various operating units is a certain level of profits and/or return on investment and cash flow. The rest is left to the managers of the individual businesses. To that extent each business has its own fully-fledged structure with all the appropriate levels of management. The 'centre' can be described as a 'strategic' level without a body. The whole empire tends to be managed through rigorous financial controls.

These are simple conceptual models of the way international companies are organised. In practice few companies adhere to any of these pure models—a hybrid compromise among the various extremities is normally reached. Nevertheless, if one accepts that these pure models exist one can explore the barriers that each places in the path of the successful development of corporate creativity and innovation.

In a macropyramid structure, creativity and innovation tend to suffer from:

(a) The remoteness of the 'bosses' from the field. Good ideas generated in some distant land have little chance of filtering through to the people who matter.

(b) People at the 'centre' often adopt the so-called 'not invented here' resistance to ideas from subsidiaries abroad (or even at home).

(c) The motivation to generate ideas and innovate gradually disappears. A 'why bother?' attitude sets in.

Clearly, the company can neutralise all these barriers, but positive steps to do so must be developed in an imaginative and integrated way. Without such steps the risk is that the company will gradually starve itself of ideas from the field. This is particularly regrettable, bearing in mind that the scooping of ideas from distant and heterogeneous markets can be the life-blood of any organisation.

Turning now to the umbrella structure, one needs to consider the following problems and opportunities:

(a) Creativity and innovation can exist quite happily in specific operating units. The fact that they are self-contained and fairly autonomous augurs well for a creative existence. The quality and intensity of creative thought and activity will depend on the individual managers of each unit. In other words some units will be more innovative than others.

(b) The cross-fertilisation of ideas and innovations among operating units is likely to be a problem. Unless specific steps are taken to improve the infrastructure for communicating ideas people will keep their successes 'close to their chests'.

(c) Innovations are likely to be market-orientated especially in relation to problems associated with product design and quality. These will normally be dealt with in response to local needs rather than international needs. This in turn often means that products will become more and more differentiated from country to country. Good for the customers but not always good for the overall corporation.

Regrettably talking about creativity in 'conglomerates' is often like a red rag to a bull. The last time I asked the Chairman of a large conglomerate what steps he was taking towards stimulating creativity in his group of companies he gave me a simple answer: 'managers who make money for us are creative; those who don't are not'. A pretty simple formula. Yet I would like to know how much better they could all do if they found a way of communicating creative ideas and innovations throughout the complex enterprise.

Understanding the impact of structures on the creative process is a valuable input to the successful organisation development task. Personnel and management development people must be consulted about the positive and negative influences that a new structure can have on the creative processes in the firm before a new organisation is finalised. Moreover, those responsible for planning and organising the development and training activities of the company must consider what educational steps can be undertaken in order to reduce the impact that a new organisation can have on the creative output of the team in its new structure.

Poor lateral communication

In the chapter dealing with the 'Creative Organisation' it was emphasised that an effective communication system is an essential ingredient for creativity in an organisation. Steps for improving the communication of ideas among functions, operating units and market environments were explored. Unfortunately, it was assumed throughout our discussion of the subject that (*a*) the company is capable of improving its communication system, and (*b*) the goodwill to ameliorate communication among people, departments and functions is in existence.

In reality, many organisational environments exist in which the lack of communication is almost man-made. The desire to communicate has been mutilated over a long period through a number of behavioural misfeasances perpetrated from the 'top'. Communication is a voluntary act among people who share goals, interests and values. It is based on an open-hearted and open-minded mutual respect among members of an organisation who believe that the transmission and receiving of data, information or ideas is for the common good. Effective communication in a company is a manifestation of a co-operative and purposeful group of people at work. Poor communication, on the other hand, is often a sign of an unco-operative, suspicious, insecure and ill-motivated bunch of individuals. At the risk of almost stating the obvious: in the former type of company creativity can flourish; in the latter the chances are very low.

If one seeks to improve the creativity and innovation activities and processes of a firm it is important that an internal 'communication audit' is undertaken. It may help matters if one knows precisely how effective or ineffective the internal communication system is and what the blockages are. It is almost futile to attempt to improve the innovative output of a firm when the communication system is hopelessly defective. At the same time it is difficult to ameliorate the communication system if one does not fully understand the overt or covert reasons for such a shortcoming. A thorough 'audit' of the firm's communication should highlight the reasons for such a weakness and also reveal the obstacles that must be overcome before corrective measures can be successfully undertaken.

Internal, as against external, communication encompasses the flow of information and ideas, (a) vertically, from the top of the organisation downwards and from the bottom/upwards, and (b) laterally, among departments, functions and operating units (at home and abroad). Clearly poor communication in any direction is an obstacle to creativity. However, it is the lateral communication which is the main barrier to corporate creativity. I recently advised an electronics company with manufacturing units in the US and in the UK. The products they market and manufacture are almost identical. The problems they have encountered during the development of the products and manufacturing process have been similar. Yet solutions worked out in the UK have not been communicated to the US company and vice versa. The managers of the two units meet fairly frequently and on the face of things get on reasonably well, however, as far as solutions to problems and ideas are concerned a 'wall of silence' exists between them. The main reason for this unhelpful lateral communication is the fact that the boss has developed a competitive 'divide and rule' policy throughout the firm. Individual success is rewarded and the only way he measures success is on the basis of a comparative 'hit parade' among the various profit centres. The last thing the UK managers want to see is an improved performance in the US company! It may sound shocking, but in reality such a situation is not so rare. Wherever human beings are being manipulated by unscrupulous or unintelligent superiors, the risk is that lateral communication suffers. The main victim of such situations is the organisation's creativity and ultimately its innovation.

Lateral communication can be damaged by a number of pressures.

(*a*) The manipulative practices of top management. It is worth recalling that an effective communication system is an integral part of the firm's inventory of attitudes. To want to communicate is part of the organisation's 'shared values' system. If the boss himself is reluctant to communicate or holds information back from his colleagues, the message transmitted to the firm is loud and clear: 'I do not believe that effective communication is an important part of our corporate attitudes . . . ' Obviously communication will suffer from such an example.

(*b*) Conflict of objectives. The objectives of the various functions and/or departments can be in a state of conflict thus creating an atmosphere in which people do not wish to communicate. If, for example, the distribution department is charged with the task of reducing inventory by 30 per cent and the marketing department has adopted an objective of shortening delivery time, the two departments are on a collision course which is unlikely to enhance communication among them. Similarly, if the controller's department takes steps to reduce outstanding debts and upsets the sales department in the process, communication between them is sure to suffer.

(*c*) Heterogeneity of attitudes. One of the tasks of good management is to ensure that members of the team develop a cluster of cohesive attitudes. When every member of an organisation believes in the same values and shares the same attitudes there is a strong probability that they will also communicate well with each other. 'When everybody in a congregation sings from the same hymn sheet' communication among them is likely to be effective. An organisation may consist of a diversity of people from a variety of educational and cultural backgrounds, possibly from different countries, with each individual manifesting different attitudes to life, to work and to colleagues. It seems fairly obvious that one of the penalties will be poor lateral communication. This is particularly regrettable inasmuch as heterogeneity of backgrounds can be a powerful source of many valuable ideas. However, such a potential strength can only be exploited if steps are taken to remove the barrier to communication that such a heterogeneity of attitudes creates in its wake.

(*d*) Lack of training. Poor communication may simply stem from the fact that the people in the organisation have not been alerted to the importance of communication and the value which an effective system can impart to the firm. Communication is one of the skills that an effective manager requires. Whilst anybody with commonsense recognises that it is not possible to perform one's job successfully without the cross-fertilisation of data, information and ideas, the subject must form part of training and development work at one stage or another in a person's career, and normally the earlier the better.

The 'imported talent' syndrome

A serious barrier to the development of a climate in which creativity can develop and flourish is the notion that progress and innovation can only be achieved through the importation of external talent. It is not uncommon for top management to convey the feeling, in an expressed or implied way, that people in the firm are incapable of being innovative and that only the injection of fresh blood can remedy the situation. New managers, consultants, other experts are brought into the organisation at frequent intervals to underpin existing resources. The impact on people's ability or willingness to innovate can be disastrous for two main reasons:

(*a*) Newcomers come and go and the 'old guard' takes the view that it is safer to close the hatches down and wait for the storm to subside. Meanwhile nobody wants to take any risks. 'Let the new boys stick their necks out' is the motto of the day.

(*b*) The full rigours of 'transactional analysis' take their toll: when people are treated as rats they tend to behave in that fashion; when people are constantly being branded as uncreative they respond by behaving in an uncreative way.

Altogether, the notion that the only creative individuals are the ones that exist outside the organisation is not only humiliating for the people in the firm, it also helps to demolish their confidence and motivation.

'Bean-counting'

This is an uncharitable description of the way accountants and controllers often behave in an organisation. Nobody disputes that they have a vital role to play in every company. They are the custodians of the way funds are managed, costs contained, profits produced and financial resources allocated and controlled. Few companies have achieved excellence without a strong and prudent control function.

At the same time, it is not unusual for people belonging to this function to be in a state of semi-conflict with members of other departments. The fact that one's plans, decisions and activities are constantly analysed and evaluated in financial terms is not always conducive to mutual affection. The accountants have a job to do and if they do it well they are bound to generate a certain level of unpopularity. This is understandable and, in fact, in many respects desirable. Controlled conflict of this nature is part of the 'checks and balances' that ensures that the husbandry of the firm's resources is managed in an optimum fashion. Accountants are normally asked to behave in a sensitive and circumspect manner towards their peers from other departments and if they are wise they adhere to such norms of behaviour. It all helps to keep the potential conflict within bounds.

The problem arises when the firm is run by accountants who insist on translating every item of expenditure, and in every department, into monetary cost-benefit terms. 'What did you do last week to produce profits for the company?' is a question that a Chairman of a well-known company used to ask every manager in sight, including people responsible for staff functions. 'Every department must become a profit centre, including the R & D department and the legal department' is the opinion of another chief executive/ accountant of a large public company.

Such remarks are fine if the main objective of the firm is to improve the profitability of the enterprise. In certain circumstances it may be the only sensible mission to have. However, in the context of this book it must be emphasised that the inflexible 'bean-counting' approach is not a helpful one for stimulating the creative process. Creativity and innovation demand a certain level of intellectual adventure and financial risk. Innovation, by definition, seeks to mitigate the risk and ensure that selected activities will entail 'doing things differently, better, cheaper or more aesthetically.' However, when those responsible for the purse-strings breathe down one's neck it is difficult to be creative. I have seen excellent projects flounder because the 'bean-counters' kept counting beans when the project needed the full support and backing of the firm's total resources. 'Are you making profits?' the boss/accountant kept asking the project team literally a few days after the project, which entailed a revolutionary concept in logistics was launched!

A number of barriers in the path of a successful implementation of creativity and innovation in an organisation have been explored. Understanding these barriers is a valuable input to the ability to overcome them.

5 From 'quality circles' to 'creativity circles'

Quality circles are not new. They have been in existence in many manufacturing companies throughout the world for quite a few years. They have triggered the imagination of the industrial community, especially in the more advanced industrial nations, for over two decades. The falling levels of productivity in most Western countries have contrasted sharply with Japan's remarkable success in improving both the quality and quantity of its industrial output. The secret of this success has been attributed to a great extent to the most imaginative establishment of a widely spread system of 'quality control circles' which have become the driving force for the improvement of industrial quality and quantity among companies that have adopted such innovative methods.

'Improved quality' and 'greater quantity' are the two expressions that describe the underlying aims of the quality circles movement. 'Better', 'cheaper', 'more aesthetic' are among the aims of 'innovation' as defined earlier. The parallel between the activities of the quality circles and the much broader role of innovation is obvious and the potential synergy between the two strands must be explored in some depth. The history of the quality circles movement is worth exploring as it provides a most valuable lesson as to how creativity can be developed and fostered in a corporate climate.

My personal opinion is that quality circles represent only a partial attempt at institutionalising corporate creativity and innovation. On the whole these circles, in most companies, have operated within a fairly narrow remit. Their main objectives and activities have tended to place a heavy emphasis upon manufacturing issues. Clearly these were the problems of the seventies and early eighties. Once quality and productivity problems have been reduced or even obliterated many quality circles have seen their roles narrowed to routine problem-solving sessions. This is regrettable because the whole notion of quality circles lends itself to a much wider scope of strategic and functional excellence searching activities. It is not difficult to produce a whole list of areas which could benefit from the 'quality circles' approach, for example:

— searching for and selecting a corporate strategy;
— developing a sustainable competitive advantage;
— developing new and better marketing strategies;
— selecting new and better brand names and/or a name for the company itself;
— planning for better and/or cheaper mass-training systems;
— identifying more effective distribution system;
— designing more attractive and more effective packaging;
— enhancing and communicating the firm's corporate image;
— the successful placing of a company's shares with under-writers.

Or, at a much more operational level:

— improving the quality of the firm's switchboard;
— planning for a more welcoming reception area;
— landscaping the offices so as to improve morale and general feeling of well-being.

These are just a few challenges—one could list others ad infinitum. But how many members of the quality circles movement could claim that their respective circles have actually dealt with such challenges? It is fair to say that champions of the quality circle concept will assert that there is no reason to confine the whole approach within the narrow orbit of manufacturing quality and productivity. Indeed, experts in the field would suggest that the movement has a much wider role to play in the life of an organisation and can offer a most valuable 'infrastructure' for total problem-solving, innovation and communication procedures. This is a most attractive notion, but few companies have managed to escape from the narrow field of work practices associated with the present modus operandi of quality circles. In fact the very name often acts as an intellectual barrier to the broadening of the creative scope of the teams in their circles.

My purpose here is to spur companies which have quality circles to reflect upon the whole subject and try to galvanise them into transforming existing quality circles, wherever they may be located, into task-forces with much broader terms of reference in the life of their respective firms. 'Quality' means different things to different people. Redefining 'quality' to include general excellence in whatever a firm seeks to achieve takes us into richer and more fertile pastures.

The history of 'quality circles'

'Quality Control Circles', the forerunners of the wider 'Quality Circles', started life in Japan in the early fifties. Ironically enough the concept was not a Japanese invention. It emerged from the work of two well-known American academics Dr W E Deming and Dr J M Juran, whose influence had caught the imagination of Japanese management. Japanese industry took to the quality control circle concept like fish to water: from small beginnings (23 circles in 1962) it grew to a massive movement (over 115,000 circles in 1980). In fact, it is estimated that one out of every eight Japanese employees is participating in a circle! Moreover, nobody can deny that the impact of these circles on Japanese industry has been most remarkable.

Quality circles represent an institutionalised and participative mechanism for diagnosing and solving productivity and quality problems. The process is centred around a small group of voluntary members who meet at regular intervals in order to:

(*a*)   identify, diagnose and solve problems; and

(*b*)   improve communication and commitment and quality among the various parts of the organisation which are responsible for productivity and/or quality.

Typically circles consist of a leader and eight to ten employees from a given work area. The group may be smaller or larger—the size of the teams depends on the personal preference and experience of the leaders and/or facilitators. Meetings take place at regular intervals, typically one or two hours per week.

The routine activities of circles follow the following cycle.

(*a*)   Circles select their own problems for analysis with the view to identifying causes or sub-causes. Alternatively, the circles respond to problems submitted to them by other parts of the firm;

(*b*)   Solutions to problems and/or removal of causes are generated and evaluated.

(*c*)   'Best' solutions are selected and action plans developed and communicated.

(*d*)   Solutions are implemented.

(*e*) Circles check that problems have been eliminated or solved.

(*f*) The process of tackling the next problem commences.

The quality circle took a fairly long time to emerge in the United States in spite of its original American parentage. It was not until 1974 that Lockheed and Honeywell adopted the full 'QC' approach. Since then, hundreds of companies in a variety of industries, including service organisations, have accepted the whole idea.

As one would expect, each company has developed its own approach to quality circles. Whilst a plethora of training programmes and consultancy services on the subject can be obtained, it is only right that each organisation develops its own system and procedures. It is not intended here to indulge in a detailed description of the various approaches to the subject, nor to the listing of successes and failures. The subject has been tackled by many authors in excellent textbooks. Like most managerial techniques, the subject is currently the subject of controversy between its faithful supporters and non-believing detractors. As long as the debate is constructive a useful evaluation of the quality circle movement can be attained.

Looking at it in the much broader perspective of innovation the following benefits can be ascribed to the quality circles concept:

(*a*) they have helped to create a climate in which the search for quality and productivity excellence have been greatly enhanced;

(*b*) they have increased employee motivation and morale;

(*c*) they have improved communication among employees, functions, management and, in some companies, with unions;

(*d*) they have acted as a valuable catalyst in enhancing managerial skills through the intensive training involved and practical experience gained during the problem-solving exercises;

(*e*) in many instances, they have helped to improve financial performance.

From quality circles to creativity circles

This is a good moment to stop and reflect upon what has just been said. If one were to refer throughout to 'creativity circles' instead of 'quality circles', everything that has been said still makes sense. The whole modus operandi, the structure of the terms and the sub-routines are perfectly appropriate to the more ambitious and all-embracing task of responding to the firm's need to innovate.

Two main conclusions can be drawn from this.

(*a*) Firms that have successfully adopted the quality circles concept are in a good position to extend the system to encompass the total creativity and innovation cycle by turning their circles into creativity circles. This will mean that they will be able to exploit all the development and training work invested so far in a much more comprehensive way.

(*b*) Firms that wish to develop creativity circles from scratch can derive many lessons from the experience of organisations that have been operating quality circles. Clearly, one can learn from both successes and failures in this regard.

The collective experience in this field is vast and the literature extensive. The creative reader who bothers to probe into the experience that companies have had with quality circles can derive a wealth of ideas as to how to organise and develop a fruitful network of creativity circles. The bibliography provided at the end of this book incorporates a number of books on the subject of quality circles. Anybody entrusted with the task of having to develop a programme of work aimed at introducing a fully fledged creativity and innovation system in an organisation would be well advised to study the literature with some care. Valuable lessons can be extracted from such an analysis.

Quality circles at work

At the risk of repeating what has already been said it is worthwhile looking at the components of the quality circle concept in greater depth and exploring the practical aspects of the whole process.

Quality Circles were defined as:

'Small groups of company personnel who do the same or similar work, voluntarily meeting together at regular intervals, for about one hour per week in paid time, usually under the leadership of their own supervisor, and trained to identify, analyse and solve some of the problems in their work, presenting solutions to management and, where possible, implementing such solutions themselves'.

Reviewing each element of this definition in some detail will help to grasp the overall purpose and workings of the circles .

'Small groups'

Experts in the field seem to be somewhat divided as to the exact meaning of the word 'small'. Groups as small as three and as large as 12 have been used successfully. On the whole, larger groups, say of eight upwards, appear to be popular inasmuch as one can get a broader range of experience and creative input from such groups. However, experience has shown that the exact size of the groups should be left to the decision of the group leaders and the facilitators. Personal choice has to play an important role in this regard. The important point is that groups should not be so large (in excess of 12) that proceedings become fraught with inter-personal communication problems.

At the same time it is appropriate to mention that sometimes one has to content oneself with small groups because the area of work which the circle is seeking to serve is so small that it is difficult to field more than a small team. Moreover, where the team consists of very experienced and very enthusiastic quality circle members, a small group can perform wonders.

'Same or similar work'

Experience has shown that people from the same work environment and with fairly similar work experience are able to communicate effectively during problem-solving activities, especially when the problems relate to their specific area of operation.

Team members who come from a heterogeneous range of disciplines and/or work areas are less likely to speak the same work language and often find it difficult to identify projects of interest to all members of the team.

Obviously when specific expertise is required one can attach an external resource from outside the work area with the view of providing the appropriate help and advice. Thus if the problem relates to the need to improve the quality of the packaging of tomato ketchup, if the team requires special knowledge about plastics, an expert from the field can be invited to participate in the group proceedings.

'Voluntarily'

One of the major characteristics of quality circles is the fact that participation is a voluntary activity. Forcing people to join is contrary to the whole spirit of the concept. People join a circle because they want to join it and are stimulated by its role and objectives. The simple psychology is that people who are ordered to participate in such an activity are less likely to develop the enthusiasm and urgency which the quality circle concept envisages. Obviously, in the first place when the whole system is being established members of the company will be invited to join. However, the voluntariness of participation must be emphasised and no stigma should be ascribed to somebody who decides not to join. The ideal situation occurs when members of the organisation express their desire to join a circle because they have heard how interesting and useful such activities are.

One important implication of the voluntary nature of team participation is that an individual can choose to leave a circle without criticism or pressure. It may be appropriate for the group leader to enquire about the reasons for this departure, but only in order to derive some motivational lessons for the future effectiveness of the group.

'Meeting together at regular intervals'

The essence of quality circles is that meetings should take place at regular intervals rather than in a spasmodic fashion. The regular nature of the meetings imparts to the whole concept a certain level of ritualistic dedication. The meetings can be short, say one hour, but the regularity is important. A friend of mine refers to these meetings as the 'Friday morning prayers'. When meetings are not held at regular intervals it is quite easy for members of the team to find excuses for postponing them and gradually the whole system tends to fizzle out. Regularity provides a sense of urgency and commitment.

'In paid time'

The underlying meaning of this phrase is that participants in quality circles must not expect additional financial rewards for attending meetings. It is part of their job and an integral part of their personal commitment to the success of the company. Naturally, if the members of the team comprise of individuals who span different shifts, overtime payment may be involved for those attending outside their regular shift time. However, the participation is still done in company 'paid time'.

It is appropriate to mention in this connection the question of personal rewards. This subject has evoked lengthy discussions among experts in the field. The consensus in this regard is that financial rewards are totally inappropriate. The greatest reward that participants will receive is the realisation that they have made an important contribution to the success of their organisation. The whole rationale of the quality circles is based on the philosophy that people who work for a firm are totally committed to its success and excellence and are willing to harness their personal creativity towards solving problems that impede its continued success. Having helped to achieve such an objective is an adequate reward. Obviously, non-financial rewards such as award certificates, achievement announcements, personal gifts from the boss or award medals are perfectly legitimate items. Indeed, it is normally felt that a vital aspect of the quality circles programme is the personal commitment and involvement of top management in recognising circle achievements.

'Under the leadership of their own supervisor'

This is another sensitive item which has preoccupied the quality circle movement. A circle needs a leader who is responsible for conducting meetings and coordinating the activities of the individual circle. In most cases, under the supervision of a facilitator, the leader conducts the training of circle members to ensure that they are knowledgeable in the various methods of identifying, analysing and resolving problems brought before them.

At the same time it is important to remember that the leader's role is not a hierarchical one. He or she 'leads' the proceedings in the sense that they provide the focal point for group discussions and activities. Is it imperative for the leadership to be assumed by the supervisor? In theory the answer must be in the negative. On the other hand, one must recognise the behavioural implications: the supervisor is a person who can help 'things to happen' and his support, commitment and dedication can be of great help in creating an effective circle. To that extent the general feeling has been that the supervisor of the group who does the same or similar work is a useful person to act as the circle's leader.

'Identify, analyse and solve some of the problems in their work'

This phrase covers the salient ingredients of the quality circles' activities. Each component deserves a brief exploration:

(a) *Identify problems.* The choice of problems for analysis is not as easy as it may sound. A group of people invited to identify problems for analysis can generate a large number of problems. At the same time one has to recognise that:

   (i) A distinction has to be drawn between problems and symptoms. Removing symptoms does not solve the actual problem. It is important that a thorough cause-and-effect analysis is undertaken.

   (ii) Problems can be large and small. Clearly, it is important that larger problems receive more attention than small ones.

   (iii) Problems may require urgent attention or be less urgent. Once again in selecting a problem for analysis the more urgent ones deserve priority attention. The slight dilemma is that in the early stages of a circle's life it is wise to select simple problems inasmuch as the group needs to chalk up a few successes in order to enhance the image of the circle and boost its own confidence.

Various simple problem-selection methods are in existence to help the circle to choose the most appropriate problem for attention.

Before undertaking any problem-solving discussions and/or exercises it is vital that a clearly-defined problem statement is reached. The wording must be succinct and meaningful. Vague terms such as poor productivity is less meaningful than output per worker in the tool room is 20% less than identical units in a competitor's plant.

(b) *Analyse problems.* At this point the circle is ready to explore the true causes of the problem by using a number of helpful techniques which will be discussed in subsequent chapters. Data pertaining to the various causes is collected and considered carefully.

(c) *Solve problems.* The team is now ready to commence generating ideas aimed at solving the problems defined and remove the causes that are responsible for the existence of the problem. The kind of techniques which are normally used in generating ideas in any creativity session are extensively used in quality circles as well. Brainstorming, force-field analysis, synectics, spider diagrams are well known methods used both in creative sessions and also in quality circles and will be discussed in some depth in subsequent chapters.

'Presenting solutions to management'

In most cases quality circles must 'sell' their solutions and recommendations to management before they can be implemented. In a few instances all that is required is a written report or for the leader to talk to the appropriate manager in charge of the unit whose problem the circle is attempting to solve. However, in most cases a more formal presentation to management is to be preferred. It is worth remembering that the importance of the presentation is multifold:

(*a*) it is an 'image-building' tool for the circle itself;

(*b*) it can help to gain approval of the circle and its programme of work;

(*c*) it can provide a forum for a thorough understanding of the solution that the circle is recommending and full ventilation of the supportive evidence;

(*d*) it can gain future cooperation from management.

In other words the presentation is a valuable stage in the activities of the quality circle and full attention must be devoted to the quality of the presentation itself. If necessary, the training of the teams can include a short module on effective presentation techniques.

'Implementation'

The circle is normally expected to develop an implementation plan in writing and submit its details during the formal presentation. The plan should show that the circle has thoroughly evaluated the solution, include a schedule for implementation, also highlight benefits and follow-up actions which may be needed. Moreover the plan should contain dates for completion of each action and list the persons responsible for implementing them.

Once approval is gained from management the implementation plan can be put into effect.

Creativity circles

The benefits that quality circles have brought to companies that have championed them are equally germane to those companies which decide to introduce the much broader concept of creativity circles. Nevertheless, we are not talking about a cosmetic change of name only—creativity circles could encompass a much wider range of terms of reference and activities.

Before proceeding to highlight the potential differences between quality circles and creativity circles it is important to recall that creativity (and its ultimate result: innovation) can take one of three forms:

(*a*)   normative creativity;

(*b*)   exploratory creativity; and

(*c*)   creativity by 'serendipity'.

Normative creativity

In simple terms 'normative creativity' refers to the process of applying creative ideas towards solving a problem. The root of the word is 'norm' which means 'standard quantity to be produced or amount of work to be done'. Thus 'normative' means responding to a defined goal, need, desire or mission. The measure of success or achievement in this respect is when the problem has been solved and innovation attained. 'Creativity by objectives' is another way of describing the process.

Problems can only be solved if their precise nature and causes are known. To that extent groups entrusted with the task of solving problems must devote time towards collecting data, analysing, diagnosing the causes and finally generating ideas likely to solve them. Very often the sheer activity of trying to understand the problem and its underlying causes paves the way towards identifying possible solutions.

If a television set ceases to work it is not possible to repair it until the cause of the problem has been established. It is easy to assume that the problem is associated with a broken tube but the owner of the set will not be too happy if after the replacement of the tube the television is still not functioning. Clearly, the owner or the electrician who tries to repair or replace every component listed in the manual needs his head examined. A careful analysis of 'cause-and-effect' has to be undertaken and only when the real cause has been established and defined the problem-solving process can commence.

A number of valuable tools and techniques designed to assist problem-solvers at work are available. The majority of these tools are well-known in the quality circle fraternity and often used in their activities.

Exploratory creativity

Exploratory creativity occurs when ideas are generated to develop future opportunities which are not necessarily related to known requirements or recognised demand. It attempts to extrapolate from present day knowledge and technology towards a futuristic scenario which may or may not meet future needs. Exploratory creativity highlights opportunities which are not always exploitable in commercial terms. If the management of a bank devotes some 'creativity' time to generate ideas as to the kind of services that the bank may render to its clients in twenty years' time, such an activity can be described as 'exploratory creativity'. It is difficult to measure the quality of the output inasmuch as one is not responding to a specific marketing or technical need. On the other hand, the impact of this type of creative session on an organisation's thinking or over-all direction can be of the highest value. Exploratory creativity can help an organisation to extract itself from a strategic rut in which it has found itself stuck.

Whilst 'normative creativity' can be described as results-orientated, 'exploratory creativity' is opportunity-seeking. The former is deemed successful when problems are solved. The latter can be said to be successful when the mould of present-day thinking has been broken and unorthodox opportunities presented to management. It is only when the best opportunities have been identified, quantified and exploited that innovation can be said to have been attained.

The difference between the two types of creativity described above is quite subtle. The main importance lies in the fact that the techniques used for generating ideas in normative creativity are different from those that one tends to use in exploratory creativity. In the former case, one uses techniques like brainstorming, synectics or trigger sessions. In the latter, one uses morphological analysis, scenario writing or scenario daydreaming. In normative creativity one tries to focus the idea generation activity upon a defined problem. In exploratory creativity one tries to direct the creative process in an outward direction towards a futuristic dream-world with the hope of striking gold at the end of the cycle.

Figure 26 attempts to describe the conceptual difference in the two strands of creativity in a diagrammatic way.

Figure 26.   Normative and exploratory creativity compared.

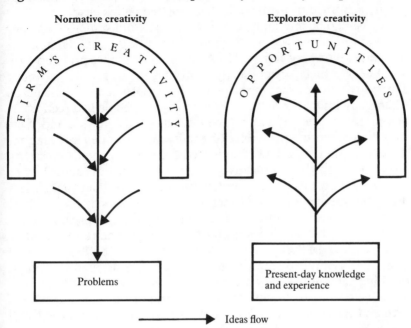

Creativity by serendipity

'Serendip' was the ancient name of Ceylon or Sri Lanka used by Horace Walpole in his fairy-tale 'The Three Princes of Serendip'. The heroes of this book 'were always making discoveries of things they were not in quest of '. They simply floated over the waves of destiny and allowed chance to ordain the events that directed their daily lives. The word 'serendipity' has been introduced into modern use to mean discoveries or events occurring by some happy chance or by accident. Thus creativity and innovation are said to take place by serendipity where the ideas underlying the innovation are discovered by an unexpected accident.

Many famous discoveries and innovations from the annals of human inventiveness represent examples of creativity by serendipity. They all make for interesting reading and amusing if apocryphal story-telling, for example, the story of how Archimedes stumbled upon the notion of water displacement whilst he entered a full bath and watched the water overflow, or how James Watt's invention of the steam engine was based on the accidental observation of a boiling pot, the lid of which kept rising as the steam escaped, or, most famously, that Isaac Newton's discovery of gravity stemmed from an apple that dropped on his head.

One can go on and on recounting stories of innovations by serendipity, but in what way are such innovations different from normative and exploratory activities? Potential lucky strikes probably face us all at one stage or another, yet very few of us hit the 'jackpot'. There is no doubt that many people had apples fall on their heads when lying under apple trees. Equally, many people had seen water boiling in a kettle and raising the lid, but it was Newton and Watt who discovered the principles of gravity and steam energy and not the many others who had experienced the same events. Is creativity by serendipity the prerogative of those that can be described as geniuses? The answer is definitely 'no'. Many brilliant, albeit less dramatic, innovations have emerged over the years as the result of ordinary, average individuals in small and large organisations. Three main characteristics typify those who generate this kind of creative idea: (*a*) they possess an acute observing skill; (*b*) they also manifest an inquisitive mind, and (*c*) they have developed a lateral thinking capability—they are able to extrapolate a set of facts from a chance event to a totally different environment. The person who invented the 'cat's eye' road safety reflector probably possessed all these characteristics without realising it.

This is the point at which quality circles and creativity circles diverge. The main rationale of the quality circle is the development of a corporate system designed to solve problems. Its aim is to institutionalise normative creativity in such a way that an infrastructure exists to 'identify, analyse and solve problems at work'. Few quality circles undertake exploratory creativity activities in areas outside the immediate work environment of the circle members. Moreover few circles attempt to develop the personal wherewithal of individual members with the view of increasing their propensity to exploit 'serendipity' situations.

'Creativity circles', whether one opts to call them by this title or by any other name, are the logical extension of the quality circle concept to the management of modern operations. Companies that have benefited from the development of quality circle networks are the obvious candidates for undertaking the enlargement of the circles' scope and terms of reference. Developing an effective network of quality circles necessitated an arduous and dedicated programme of management development and training. Likewise, the development of more broadly-based creativity circles requires an imaginative and relentless programme of work. However, firms that have gone through the process once are well on the way towards being able to equip their respective organisations with an even sharper cutting edge.

The differences between quality and creativity circles

Quality circles	*Creativity circles*
1 Main purpose is to identify, analyse and solve problems at work.	Terms of reference can be broadened to encompass exploratory creativity, at all levels, and the development of the appropriate skills that make managers alert to accidental or chance innovations ('serendipity').
2 Mostly concerned with problems affecting immediate work area.	Can be invited to generate ideas and/or solutions to problems outside direct area of responsibility. Act as a Think Tank for other parts of the firm.
3 Tendency to concentrate upon manufacturing, quality, productivity matters.	Can deal with every facet of the organisation, commencing with the search for strategy, mission statement, marketing strategies, product development, etc, etc.
4 Quality circles, in the main, are conducted under the leadership of a department's supervisor.	Creativity circles can be led by any member of the organisation. The important element is that the individual has had experience in leading creative sessions.
5 Emphasis normally on a 'bottom up' approach. Most group sessions are held at operational level. Whilst top management often expresses total support of the QC movement and its activities they seldom take part in circle meetings.	Successful implementation demands a 'top down' strategy. Top management must be seen to participate in group activities and support their efforts at all times.

Quality circles	Creativity circles
6 Whilst participation is normally voluntary it often tends to be ritualistic. This can generate some boredom with the proceedings.	Participation must be voluntary as in the case of QC. However the meetings of the creative circles can be more varied by being entrusted with problems unrelated to the participant's immediate work environment. Thus they can bring a fresh perspective to problems and altogether find the task more interesting.
7 Tend to deal with short-term issues and problems.	Can handle issues of longer-term importance to the organisation. This means the CC can have a higher impact upon the future direction of the firm.

The rewards

The rewards of the quality circle movement are indisputable. On the financial side, substantial ratios have been quoted by QC champions. The benefit ratios improve once the cost relating to start-up, training, salary of facilitators and other associated items are out of the way. Moreover, it is important to remember that in many instances the non-tangible benefits can outweigh the ones that can be measured in financial terms, eg:

(a) greater customer satisfaction with company products;

(b) an enhanced corporate image;

(c) higher morale;

(d) general improvement in productivity;

(e) a happier labour force;

(f) lower level of absenteeism.

The success of the whole concept in Japan has been legendary. On the other hand the success of the QC concept in the West has been more patchy. Many companies in Western countries have derived outstanding benefits from the adoption of the process. However, quite a few firms have expressed some doubts about the long-term value of the whole effort. The secret of the Japanese success can be attributed to a number of ingredients associated with Japanese culture and environment. For example, the QC concept gained the total and unequivocal support of the Japanese Government. It was the Japanese Government that invited the American expert on statistical quality control, Dr W E Deming, to visit Japan and help in introducing the method into their industry.

Japanese industry itself accepted the whole idea with total dedication and commitment. The Japanese Union of Scientists and Engineers (JUSE) supported and promoted QCs in a steadfast way. It was JUSE that established a Deming Prize for winners of a quality achievement. In Japan that prize has the same prestige among businessmen as the Queen's Award given to exporters in Britain.

Other bodies such as the Japanese Standards Organisation and the Japanese Management Association provided additional support to the whole campaign to develop the QC movement. They provided training programmes and other support to firms that sought to introduce a QC system.

An imaginative crash programme of mass-training was established on radio and the mass media to spread the Deming ideas among the masses of workers in manufacturing enterprises. The idea of a 'Quality Month' was introduced, supported by a large number of 'quality' conventions, seminars and other functions throughout the country. A 'Q' symbol for 'Quality' was introduced and 'Q' flags adopted. The full panoply of mass communications was placed at the disposal of what Japanese industry considered almost as a religion.

The Japanese industrial environment and culture are in harmony with the QC philosophy. In particular one needs to highlight a few points in this connection.

(a) The blending of one's life goals with company's goals is one of the characteristics of the average Japanese worker. Success of the organisation, for a Japanese, represents his or her own success.

(b) 'Groupism' makes the Japanese worker feel happier and more secure. Quality circles provide an excellent opportunity to belong to such groups.

(c) Japanese unions co-operate with management and are more willing to negotiate favourably on ticklish issues such as innovations based on robotics and other types of modern technology. To that extent getting them to co-operate in quality circle development is less adversarial than it has been in many Western organisations.

Japanese managers and workers alike have come to appreciate the importance of quality for success since the war. Commitment to quality has become a national, corporate and individual attitude or, to use the expression described earlier, has been adopted as a 'superordinate goal'.

Quality circles have yielded rich rewards for the dedicated and imaginative organisations which have invested development work and managerial effort in their installation and continuous stimulation. Creativity circles can offer even richer rewards—it is a religion based on a broader church and can help to catapult a mediocre firm into the range of excellent companies.

Establishing a creativity circle

Where does one start? The process to be undertaken is described in Figure 27. It represents a programme of work which calls for single-minded dedication from the top of the organisation, supported by a multi-faceted and integrated series of steps. It is not a job for the faint-hearted, nor should it be attempted by anybody who is not prepared to see it through regardless of the obstacles that cynical and less-than-helpful colleagues are likely to place in the way.

An integrated approach

The establishment of a company-wide creativity circles network is an ambitious programme which requires careful planning and systematic implementation work. It may take years to develop—but so did the introduction of quality control circles in Japan and quality circles in the rest of the world. It is not a process that can emerge as a result of an edict from above commanding. 'Thou shall establish a network of creativity circles'. It needs a carefully-planned programme of work headed by a 'project champion' whose full-time task is to plan, direct, enthuse and control the process of developing the network.

Figure 27.   Developing 'creativity circles'.

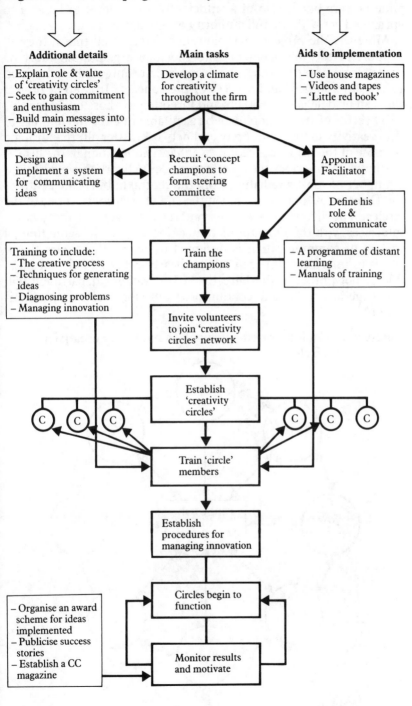

It is recommended that the project champion is not only given wide powers but is also of a sufficiently senior level to be able to speak and act with the full authority of top management.

Morever, the project champion must have, at all times, the full support of top management, and the total organisation must be made aware of the fact that the bosses are unequivocally committed to the development and success of the concept. It is not a project that can be delegated to others and forgotten by those in charge.

'Director of Innovation' may be a suitable title for the founder of the creativity circle philosophy and network. After all, the ultimate purpose of the whole concept is to enhance innovation in the firm!

Figure 28 describes the creativity circles network as a wheel with a number of spokes radiating from the central hub. At the centre is the Director of Innovation and at the end of each spoke is one of the circles. The arrows seek to illustrate the way each creativity circle interfaces with the Director of Innovation and, at the same time, a system of communication is designed to enable the circles themselves to interface with each other. Clearly, where this is not possible or not practical, the Director of Innovation's department will act as the focal point and conduit procedure for effective communication.

Figure 28. An integrated approach to managing creativity circles.

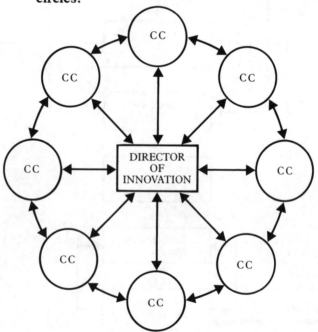

Briefly, the role of the Director of Innovation can be summarised thus:

(*a*) to plan and develop a creativity circle network throughout the firm;

(*b*) to take all the necessary steps to develop a climate in which creativity can be generated and communicated;

(*c*) to design and implement a system for communicating ideas among all operating units and/or functions;

(*d*) to invite volunteers to act as members of creativity circles and select a few of them to act as circle champions;

(*e*) develop a programme of training for circle leaders and members;

(*f*) help circles to commence to function, monitor progress and communicate lessons learnt to all other circles;

(*g*) organise a company-wide communication system to encompass:
    (i) Promoting the network concept, its value and benefits for the firm's future success and excellence;
    (ii) details of results and success stories;
    (iii) award schemes (not necessarily financial);
    (iv) training;
    (v) invitation for new volunteers to join the network.

The full gamut of communication tools can be used by the Director of Innovation in achieving his or her objectives, for example: house magazines; films, videos and tapes; posters and billboards; special booklets, brochures and other printed matter; conferences, seminars and workshops; badges, certificates, flags— plenty of scope for creative thinking.

All this represents an enormous challenge for management. It involves a lot of hard work and imaginative effort. Yet the rewards for the creative and visionary organisation can be truly substantial.

6 Problem-solving and creativity

'It isn't that they can't see the solution. It is that they can't see the problem.'

G K Chesterton

In this chapter we shall explore the way creative thinking can assist in the development of solutions to problems. The content of this chapter should be of value not only to managers in organisations, but also to people not connected with the business community. Problem-solving activities are not the sole prerogative of individuals in the commercial and business world. When water gushes down the wall of one's house one is facing a problem. When one cannot start one's car in the morning it is another problem. When a lawn gets covered with weeds, for some individuals it is a horrific problem. At the other extreme, in the 'big' commercial world, the breakdown of a computer can present a company with a very serious problem. A strike can create for the company's management another devastating problem. Being sued under product liability for having caused injury to a customer is not great fun either. Life is full of problems, and the average individual, both in the business world and in private life, spends a considerable amount of time grappling with large or small problems. Clearly, if somebody could obliterate all problems it would be a giant step towards turning the world into a paradise.

Coping with problems

Alternatively, if somebody could turn the whole process of problem-solving into a fun activity this would be another step towards making life truly enjoyable. Unfortunately 'problems' cause people anxiety and anxiety can drive some individuals to the point of despair. If one can find a rational way of looking at problems and de-emotionalise them it can certainly ease the pressure and help to remove the surplus stress that they can cause. Trying to solve problems when one is not under stress is usually easier than when one is

121

close to a nervous breakdown. In other words if one is facing a problem, large or small, it is best to try to approach it in a relaxed state. This is an easy piece of advice to give to others—a difficult one to apply.

In common with most people I have to deal with problems every day of my life. In addition to my own problems, I have to try to solve the problems of others because it is part of my job. Over the years I have assembled a number of very helpful aphorisms which have virtually changed my life in relation to the problem-solving task by helping to remove the stress factor. Here they are:

'We have no problems—every problem is an opportunity in disguise'
I do not even recall who coined this phrase. All I know is that a number of companies worldwide have adopted it as part of their 'superordinate goals'. In such companies members of the organisation are simply not allowed to whinge about 'problems', as it is passionately believed that if you dig deep enough into any problem it might turn into an opportunity. Moreover, if three companies face the same problem the one which manages to solve it has gained an opportunity, a competitive advantage.

The main impact that this aphorism has had for me was the realisation that problems can be approached from two perspectives: an optimistic and positive one, or a pessimistic and negative one. I discovered that trying to tackle a problem from the vantage point of optimism and positive attitude facilitates the search for solutions. In the case of an individual this statement entails self-discipline and a determination to look at a problem/opportunity from a positive viewpoint. One must reassure oneself that the problem, as seen at first glance, cannot be quite as bad as it appears, and that some good may lie somewhere underneath it.

The message is: as a first step try to approach the problem-solving process with a positive mind. Whether you are a businessman, a civil servant, a politician or an ordinary citizen, remember that solving problems must not be a trauma. It is a challenge which the optimist is more likely to solve than the pessimist.

'A problem well stated is a problem half solved'
This very simple statement encapsulates fundamental wisdom. The trouble with any problem-solving exercise that one undertakes is that very often we do not know what the precise nature of the problem is. We know something about the symptoms; we may know a little about some of the causes, but we seldom possess all the relevant information that makes the problem-solving task a relatively simple one.

Whatever one can do to understand the cause-and-effect relationship between symptoms and their underlying causes can help in moving towards the development of solutions. I have discovered over the years that in many situations the thorough analysis of the problem itself can pave the way towards the identification of possible solutions. In other words, the analysis of a problem can form an integral and valuable part of the creative process.

Edward Hodnett summarised this notion most succinctly by saying: 'A good problem statement often includes (*a*) what is known; (*b*) what is unknown; and (*c*) what is sought'. This means that a tremendous amount of work must be undertaken by problem solvers before they even start attempting to generate creative solutions.

In a previous chapter we referred to 'normative innovation' as the process of solving problems by defined objectives. In such situations innovation is achieved when a well-defined problem has been solved and the firm's financial and other objectives have been met. In the case of normative innovation it is particularly important that diagnostic work is undertaken before creative resources are allocated and used. Attempting to solve ill-defined problems is not an effective way of using creative brainpower.

'A problem is an undesirable deviation of what is happening from what should be happening'
This is a very simple and concise definition of the word 'problem' but, on reflection, it represents perfect commonsense. I first came across it in the excellent book 'The Rational Manager' by Charles Kepner and Benjamin Tregoe, whose work has made a tremendous impact upon my thinking and work. Moreover, they have helped me to deal with awkward problems in a relaxed fashion mostly because they added another condition to the existence of a problem: a person has to *want* to find the cause of something that is wrong and correct it. If a person knows that a deviation exists, but has no wish to solve it, no problem exists for him. This means that a problem has a certain level of relativity to the beholder's circumstances. If water gushes down somebody's wall when it should not, it is clearly a deviation from normality. However, if the owner of that wall does not care about it or has no desire to solve it, no real problem exists.

I feel that there is another dimension: a problem only exists when a person can do something about it. This is where I have found, over the years, that I have been able to deal with stressful situations. If one sits in a car on a motorway, heading for an important meeting, an accident that stops the flow of traffic is a deviation from what should be happening. Potentially this could be a major problem for the driver whose work demands punctual attendance at the destination point. Obviously, the accident makes it impossible. The driver *wants* to reach the destination but the road is blocked and there is absolutely nothing that he can do about it. In the circumstances, in my opinion, the driver has no problem. There is nothing he or she can do. The best thing is to sit in the car and listen to music. Why bother to get an apoplectic fit when one is stuck and unable to do anything about it? This is where 'The Rational Manager' has helped me to deal with problems. Before I start spending a lot of my time trying to solve any of them I ask myself three questions:

(*a*) Is there a *deviation* between what is happening and what should be happening?

(*b*) Do I *want* to do something about it?

(*c*) Is there *anything that I can do* about it?

The answers to these three questions determine whether I shall take the matter forward to a problem-solving mode. This approach is not based on some complicated philosophy or complex methodology. It is simply an exercise in rational thinking and sound commonsense.

In summary, my assertion is that problems are not always what one assumes them to be at first. In fact, in certain circumstances, they can be valuable areas for opportunity-seeking activities. Secondly, before one can start solving a problem it is important that the true nature of the problem and its causes are fully diagnosed and defined. Thirdly, a problem only exists when somebody is willing or able to attempt to solve it. One should not waste creative time to solve problems that are not solvable.

The problem-solving process

Most people and most companies face problems of one type or another. Without problems life could be extremely dull. As stated above, a problem is first noticed when one observes a deviation between what is happening as against what should be happening. In order to identify and define a problem one must know first what should be happening. This is the fundamental benchmark against which one can measure performance. If a car can only reach a top

speed of 60 mph one cannot define this as a problem until one
knows that the specified top speed is supposed to be 90 mph. It is
only at that point that one can say that a problem exists. In other
words, some homework and fact-finding activities must be undertaken before a problem can be defined and until such definition has
taken place it is difficult to look for solutions.

The other important point to remember is that what appears as a
problem is the effect of some other problem, and the latter may be
the result of a third one, and so on. If a product fails to reach its
sales target it appears to be a problem—problem 1. On analysing
the causes of the problem one discovers that the main reason for
these poor results is the high price—problem 2. The reason for the
high price is the high unit cost of production—problem 3. That in
turn stems from the fact that the raw material is imported from the
US and involves heavy transport and duty costs—problem 4. This
can be illustrated in a simple diagram (Figure 29). Problem 1 cannot be solved until problem 4 is solved.

The example described is relatively simple and clear-cut, as the
nexus between cause and effect is easily identifiable and definable.
The same case can be complicated by adding a few extra factors.

Figure 29. A problem and its underlying causes.

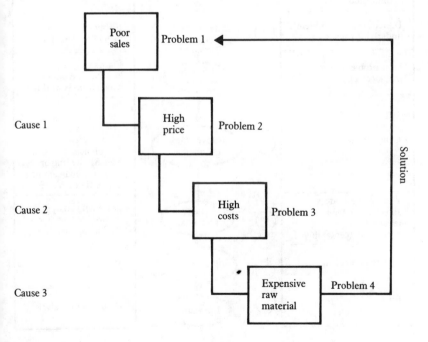

For example, problem 1 (failure to reach sales target) *may be due to a number of causes*: (i) high price; (ii) poor sales force; (iii) poor quality; (iv) end of product life cycle; (v) ineffective channels of distribution; (vi) poor company image. Each one of these causes can turn out to be the major problem-area for careful analysis and creative solving exercise. Undertaking a problem-solving exercise in the second case is much more demanding and reaching an innovative solution more difficult.

Problem-solving activities can either be carried out on an ad hoc basis or as a matter of regular routine associated with a mechanism for solving organisational problems such as creativity circles, quality circles, think tanks, etc. The process in both situations is more

Figure 30. The problem-solving routine (an ad hoc model).

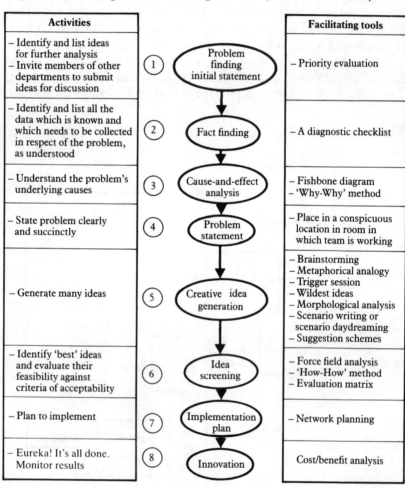

or less identical, except that in the latter case the cycle is a continuous one: when the group finishes dealing with a problem and achieves a solution (innovation) the next problem on a list is tackled.

Figure 30 describes the problem-solving process in a firm that deals with such activities on an ad hoc basis. Figure 31 describes the same process in organisations that have developed a continuous cycle of problem-solving routine.

The various components of the process deserve some elaboration and a number of helpful tools that can be used during a few of the steps explored.

Problem-finding

This is purely an exercise at defining the problem given and considering whether it is worth pursuing the matter further. At this stage no attempt must be made to solve it but the group must simply decide whether the allocation of valuable group time can be justified.

The kind of information which is likely to convince the group that a problem ought to be rejected or put aside for the time being may consist of one or more of the following elements:

(*a*)   the problem appears too small or trivial, hence of low priority;

Figure 31.   The problem-solving cycle—a continuous model.

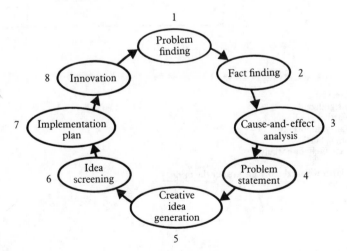

Figure 32.   Problem-solving—priority evaluation.

	0	1	2	3	4	5	Score
Is the problem considered large?							
Does it involve company in losses or added costs?							
Is a solution deemed urgent?							
Will customers appreciate the removal of this problem?							
Will company's image be enhanced?							
Will company's internal morale benefit?							
						Total Score	

Score:

0 = Irrelevant
1 = Insignificant
2 = Worth recording
3 = Fairly important
4 = Important
5 = Extremely important

The higher the total score the greater the priority

(*b*)   its nature is such that the impact on the firm is not likely to last beyond a short period of time;

(*c*)   strong evidence exists to show that there is nothing one can do to solve it (eg legal constraints);

(*d*)   it is the outcome of top management past misdeeds and politically it is unwise to start delving into it;

(*e*)   solutions are likely to be extremely costly and the firm is unable to allocate such funds.

Subject to these screening constraints a problem is stated and selected for further analysis. At this stage one does not attempt to go beyond the initial definition of the problem and one does not yet commence to probe into the various cause-and-effect sub-routines mentioned earlier.

It must always be recognised that problem-solving activities are time-consuming and entail the organisation in expensive costs, especially in terms of managerial time. It is therefore wise to develop a simple methodology for identifying the relative priority of problems submitted for creativity treatment. Figure 32 illustrates such a screening method. Its precise details need to be developed in relation to the specific needs of each organisation.

Fact-finding

This is an important sub-routine in the problem-stating/problem-solving process. Its aim is to assemble all known data pertaining to the problem and also identify unknown data which must be collected. Two major benefits can be derived from carrying out this activity thoroughly and conscientiously:

(*a*)   the availability of a large volume of facts can, in itself, help to diagnose the true causes of the problem—it has been known for problems to be solved as a result of this phase of the cycle;

(*b*)   a thorough analysis of all the facts surrounding a problem can start the 'creative juices' working towards the development of solutions.

In attempting to define the fact-seeking needs surrounding a problem the following checklist can be of great help:

WHAT?

Into what parts can the problem be divided?

To what other problem(s) does this problem relate?

What is the total situation of which this problem is part?

What is the dimension of the problem? Large, medium or small?

What will happen if the problem is not solved?

What will happen if a solution is delayed?

WHY?

Why did the problem occur in the first place?

Why was the problem not recognised earlier?

Why did the firm not attempt to solve it earlier?

WHEN?

When was the problem first noticed?

Does the timing of the appearance of the problem have any significance?

Is there any seasonal pattern to the occurrence of the problem?

HOW?

How did the problem come to be recognised?

How does it affect the firm's performance?

If it is an old problem how was it dealt with on previous occasions?

How was it prevented from recurring in the past?

WHERE?

Is the problem confined to one part of the organisation only?

Is the problem confined to one part of the world/country only?

If the answer to the above question is 'yes'—is there any significance in this fact?

Is the problem associated with one distribution outlet only?

WHO?

Who identified the existence of the problem in the first place?

Who was responsible for its occurrence?

Who could be made responsible for solving it?

> Who is the person and/or which is the department worst
> affected by the continued existence of the problem?
> Who is most likely to benefit from a solution to this prob-
> lem?
> Who should be consulted in order to solve the problem?

These questions represent a simple checklist but the sheer effort
of responding to all or most of them can have a salutary effect upon
the problem-solving process. It is not unknown for companies to
face problems which were identified and solved in previous years by
managers who had left the company. Re-inventing the wheel is not
the most profitable activity for any organisation!

As was stated earlier, a thorough analysis of the facts which are
available or can be obtained without too much effort can be
extremely valuable. With some luck they may even point at solutions without having to proceed to the other time-consuming steps
discussed below.

In practice it often happens that during the fact-finding activity
one encounters obvious solutions to problems which hitherto
appeared intractable. The fact that a problem keeps cropping up at
a certain time of the year with boring regularity may be a helpful
signal. I have come across many situations where members of the
organisation tried to solve a problem which had been identified and
solved previously by colleagues who were subsequently moved to
other departments. The firm's so-called 'corporate memory' was so
short that nobody in the new organisation had any recollection of
such an event.

Cause-and-effect analysis

This is an important part of the problem-solving process. As
stressed earlier, a major difference often exists between a problem
and its symptoms. Removing the symptoms of a problem is no
guarantee that the problem itself will be solved. It is therefore
necessary to analyse, in some depth, the underlying causes of each
problem. Moreover, such an analysis often leads to a whole chain of
cause-and-effect relationships. Let us consider a simple problem:

'People are complaining that our switchboard is incompetent. When customers telephone
they normally have to wait for about 20 rings before they obtain an answer. Once the operators answer they tend to be short and unhelpful.'

This is an initial statement of a problem. Customers are unhappy and that represents an unsatisfactory state of affairs. However, the fact that customers have to wait before the telephone is answered and that the operators are short and unhelpful may be the result of a whole chain of causes such as:

(a) the number of operators is inadequate;

(b) the wages paid to telephone operators in the company are too low;

(c) none of them has been properly trained—hence they do not know how to deal with the pressure;

(d) their work environment is unpleasant;

(e) they are expected to perform other tasks such as make tea, file documents and shred papers;

(f) the equipment itself is antiquated;

(g) the offices are located in an area which is poorly served by BT and it is impossible to get a better service from them;

(h) customers tend to phone all at once between 14.30 and 16.00 thus creating an enormous pressure during a short period of time;

(i) managers talk too long on the phone thus clogging the very few lines available;

(j) the telephone is being used for transmitting data to the computer centre and this is currently done more or less at the same time as the 'rush-hour' for phone calls from customers.

Each one of the causes listed can probably be broken down into one or more sub-causes and somewhere along that analytical route one can identify the real problem that one must try to solve.

During the 'cause-and-effect' analysis one can use one of the following valuable techniques:

(a) the 'Fishbone Diagram' (also known as the 'Ishikawa Diagram' or the 'Cause-and-Effect Diagram');

(b) the 'Why-Why Diagram'.

The 'Fishbone Diagram'

The 'Fishbone Diagram' was first developed by Professor Kaoru Ishikawa of the University of Tokyo. The method is also often referred to by his name. The main aim of this technique is to help to identify and list all the possible causes that have brought the problem about.

It is called the 'Fishbone Diagram' because by the time one completes the exercise one has a diagram that is reminiscent of the bones of a fish—a head, a spine and little bones stemming from it. One starts the diagram by placing the problem under discussion in a box that depicts the head of the fish. A straight line describing the backbone is drawn along the sheet of paper (see Figure 33). The next step is to draw stems at about 45 degrees. Each stem should identify every likely cause of the problem that the problem-solving group can think of (see Figure 34).

Once this is done, one can place additional branches on each stem to represent a further breakdown of each cause. It does not matter if any particular cause appears more than once. On the contrary, it ought to be highlighted because it may prove to have some special significance (see Figure 35).

The 'Fishbone Diagram' can be prepared over a number of sessions. Ishikawa himself described it as a method where 'you write your problem down on the head of the fish and then let it cook overnight'. The whole process is a useful trigger point for further creative thinking. By building the diagram over more than one session the following additional benefits can be derived: (*a*) fresh ideas regarding possible causes can arise during the interval; (*b*) members will forget who originated every idea, thus making subsequent discussions less inhibited; (*c*) the team develops a total immersion in the problem and its underlying causes and that encourages the members to continue to think about the whole subject, day and night, and the nights can be particularly fruitful in this regard.

When the diagram is deemed to be fully 'cooked' the group commences the process of discussing, in some depth, each spur and/or sub-spur. The idea is also to list the various causes in an ascending scale of complication. Obviously, if the cause of a problem is a simple one it is best to identify it first and remove it rather than grapple with the more complicated causes at the beginning of the cycle. Moreover, if during the discussion the group comes to the conclusion that one or more of the causes shown on the diagram are more important, circles are placed around them. These are the causes that will receive more attention at the 'idea generation' stage of the proceedings.

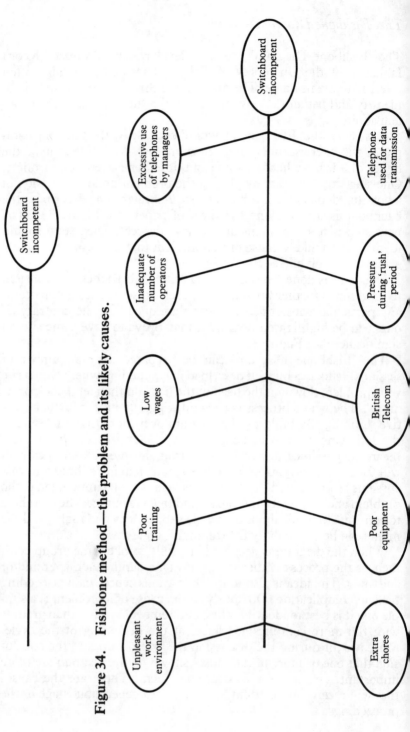

Figure 33. Fishbone diagram—the problem and its spine.

Figure 34. Fishbone method—the problem and its likely causes.

Figure 35. Fishbone diagram completed in relation to the problem: 'switchboard incompetent'.

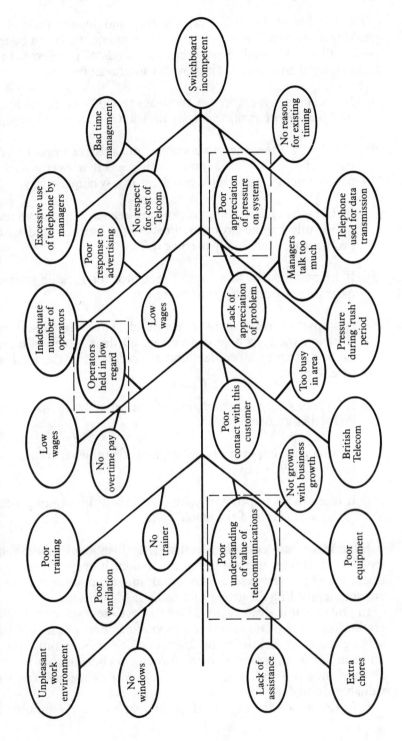

The 'Fishbone Diagram' is a simple and logical process for breaking a problem down into its main components. It can be used in all walks of life and in relation to all kinds of problems. In an organisational environment it provides additional benefits.

(*a*) It encourages members of the team to study every angle of a problem before making a hasty decision as to what is wrong.

(*b*) It helps to show the relationships and relative importance of parts of a problem—a point which is often overlooked by people attempting to solve problems in a systematic way.

(*c*) It starts the creative process working insofar as it focuses one's mind fully on the problem. People who are obsessed with a problem are more likely to solve it.

(*d*) It helps to establish a logical sequence for handling various parts of a problem in a systematic way.

(*e*) It stops 'squirrel caging' one's mind. This term describes a situation where people concentrate all their attention on one cause or part of a problem and are oblivious to the total picture.

(*f*) It forces a group to explore everything possible, so that there is no further excuse for delay.

(*g*) It offers an opportunity to explore a problem from a total approach perspective.

(*h*) It often helps to produce solutions without having to proceed to the next stages of the whole cycle.

Experience has also shown that the 'Fishbone' method has another advantage: used in group discussions it keeps everyone on track, it brings every relevant factor out into the open and prevents anyone stampeding the group into half-baked decisions.

In practice, it is always a good idea to place the result of the deliberations in a conspicuous position so that members of the problem-solving team can scrutinise the diagram at leisure and mull over its outcome. It is a method that can provide a considerable prod to creative thinking and, with experience, can provide an extremely valuable aid to diagnosis.

It is recommended that readers attempt to draw a number of

'Fishbone Diagrams' pertaining to current problems that confront them. Ideally, one should start with relatively simple problems and gradually build up one's experience towards more complex ones. With experience one will discover that it is a most helpful device for concentrating one's mind on the full picture surrounding a problem and the causes that have brought it about.

The 'Why-Why Diagram'

This method is a variation on the same theme as the 'Fishbone Diagram'. Its purpose is to delve into the root causes of the problem in a systematic way. It is best undertaken in group work with members of the team challenging every cause put forward by asking the question 'Why?'. If it is suggested that the switchboard is being incompetent because the operators have not been trained the question 'Why?' is immediately raised. If the answer given is: 'We do not have a trainer' the question 'Why?' is raised again. Once again the answer can provoke the 'Why?' question again and so on. All this has to be done in a persistent but good-humoured way, otherwise it can become a tiresome process smacking of pedantic catechism. If carried out in the right spirit, it can be an extremely valuable analysis of the causes of a problem.

The route which the group's questioning follows can normally be written up in a flow-diagram like the one described in Figure 36.

The 'Why-Why' method carries many indirect benefits similar to those listed under the 'Fishbone Diagram'. In particular, it provides an opportunity to think in a divergent way rather than manifest the characteristics of a 'squirrel-caged' mind.

This simple technique can be a most enjoyable activity, especially when it is conducted in groups under the supervision of an experienced facilitator.

In summary, at the end of the 'cause-and-effect' analysis phase, with or without the aid of the two techniques described, the problem-solving team should be in a better position to understand the exact nature of the problem and the underlying cause or causes that have brought it about. One often discovers that on reaching the end of this phase the problem statement that emerges differs substantially from what it was believed to be at the beginning of this analysis. This is all to the good inasmuch as the whole aim of the exercise is to solve the root cause of the problem and not just one or two intermediate manifestations thereof. At this point, the group should be able to address themselves to the task of producing a 'problem statement'.

Figure 36.   The 'Why-Why' method

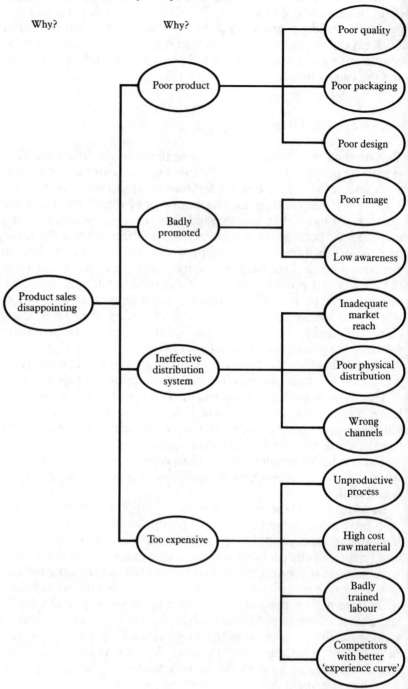

Problem statement

This is a vital stage in the problem-solving cycle. In some situations the group may reach this point fairly easily and quickly. In other circumstances it may prove to be a lengthy and agonising experience. The essential point is that at the end of the deliberations the team reaches a unanimous decision as to what problem they are trying to solve. If the group cannot agree on this point they must continue to discuss and debate the issue until they come to some concurrence. It is appropriate to remember that such discussions in themselves are valuable in stimulating potential creativity which will form part of the next stage.

A well-defined 'problem statement' can be extremely useful during the idea-generation phase that follows. Ideally it should be (*a*) stated in short and precise words; (*b*) clear and unambiguous; and (*c*) defined in terms that will facilitate the ultimate measurement of results.

If we return to the example illustrated in the 'Why-Why Diagram' (Figure 36) we can look at two alternative problem statements:

Problem Statement Number 1: 'The sales of product "X" are disappointing. We believe that the reason for such poor results is partly due to poor design and packaging and partly due to poor salesmanship. The creative team is invited to solve the problem and recommend a strategy for improving the packaging/design and salesmanship.'

This is a poorly-stated definition of the problem. It is vague, it covers too many sub-causes, it is badly-focussed and at the end of the exercise the team will not be able to establish whether they have been successful or not.

Let us look at an alternative problem statement:

Problem Statement Number 2: 'The sales of product "X" are disappointing. The analysis of the problem has shown that the root cause is unsatisfactory packaging (difficult to open, it leaks and the user cannot see how much is left inside). The team is invited to solve this problem. It is hoped that as a result of such packaging improvements sales of the product will increase by 10 % within one year.'

This definition of the problem is more precise, it is unambiguous and in the final analysis is also measurable in terms of the ultimate results.

Creative idea-generation

Having reached this point without having solved the problem, the time has come to start generating ideas. It may be recalled from earlier chapters that what one needs now is a volume of ideas on the basis that, on average, out of every 60 ideas one would be a winner! The problem itself has been well defined and when one attempts to solve it in group work it is useful to write it up on a flip-chart or some other visual aid. It is an effective reminder to the collective brainpower as to what one wants to achieve.

The idea-generation phase is the fun part of the whole cycle. This is a point at which the leader/facilitator has an important role to play. The group should be relaxed and whilst they have an important problem to solve they should behave as if they do not have a care in the world. The creative juices work better when one is not ridden by anxiety. The leader himself should be a person who possesses a very positive and tolerant 'attitude spectrum' (see Chapter 3). His main task is to ensure that the proceedings run smoothly and that every idea, however bizarre or improbable, is allowed to be voiced and discussed. This is a moment of time when the 'Intermediate Impossibles' must be treated as gold dust. Dr Edward de Bono in his writings on lateral thinking describes the concept of the 'Intermediate Impossible' as a stepping stone between conventional thinking and new insights which at first glance appear to be based on wishful thinking. It happens quite often that such impractical, or even ridiculous, ideas are the ones that trigger the imagination of the group and stimulate them towards developing remarkable and down-to-earth solutions.

A large number of useful techniques are available for groups engaged in generating ideas. Many of these techniques are similar in approach and purpose, but bear a diversity of fancy titles that creative group organisers have ascribed to them over the years. One of the earliest and most frequently used methods is 'brainstorming' which was first popularised by Alex F Osborn, the 'O' in BBDO— the well-known advertising agency Batten, Barton, Durstine & Osborn Inc. His book 'Applied Imagination' contributed to the understanding of creativity in the forties and fifties as much as Edward de Bono has contributed to the understanding of 'thinking' in the seventies and eighties. In this chapter the main techniques that one can use during the 'idea-generation' phase of the problem-solving cycle will be described briefly. The more important ones, like 'brainstorming', 'synectics' and 'morphological analysis' will be dealt with in greater detail in subsequent chapters.

The following are the techniques that can be used to generate ideas in response to well-defined 'problem statements':

(*a*) brainstorming (see Chapter 7);

(*b*) metaphorical analogy;

(*c*) trigger session;

(*d*) wildest ideas session;

(*e*) morphological analysis (see Chapter 8);

(*f*) scenario writing or scenario daydreaming (see Chapter 9);

(*g*) suggestion schemes.

Brainstorming

Alex Osborn defined brainstorming as 'a conference technique by which a group attempts to find a solution for a specific problem by amassing all the ideas spontaneously contributed by its members'. Osborn derived some inspiration from a procedure that had been used in India for more than 400 years by Hindu teachers working with religious groups. The Indian name for this method is Prai-Barshana. 'Prai' means 'outside yourself' and 'Barshana' means 'question'. During such sessions one does not discuss or criticise. All evaluation of ideas takes place at subsequent meetings of the same group.

The modern brainstorming session is nothing more than a creative conference for the sole purpose of producing a checklist of ideas which can serve as leads to problem-solving—ideas which can subsequently be evaluated and further processed. The crucial point to remember is that the main task of brainstorming is to generate ideas and not to evaluate them.

The main rules pertaining to an effective brainstorming session are:

(*a*) Judgement must be suspended. During the sessions participants must withhold criticism of other people's ideas and must not express adverse comments. Ideally, they should even suspend judgemental thinking. Everything that is said by others is acceptable. At first it is a difficult discipline to come to terms with but under the watchful eye of an experienced leader groups learn how to comply with this rule.

(*b*) 'Freewheeling' is welcome. The wilder the idea, the better; it is easier to tame down than to think up. Freewheeling means that ideas flow smoothly from each other in an associative fashion. An example of freewheeling is when one tells a group of friends a joke about the 'elephant who decided to have a sauna . . . ', and that joke immediately triggers other jokes about elephants or about saunas.

(*c*) Quantity is wanted. The greater the number of ideas, the greater the probability of good ideas being included in the list.

(*d*) Combination and improvement should be encouraged. In addition to contributing ideas of their own, participants should be encouraged to suggest how the ideas of others may be combined to yield yet another idea.

An effective leader of a brainstorming session must explain the rules to the group in simple and informal terms. He must ensure that these rules are adhered to at all times, especially the one relating to the suspension of judgement. It is important that the proceedings are held in a relaxed and informal atmosphere. Osborn quotes one of his most effective leaders as saying: 'when I can make my brainstorming team feel they are playing, we get somewhere'.

The only strictly formal feature of the proceedings is the written recording of all the ideas. This is usually done by a scribe. The person who fulfils this role must be able to write quickly and if necessary paraphrase the ideas into concise terms. At times, the ideas cascade at such a fast rate that even a shorthand expert could hardly record them verbatim.

The size of the group normally depends on the personal preference of the group leader and on the available resources. However, in practice it must be borne in mind that too large a group (in excess of ten) is difficult to manage and too small a group (fewer than six— including one leader and one scribe) may prove less productive.

Chapter 7 will deal with the organisation of successful brainstorming activities and the mechanics of this method in greater detail.

Metaphorical analogy

This method derives its origin from the work of William Gordon and George Prince who developed between them the technique that we know today as 'synectics.' Under the title of synectics a number of proprietary programmes are conducted, aimed at developing creative solutions to problems. The word originates from the Greek, meaning the 'joining together of differently and apparently irrelevant elements'. Synectics seeks to integrate diverse individuals and disciplines into a problem-stating/problem-solving group. Members of a synectics group should ideally represent as many disciplines, functions or activities as possible. To that extent it has always been felt that a person who has held a number of jobs of diverse experience is better equipped than the person whose career concentrated on one job.

The approach prescribed by the synectics method is complex and I have always encountered some resistance from group participants to its use on a regular basis. Moreover, Gordon originally suggested that a full-time synectics group should be selected after a long interview with each member in order to establish their suitability for participating in such activities. Inevitably, such a procedure tends to impart a certain level of elitism to the selected few and this, in my opinion, is incompatible with the total creativity circle philosophy that one should strive to develop in an organisation.

Nevertheless, to give credit where credit is due, the Gordon approach has alerted me to the opportunity of using a simplified version of synectics which I prefer to call the 'metaphorical analogy' method. It is easy to understand and valuable when attempting to generate ideas in response to a specific problem. The underlying theory is that if one can identify areas of any commercial endeavour or of life in general or of nature, where similar problems to the one in question have occurred, one can draw a parallel between the two situations and attempt to derive lessons from the way the same problem was solved in such other areas.

The idea is to attempt to draw an analogy between a problem for which at the moment one does not have a solution, and a comparable problem from a totally different sphere of activity for which an answer does exist. In its simplest form one tries to draw an analogy between a problem identified in one type of business and a proven solution in another business. At a higher level of sophistication one can compare a problem in industry or commerce with a well-known solution in remote spheres like nature at work.

Thus if the problem is to protect a car or a house against thieves, one can draw a metaphorical analogy with the way the skunk protects itself against predators by producing a nasty smell. An unbearable stench spreading around the car or the house when the lock is interfered with can be a worthwhile idea to consider further, although in the short term it appears to be an 'intermediate impossible'. How about combating hijacking by the same method? At a crucial moment the pilot presses a button and a horrific, but harmless, stench engulfs the passengers and terrorists, thus making the latter incapable of pursuing their evil deeds.

More recently I was invited to help a tour operator to solve the following problem. A brochure pack consisting of an attractive counter display box with brochures inside was delivered to travel agents. Most travel agents placed the display unit on the counter as a very useful promotional tool. Unfortunately, as soon as the last brochure had been picked up by a customer the box remained empty and after a while the fairly expensive display unit was thrown away. Very few travel agents bothered to phone and ask for additional brochures to insert in the box. A simple problem, but a solution eluded the marketing team. The problem was defined as follows: 'How can we encourage the agents to apply for refills?' A creative session was set up during which a number of techniques for generating ideas was used. The 'metaphorical analogy' was the one which seemed to have triggered the imagination of the team on this occasion. The members kept searching for analogous situations where the need for refills occurred at regular frequency. A large number of ideas was generated, but the one that seemed the most appropriate was the way customers obtained new cheque-books. Around five or six cheques before one reaches the end of a book there is a 'Cheque Book Request Slip'—once completed and sent to the bank a new cheque book follows very quickly. The group drew an analogy between their problem and the cheque reordering system, and subsequently managed to develop a suitable solution to their problem based on the same principle.

Trigger session

Unlike brainstorming, a trigger session commences with every member of the group being asked to generate a number of ideas independently of each other. Each member is given a card on which he or she is invited to place ideas as to how the stated problem could be solved. In the case of brainstorming it is the freewheeling interplay between the participants that helps ideas to cascade. In the case of trigger sessions one does not get the benefit of this stimulation. To some extent it means that participants have to produce ideas in a competitive atmosphere inasmuch as each member of the team is under some emotional pressure to generate 'good ideas'. In some situations this kind of pressure can be instrumental to a fruitful output.

Members of a well-briefed and well-led trigger session should be able to generate around ten ideas in a matter of five to ten minutes. Experienced and creative people can generate as many as thirty or more ideas during that time. Following the individual work, each member reads his or her ideas aloud—they are all recorded and time is allocated towards building on the various ideas by 'joining' a few of them into additional ideas or embellishing others. The results are comparable to what happens in brainstorming, but by using this two-pronged approach a large and diverse quantity of ideas can emerge.

Wildest ideas session

This is a systematic attempt at generating outrageous ideas and then endeavouring to bring them 'down-to-earth' and closer to the realities of the problem under discussion. It is an excellent way to lubricate peoples' brain cells and encourage them to generate and cope with obvious 'intermediate impossibles'. Members of a creative group who have not had much experience with team idea-generation activities normally tend to be conventional in the ideas they usually produce. The 'wildest ideas' routine can shake them out of such an inhibited posture, encourage them to think more broadly and, if necessary, in an eccentric fashion.

Let us imagine that the problem statement says: 'How can we reduce the cost of photocopying which is deemed to be too steep?' This is a fairly common problem in most organisations. The wildest ideas sub-routine may put forward the following wild ideas:

(*a*) electrify the button of the photocopier so that every person who attempts to use the machine gets electrocuted;

(*b*) only people who want to make 1,000 copies at a time can use the machine;

(*c*) as one uses the machine a photograph of the user is taken and the number of copies made shown on his forehead;

(*d*) as one uses the machine the number of copies made is tattooed on the person's forehead.

Some of these ideas are obviously outrageous. The concept is to choose the wildest of the lot and try to save it. Initially, it may prove difficult, but with some experience the group learns how to think laterally and find some positive angle which makes an intermediate impossible possible.

Morphological analysis

This is a very useful technique for generating a vast number of ideas in a very short space of time. Essentially it is a method for generating 'exploratory' creativity rather than ideas for 'normative innovation', which is what we are discussing in this chapter. Nevertheless, there are certain circumstances where it could be a useful technique for generating ideas for problem-solving activities as well. Morphological analysis, also known as morphological method, is such an important technique that it will be discussed more fully in Chapter 8.

This method aims at singling out the most important dimensions of a specific problem and then examines all the relationships among them. 'Morphology' means the study of the structure and form of things. In this connection it means the study of the interrelationship among a number of independent parameters. The best way to describe the technique is by exploring a practical example.

'A firm operating in the immensely competitive portable radio business is seeking to develop a product which none of its competitors currently has. Put briefly the problem defined is: "We want to develop a unique product with minimum competition" '.

It is appropriate to mention that the challenge is more exploratory than normative in character. Yet it provides a simple example of the technique in use. One dimension of the problem is the shape of the radio. The second dimension is the location in which the radio might be used and the third is the way it may be carried about. The relationship between these can now be represented in a three-dimensional morphology as shown in Figure 37. Assuming that these three dimensions fully define the problem there would now be $6 \times 6 \times 5 = 180$ cells. Each cell represents an idea. Some of these ideas may be clearly useless—others may prove to be valuable and worth exploring further. Out of 180 ideas there must be one which is truly excellent!

Scenario writing or scenario daydreaming

A scenario is a logical and plausible recording of future events with careful attention to timing and correlations, especially wherever the

**Figure 37.   Morphological analysis in relation to the design of
new portable radios.**

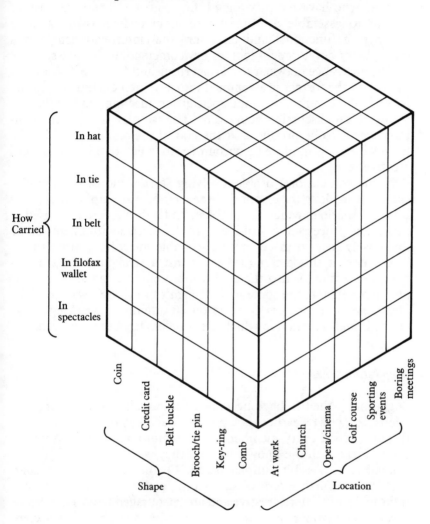

latter are especially relevant. It is a systematic attempt to write
about a 'future world' in the form of a summary of the events that
are likely to take place in relation to a company, an industry or a
specific problem. It represents an intelligent and genuine attempt at
writing a forecast for the future with a certain level of probability
built into it through using a number of extrapolative methods of
proven value. Altogether it is an excellent exercise in (*a*) helping
companies to become more proactive about the future environment

in which they are likely to operate; (*b*) stimulating a more creative climate; and (*c*) providing a superb training ground for bright recruits who have recently joined the company. The sheer task of having to assemble a futuristic scenario encompassing a large number of functional and environmental interrelationships is a most potent development tool for newcomers to the business.

The difference between scenario writing and scenario day-dreaming is that the former is assembled into a written document and the latter is done verbally, in an open group meeting, and without a record of the discussion being kept. The fact that no written document needs to be produced at the end of the session provides the team with a less inhibited environment in which to think freely and creatively.

In the context of a problem-solving session the two techniques can be valuable to the extent that the members attempt to describe a future scenario in which the problem under discussion has ceased to exist. The process of describing a problem-free environment can be immensely helpful in generating valuable ideas for getting there. The merit of this technique, as against a straightforward brainstorming session, is that the deliberations of the creative team focus on the problem in the context of the firm's future environment. The idea generation process is based on an attempt at working backwards from a situation in which the problem has been removed.

Suggestion schemes

Suggestion schemes have become quite popular in many organisations. As we saw earlier they provide a channel of communication through which every member of the organisation can transmit his or her ideas with the knowledge that they will be screened and evaluated and, possibly, implemented. Furthermore, such schemes perform the further task of stimulating a climate in which people want to become more creative and are encouraged to do so.

Some companies use suggestion schemes for obtaining a company-wide participation in generating ideas in response to specific and well-defined problems. The problem statement is circulated in the company with an invitation for ideas as to how it can be solved. Awards are offered for the idea which is found to be the most satisfactory and which is actually implemented. This way one gets the whole organisation to participate in thinking about the problem and generate ideas in response thereto. Clearly, the nature of the problem must be such that its open discussion cannot be harmful to the rules of confidentiality. There are many problems which cannot be ventilated openly among the whole mass of employees because of basic rules of prudent secrecy. On the other hand there are certain problems which can benefit from the injection of ideas from the wide catchment area of the organisation as a whole.

For instance, an airline can derive a wealth of creative ideas from its general personnel in response to the following problem:

'Passengers are only allowed one small bag on the aircraft. Many passengers ignore this rule and carry with them more than one bag. They resent being told to leave excess hand-luggage behind to be sent to the hold. This is often a source of conflict with the staff.

Therefore the problem can be defined as follows: "How can we tell passengers to desist from taking with them more than one bag without causing them an affront or irritation?"

Send us your ideas. Winning ideas will earn one week's holiday in Elba. Runners-up will get two weeks' holiday in Elba!'

Idea screening

If one or more of the techniques outlined above were used by the creativity team the 'funnel' should be full of ideas—good, bad and indifferent. They all deserve scrutiny, exploration and evaluation. However, at this stage one must match every idea to the realities of the firm's objectives and criteria of acceptability.

In Chapter 2 we discussed a set of procedures that a firm can apply in converting ideas into reality. Now is the moment to start invoking them with a careful eye on the practicality of each idea and its compatibility with the firm's specific needs.

In particular the following methods were considered:

(*a*) the application of the portfolio management matrix to the idea screening process;

(*b*) a screening algorithm;

(*c*) a quantified approach to criteria evaluation.

A conscientious and thorough adherence to these procedures will help to ensure that an effective screening process takes place and that the most promising ideas move down the funnelling cycle towards the identification of the best solution to the stated problem. During the idea screening stage two additional methods can be used with great effect:

(*a*) force field analysis;

(*b*) the 'How-How' diagram.

Force field analysis

Force field analysis is frequently used by creative groups in trying to establish what impact a proposed solution is likely to have during implementation. Any attempt at implementing a solution to a problem is bound to be subject to a myriad of forces—some helpful and some unhelpful. It is important that all these forces, both supportive and otherwise, are identified and their relative impact evaluated. Helpful and supportive factors are referred to as 'driving' forces. The unhelpful and constraining factors are often called 'restraining' forces.

Listing all the driving and restraining forces is an excellent discipline because:

(a) It helps to determine whether a proposed solution is practical or not. If the intensity of the restraining forces is overwhelmingly powerful the chance that the solution could be implemented is greatly reduced. A solution with a better relative balance between the driving and restraining forces should be preferred.

(b) It provides the team with an inventory of the factors which are likely to facilitate and/or impede implementation, and with such knowledge steps can be taken to enhance the former and remove some of the latter. Altogether, it can assist the team to develop a strategy for amending or improving a solution to take account of the forces identified during the force field analysis.

The procedure used is for the group to list and discuss their perception of the driving and restraining forces. The group leader places all the driving forces as arrows facing upwards above a horizontal line and all the restraining forces as arrows facing downwards below the line. Having identified all the driving and restraining forces applicable to the solution the team tries to determine the relative impact of each factor. They must try to reach consensus on the subject. Once this is achieved, it is normally shown by the relative lengths of the arrows on the diagram. It is important to remember that it is the *relative* lengths of the arrows that matter. The longest arrows represent the fact that either the driving forces, above the line, or the restraining forces, below the line, are the most powerful factors.

Figure 38 illustrates a typical example of the outcome of such an analysis.

Figure 38.   Force field analysis of a project to improve the packaging of an existing product the sales of which are declining.

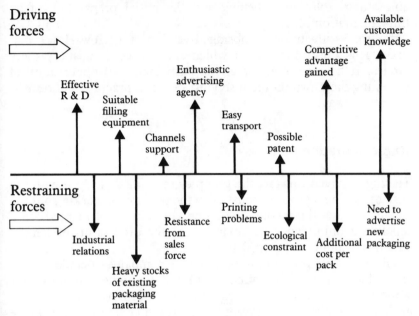

The 'How-How' diagram

The 'Why-Why' diagram was described on page 137.

The 'How-How' diagram is similar in approach except that it seeks to identify the various steps that should be undertaken when implementing a solution. Like the force field analysis it can help to test the solution against specific action plans. Against every step one can pose the question 'How?'—thus forcing the participants to respond to the practical challenges of implementation.

The question 'How?' must be posed and repeated persistently until such time as a specific solution route becomes so clear and acceptable that continuing to ask the question 'How?' becomes an exercise in hair-splitting.

The procedure commences with an agreement among the participants as to the favoured solution. At this point they ask themselves 'How?' it could be implemented. A few routes are identified and each route will have a number of alternative sub-routes in response to the 'How?' challenge. During thorough discussion of each chain, a convergent process can be used to narrow the list of alternatives.

The 'How-How?' can then restart on the narrower field of analysis but proceed to a few additional and more detailed steps of implementation. Properly managed and led, it can be an extremely valuable aid to solution screening and the initial preparation of an implementation plan.

Figure 39 illustrates an abridged version of a 'How-How?' diagram. It is a useful technique which can be used in most creativity circles. It has the merit of giving participants an opportunity of screening their own problem-solving ideas in a practical and results-orientated way.

Implementation plan

Having survived this far, the group or individual charged with the task of solving a problem must be in the position of working out the details of how the favoured solution could be implemented. In a small and unbureaucratic environment the process of implementation can commence forthwith.

In large and procedurally-orientated companies detailed plans must be prepared and often submitted to higher authority for approval. In the latter situations it is not uncommon for the teams to have to make formal presentations summarising the gist of the work and thinking they have pursued in trying to analyse and solve the problem.

In this connection it is worth remembering that such a presentation fulfils a number of functions.

(*a*) The preparation of a presentation is, in itself, a most valuable exercise in forcing the team to reflect upon the work they have undertaken and the conclusions they have reached. The work involved in preparing a presentation to a senior audience is often a valuable stimulus towards making the team consider a few loose ends that have hitherto escaped their notice.

(*b*) It is a 'selling' tool aimed at obtaining support from people who were not privy to the whole exercise. It must therefore be clear, succinct and capable of generating enthusiasm in the audience. A polished presentation can help to gain commitment from those who will ultimately need to authorise the project and provide the funds.

(*c*) An effective presentation can help to pre-empt objections. The fact that a team has considered so many driving and restraining

Figure 39.   The 'How-How?' diagram in relation to a decision to solve a problem through improved product.

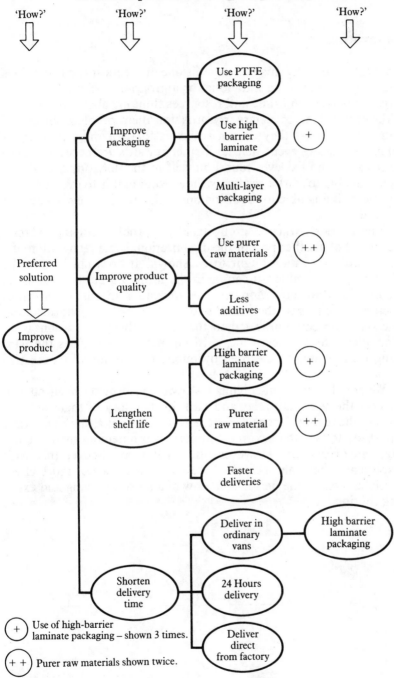

factors during its deliberations is bound to make its implementation plan more credible in the eyes of the people in authority.

Innovation

Solving a problem, small or large, is one of the most exciting things that can happen to an individual or a group of individuals. Many organisations spend time and resources thinking about how to provide physical or monetary rewards for their problem-solvers or innovators. What they do not realise is that solving a problem is such an exciting event that no further rewards are necessary. Any individual who has ever found himself in the unhappy position of being unable to start a car knows how exciting it is to overcome the problem. Being able to set off on one's planned journey is a perfect reward.

Nevertheless, where a group tackles a problem-solving exercise on behalf of another part of the organisation, some recognition of a successful innovation ought to be shown. It does not have to be monetary or tangible—it can be in the form of a public announcement or a certificate. Moreover, as innovation means doing things 'better' or 'cheaper' the benefits to the firm can be quantified and the outcome communicated to the rest of the organisation as an example of team effectiveness. In normal circumstances the winning team is amply rewarded by public recognition of its creative effort.

Where the problem-solving task was performed on an ad hoc project the team can relax and bask in the glory of their success. Where the team is a permanent creativity circle or a think tank they are ready to face the next most important problem on their list and start all over again. However, they will soon discover that with experience they can perform these tasks much faster, more effectively and enjoy the permanent glow of a most satisfying and exciting routine.

7 Brainstorming—technique or climate booster?

In the previous chapter, 'brainstorming' was briefly described. Brainstorming is an important technique and deserves a more detailed exploration.

Most managers have been exposed to it at one stage or another— some use it at fairly frequent intervals. However, my experience has taught me that people who use it without proper training or without the help of a facilitator do not derive the full benefit of this valuable method. In fact many people believe that simply sitting in a room and discussing a problem or a situation in a relatively relaxed fashion and writing ideas on a flip-chart constitutes brainstorming. If one chooses to use the technique as originated and developed by Alex Osborn one must remember that there are a number of well-trodden and well-proven rules of the game which help to optimise the outcome of brainstorming sessions. It is very useful for groups and their leaders to become familiar with these practical issues. This does not mean that a creativity group should not experiment with its own variations on the theme and evolve its own style of approach to idea generation. Nevertheless, if one wants to use an Osborn-type brainstorming technique one ought to familiarise oneself with its basic do's and don'ts.

It is essential to emphasise at the very outset that the use of brainstorming has a most valuable fringe benefit: it can help an organisation to partake in an activity which stimulates a climate in which creativity can flourish. This is a point which is often overlooked by less imaginative managers. I remember an occasion when the Chief Executive of a fairly sizeable firm invited me to assist them in solving a very troublesome problem. Among other techniques we spent some time on brainstorming sessions. All the participants found them highly stimulating and valuable. Unfortunately, and for various understandable reasons, the outcome of the various exercises proved somewhat inconclusive. 'This was a waste of time. We shall never undertake such wasteful activities again' was the decisive verdict of the boss. Whilst it is easy to sympathise with such sentiments, especially after partially abortive sessions, the point that the

155

boss in question missed was the fact that the creative sessions held in the company were not wasted. Each session provided a most valuable opportunity for members of the company's personnel to undertake excursions into a creative world which hitherto was totally unknown to them. The participants were ecstatic about having had an opportunity to explore solutions to what they all felt was a problem of strategic importance. The peremptory way in which the boss put an end to these explorations came as a most disappointing anticlimax. Brainstorming sessions, held at regular intervals, can have a remarkable impact upon an organisation's climatic welfare and this valuable side-effect must not be rejected so lightly. It is not unlike a person who decides to improve his general fitness and reduce his weight. On a doctor's recommendation he goes to a gymnasium. After one long session he discovers that not only has he not lost any weight but he also feels stiff and tired. Thereupon he comes to the conclusion that exercise is a waste of time.

It must be recalled that having the right climate in which creative ideas can be generated, ventilated and communicated is an essential condition for innovation. Brainstorming sessions, either of the Osborn type or home-made varieties, are powerful boosters to a climate which is fully responsive and empathetic to the creative process. A change in a company's climate or culture is not something that one can measure in immediate tangible results. This is a message which is not always easy to convey to hard-nosed businessmen.

I never get tired of repeating this message. Simple as it may be to understand, few companies are prepared to accept the fact that regular weekly or monthly 'creative morning prayers' can have an almost magical effect upon the firm's climate. People who have participated in the regular meetings of quality circles fully appreciate the stimulus that can be derived from these meetings, even when they are somewhat inconclusive.

Over the years I have had the opportunity of observing a number of companies, in various parts of Europe, who have been taking the creativity and innovation game seriously. Each one of these organisations has developed its own approach to group creativity. One thing that they all appear to have in common is the regularly held creative sessions in which ideas are being generated and 'kicked around'. Another element they have in common is the realisation that all these sessions and meetings have the prime task of stimulating a corporate climate and ethos in which ideas can spawn and flourish and, as a secondary task, generate ideas and/or solve problems. One more thing they have in common is above-average performance levels in their respective business sectors.

The theory of 'brainstorming'

Alex Osborn's book 'Applied Imagination' first appeared in the early fifties. Until it appeared, little had been written on the subject of creativity. Since then a considerable literature has developed, research has been conducted and programmes specifically designed to instruct students in creativity and associated techniques have been added to the curricula of many universities and training establishments. Many new techniques and modifications of well-established techniques have emerged over the years. Proprietary packages were developed and offered as the ultimate panacea for the need to innovate. Some of these packages have survived, others have vanished off the face of the earth.

The one technique that appears to have survived the test of time is Osborn's approach to brainstorming. Osborn was a modest and unassuming person who developed a personal passion for one subject: helping people, groups and organisations to become more creative. He was convinced that most people could be more creative but often fail to be so simply because they tend to 'drive with the brakes on'. He felt that all too often one allows oneself to be creative and self-critical at the same time. 'It is a little like trying to get hot and cold water out of the same faucet at the same time: the ideas may not be hot enough, the evaluation of them not cold or objective enough. The results will be tepid', was one of his famous quotes. This summarises the gist of his philosophy and approach: deliberate idea generation must take place independently of any attempt at evaluation. Moreover, quantity of ideas can ultimately yield quality. These are extremely simple notions, yet any person who ever participated in brainstorming sessions knows how hard it is to defer judgement, especially when the ideas appear eccentric or even absurd. The self-discipline demanded by an effectively-run brainstorming session is probably the hardest skill to achieve.

The principle underlying brainstorming is that a group of people applying their collective brain-power towards solving a problem or generating exploratory ideas are capable of producing a vast number of ideas provided they are prepared to suspend judgement and evaluation. A relaxed and judgement-free atmosphere provides the participants with a fluency of ideas which would be seriously impeded the minute somebody decided to raise a challenge or dissent. The fact that every participant can express his or her ideas without the feeling that 'somebody is looking over my shoulder' acts as a most valuable stimulant for creative output. In this connection it is appropriate to mention that judgement can be passed and negativity expressed without a word passing anybody's lips. Body language is a very powerful and eloquent communication tool. I have conducted brainstorming sessions where all the rules pertaining to the need to suspend judgement were fully adhered to with one exception: a participant had managed to convey negative evaluation, almost distaste, through his facial expression and the way he sat in his chair! It was made clear to everybody present that one person in the group thought that many of the ideas expressed were absurd. Yet that person did not say a word—his body language did the talking. I normally take the precaution of alerting participants to the need to withhold judgement throughout the brainstorming session, both verbally and through non-verbal communication. Often the latter is more difficult to control. Individuals who are incapable of controlling their negative body-language communication can represent a constraining effect on creative group work and one must be prepared to ask them, diplomatically, not to attend future meetings.

Composition of a brainstorming group

The size of brainstorming groups has received a fair amount of attention from writers and researchers over the years. Osborn himself was of the opinion that the ideal panel should consist of a leader, an associate leader, about five regular or 'core' members and about five guests. The 'core' members serve as pace-setters.

I have experimented with many different size groups and have found that I get the best results with groups of the following composition.

(a) *A leader or a chairman.* I have never found it necessary to have an associate leader. It is difficult to see what role such a person can play except as a leader when the regular chairman is unable to attend. Osborn appears to treat the associate leader more as an idea recorder or a scribe. Only to that extent do I agree with his idea in this connection. In situations where the brainstorming panel meets on a regular basis, I find that rotating the chairmanship is a most valuable strategy. This provides two benefits:
  (i) it provides every member of the team with an opportunity to act as the leader thus enlarging the network of experienced chairmen in the firm;
  (ii) it removes the psychological barrier that is often caused by the misplaced notion that 'chairmanship' or 'leadership' of the panel implies some hierarchical authority.

It is important that members of a brainstorming group recognise that the real role of the leader is purely to organise, stimulate and control the proceedings and not to manage the individuals. In this regard quite often the gentle, softly-spoken and non-authoritarian types make better leaders that the aggressive and domineering characters.

(b) *A scribe*. It is very useful to have an experienced scribe through-out the proceedings. A scribe is a person who records all the ideas that are generated by the group either on a flip-chart or on an over-head projector. Basically he is a member of the group, but owing to the pressure of having to record all the ideas that cascade he is fully engaged on that task. It needs a very alert mind and the ability to write quickly. Bearing in mind that a good group can generate ideas at a torrential rate a scribe has to record them at a faster rate than most people can write. It is therefore important that such a person can paraphrase the ideas into a condensed form. However, it must be done in such a way that when the screening and evaluation stage is reached, the participants can remember the exact gist of each idea, although it has been recorded in an abridged format for convenience.

Some companies have resorted to the use of audio-video equip-ment for recording group proceedings instead of using a scribe. My own experience with such equipment has been fairly disappoint-ing—most participants find the presence of a mechanical eaves-dropping device sufficiently inhibiting to stifle their creativity.

In organisations that conduct brainstorming sessions on a regular basis and as a company-wide network, a good scribe should be rotated around the 'circles' in order to demonstrate how the task can be performed effectively. Good scribes are worth their weight in gold.

(c) *Other members*. In addition to the leader and the scribe I nor-mally try to assemble eight more participants, making a total of ten. It must be emphasised again that this is not a magic number. Each organiser of brainstorming sessions should find out for himself what size group is the most comfortable one for him to manage.

Following Osborn's cue, I am keen on the idea of having half of the team as 'core' members and the other half as 'guests'. The 'core' members are regular participants of the 'circle'. They should be selected on the following criteria:
    (i) individuals who have proved themselves as capable of gener-
        ating an above-average number of ideas;

   (ii) individuals with a high threshold of tolerance for other people's ideas (a good 'attitude spectrum');
   (iii) members with a high level of conceptual fluency (see Chapter 3).

In large organisations there is some advantage in drawing people from different departments or operating units in order to stimulate a cross-fertilisation of experiences and ideas from a heterogeneous business background.

Inviting different groups of guests to complete the team is a useful concept. Moreover, the guest members should be rotated from time to time. The guests should be expected to participate in the proceedings, and not only to act as observers. This means that the main rules and procedures of brainstorming should be briefly explained by the leader/chairman at the beginning of each session.

The main advantages of inviting guest-panellists are:

   (i) if the same group is left together over a long period of time it can become stale or predictable in its pattern of thinking—the addition of guest members can neutralise this effect;
   (ii) stimulated guest members can become 'apostles' of the creativity creed and help to set up satellite groups in their respective departments;
   (iii) participation in brainstorming activities can help guests to become less cynical about their value—a most valuable benefit for the company as a whole.

One word of warning: care should be taken in selecting guest members of relatively comparable rank. When one of the guests is much superior in rank to other members it can stifle the flow of ideas and the uninhibited nature of the proceedings. This remark does not apply to organisations in which the relationship between bosses and their subordinates is relaxed and uncluttered by hierarchal formalities. In this regard I have discovered that companies in which all levels of management rub shoulders at the same canteen during lunch are less obsessed by the trappings of hierarchy. Invariably in such situations guests can be invited from any level of management without fear of ruining the game through the intimidatory presence of senior people.

Suitable topics for brainstorming

Brainstorming should focus on specific problems and/or well-defined exploratory activities. Vague and ill-defined areas of search should be avoided. Thus topics such as 'let us consider ideas for making our business more successful' or 'how can we make the average citizen of this country behave in a more responsible way?' are not useful subjects for fruitful sessions.

We saw earlier how important it is to undertake a cause-and-effect analysis in order to be able to state a problem in simple and unequivocal terms. The clearer the definition of the problem the more fruitful the brainstorming session is likely to be.

More specifically, the following guidelines may prove of some help.

(*a*) Simple or easily-diagnosable problems are more suitable for brainstorming than complex or multi-faceted ones.

(*b*) Topics or problems for which data and knowledge are available are normally more suitable than ones which suffer from a shortage of such information.

(*c*) The will to solve a problem must exist among those responsible for it to justify a brainstorming session. If there is evidence to suggest that whatever one is going to put forward to those in charge of the problem, they will refuse to 'bite the bullet' and grapple with the whole situation, it is a waste of time to brainstorm.

(*d*) Trouble-shooting problems are ideal topics for brainstorming, for example, 'how to reduce pilferage from a supermarket during school vacations'. Obviously, the problem will have to be refined and more clearly defined, but it is a useful topic for group work.

(*e*) At the 'exploratory creativity' level any situation calling for a large number of disparate ideas is suitable. For instance: new product concepts, new market/segment concepts, names for new products/brands/companies, themes for an event/conference, etc.

Unsuitable topics for brainstorming

One can extrapolate from the above what kind of topic is unsuitable. However, a number of situations merit specific attention.

(*a*) Problems which only have one or very few answers are invariably unsuitable. 'Where should we place our plant extension?'

in a company which only has one location is hardly an appropriate subject for a brainstorming session.

(*b*) Problems which need a higher authority for adjudication, for example: 'how can we replace the Chief Executive with a more creative person?'

(*c*) Subjects that require technical or professional expertise which is totally outside the understanding and capability of the panel, for example: 'how to reduce the amount of a catalyst currently used in production of a complex chemical'. This problem will obviously disappear if the participants in the group are all experts in this specific field or an expert member of the team is able and willing to explain the technical details of the task in point.

Altogether it is always advisable to start with relatively easy challenges and then proceed to more difficult tasks. The ability to chalk up a few successes is extremely valuable both for the group's self-esteem and as an aid to promoting the technique to other potential participants.

Preparatory procedures

Preparing the ground before undertaking brainstorming activities normally reaps considerable dividends and is worth the effort. I find the following steps particularly helpful.

Explaining the technique

A thorough explanation of the details of the technique, its purpose, and the various barriers that can impede success must be made to the group especially if it is their first excursion into such activities.

Moreover, the rules of the game must be emphasised, including (*a*) the need to suspend judgement; (*b*) the desirability of the 'free-wheeling' of ideas and (*c*) the need for quantity of ideas rather than quality.

With new groups I spend some time describing the need for a positive approach to other people's ideas, the 'attitude spectrum' concept and the role of the 'intermediate impossible'.

Warm-up exercises

These are an essential preamble to the actual problem-solving sessions. As in the case of physical training, where one starts with some warm-up exercises, it is important that the members of the panel are given an opportunity to relax and get into the right frame of mind. This can be achieved through a number of routines.

(*a*) The use of a number of games, puzzles and quizzes (similar to those shown in Chapter 3).

(*b*) A 'dummy' brainstorming session. This consists of an idea-generation exercise on a topic which is quite irrelevant to the participants, like 'a new use for paper-clips' or 'a self-changing nappy'. The team is invited to generate as many ideas as possible, in a freewheeling mode, whilst suspending judgement. The chairman or facilitator allows the exercise to go on for about 20 minutes without interruption, unless he or she feels that the rules of the game have been totally breached. At the end of the exercise the leader provides the group with a de-briefing chat highlighting the strong and the weak points demonstrated during the dummy run. If necessary, a second practice run can be organised to give the participants more confidence and to 'lubricate their brain cells'.

Defining the task

Every member of the team will have a perception of the specific problem to be solved, and it is important that a consensus is reached in this regard. In open discussion the group will seek to diagnose the problem and its main causes. The various techniques discussed in Chapter 6 like the Fishbone Diagram, the 'Why-Why' Diagram etc, can now be used by the team. The discussion has a dual purpose:

(*a*) to help the participants to enter into a more creative frame of mind: their brains will enter into a 'higher gear', so to speak;

(*b*) to ensure that everybody present works towards the same end.

I normally write up in very conspicuous letters, on a board or on a flip-chart, the wording of the problem that the team has agreed to tackle or the task they have undertaken to explore. The presence of this visible reminder is a useful stimulus to the brains of the individual members and provides direction for the ideas that follow.

Brainstorming at work

The group is now ready to start working 'for real'. The problem or the theme to be explored has been defined and agreed upon with everybody present. Ideas are now needed in large numbers and, if possible, without interruption. As a facilitator, when I deal with inexperienced groups, I ensure that I have a number of ideas 'up my sleeve' in order to re-start the flow when I notice that the group is drying up.

Seating arrangements

It is important that the members of a brainstorming team sit in a circle, rather than around a square or a rectangular table. The 'eyeball-to-eyeball' contact is useful and can be best achieved when people sit in a circle. Personally, I prefer the members to sit in a circle without a table. I find that a table acts as a constraint to an easy flow of communication. Without making too big an issue of the matter, the posture of the individual is important. They must be totally relaxed, but at the same time it is better if they do not slouch to the point of looking somnolent. There is a fairly delicate balance between appearing relaxed, and appearing disinterested. It is also important to remember that a group sitting comfortably in a circle and looking at each other can bounce ideas at each other and from each other in a most exciting way.

Output

With experience an effective brainstorming group should be able to generate as many as 150 ideas in less than 20 minutes. Obviously one must expect a much smaller output with inexperienced or newly-constituted teams. When a team generates fewer than 50 ideas in 20 minutes it is time to re-start, after undertaking a few more warm-up exercises. It is important that considerable patience is exercised in the early stages in order not to frustrate and de-motivate the members.

With time and experience, groups can start brainstorming without any preparatory work and briefing. They simply decide when and on what topic to brainstorm, and get on with it.

Idea supplementation

After a brainstorming session the participants are so highly stimulated that it is important to 'catch' all supplementary ideas which are brewing in their mind. This can be done quite effectively if the evaluation session is postponed for a few hours or even days.

Experience has shown that after brainstormers have 'slept' on a problem they often generate the most valuable of all the ideas collated during the session itself. The leader should alert them to this possibility and ask them to communicate all supplementary ideas that may have occurred to them following the termination of the session. Such ideas must be added to the list assembled by the scribe.

An effective leader should exhort his members to continue to incubate those ideas which are buzzing about in their minds. It should be possible to increase the total output of ideas by around 20 per cent and quite often these supplementary ideas can be even better than the mass produced during the brainstorming itself.

Finalising the list of ideas

If the leader and the scribe have done their jobs properly a list of ideas can be finalised consisting of (*a*) the ideas generated during the session and (*b*) the supplementary ideas that have emerged since the session ended. The combined list should consist of around 150-180 ideas and among these there should, in theory, be a few brilliant ones.

The combined list should be typed. I find that having it typed in triple-spacing can be useful during a subsequent evaluation session. Moreover, it is helpful to have all the ideas numbered in the order in which they were generated. This is of value during the screening activity as one can refer to ideas by their number without having to repeat whole sentences. This is particularly helpful when evaluating ideas against the matrix described in Figure 11.

This completes the brainstorming cycle. Ideas have been generated and supplemented by the post-brainstorming period of reflection. A list is now available to be screened and evaluated and the precious few converted into innovation. The procedures to be adopted in this regard will be discussed later.

Figure 40 summarises a timetable of the activities that were described in the previous pages with a recommended length for each part of the sub-routine to be used. The timetable is designed for groups which are relative novices in the use of this technique. As

Figure 40. Timetable for a full brainstorming session—(typical timetable for newcomers to the method).

Activity	Timing	Remarks
I Preparatory procedures		
A Explaining role and procedures of session, leader, scribe and conditions for a successful session	30 minutes	
B Warm-up exercises 1 Miscellaneous games/puzzles 2 'Dummy Run' 3 De-briefing	20 minutes 40 minutes 10 minutes	If appropriate two 'Dummy Runs' may be necessary
II Define problem and/or task to be brainstormed	45 minutes	
Use diagnostic tools like Fishbone Diagram and/or 'Why–Why' method		A brief rest will be needed
III Brainstorming	20–30 minutes	Aim for 150 ideas
IV Idea supplementation		
either Immediate or Follow-up	20–30 minutes continuous	Communicate via leader (over period of two days)
V Ideas list edited and typed	Scribe	Ready for evaluation session

was emphasised earlier, with experience the groups can short-circuit the whole cycle and dive into an idea-generation brainstorming session with minimum warm-up and preparatory briefing.

Below is a list of ideas which emerged from a brainstorming session which I conducted a short while ago in response to the problem: 'how can we dispose of 1 billion paper-clips profitably?'

1. Straighten them and use them as fuse wire
2. Pilot light cleaners
3. Spark plug cleaners
4. Straighten them and use them as pipe cleaners
5. As drain cleaners
6. Ear cleaners
7. Nose cleaners
8. Tooth picks
9. Back scratchers
10. Belly-button cleaners
11. Nail cleaners
12. Wedding rings
13. Brooches
13. Bracelets
15. Anklets
16. Bangles
17. Buckles
18. Necklaces
19. Ear-rings
20. Nose-rings
21. Decorative caps
22. Helmets
23. Veils
24. Bras
25. Suits of armour
26. Flak jackets
27. G-strings
28. A fashion dress studded with paper-clips like sequins
29. A gentleman's money belt
30. Money tokens
31. Luncheon vouchers in canteens
32. Tokens at game of poker
33. Design a new game called 'clippy winks'
34. Develop national championship of 'clippy winks' for managers

35. Develop a painting set with paper-clips
36. Magnetise them so that they can stick on a metal board
37. Develop a new art form with magnetised and coloured clips
38. Produce desk display units with magnetised clips
39. An anti-stress toy for managers
40. A Christmas gift consisting of a box with coloured clips in the shape of the company's logo
41. Coloured clips in a pretty display container for smart offices
42. Different coloured clips for use by managers for different levels of urgency, eg red for urgent, green for less urgent, blue for confidential, etc
43. Attach a small suction-unit to every clip so that it can be stuck on a flat surface such as a board or a filing cabinet
44. Attach to each clip a name-tag for conferences
45. Develop clips into magnetised and electrified 'homing devices' for tracing managers on their 'walkabouts'.

This is a partial list of the output that emerged in an amazingly fast session. More than another 100 ideas came from the group. Another 30 or so were added subsequently.

A few lessons can be learned from scrutinising this partial list.

(*a*) The easy flow of ideas and the 'freewheeling' effect can be seen throughout. One idea leads naturally to the next one. Occasionally, there is a change of pace but it opens a new range of 'synergistic' ideas.

(*b*) Ideas came in clusters: there was a 'repairing/cleaning' cluster of ideas; 'jewellery' cluster; 'clothing' cluster, etc. This breakdown of ideas into clusters can be extremely useful during the evaluation stage. A technique known as 'spider diagram', which will be discussed later, is specifically designed to capture this phenomenon.

(*c*) At no stage could one get the slightest feeling that the participants flinched from generating impractical 'intermediate impossibles'. The suspension of judgement was total and manifested itself by the far-ranging and sometimes 'way-out' ideas.

The group found the whole exercise great fun. However, they all admitted towards the end that having generated 150 or so 'crazy' ideas they felt totally exhausted. This is perfectly normal and one should try to avoid asking the same group to brainstorm again without allowing them to have some rest. Under no circumstances should it become a chore.

The spider diagram

As we saw above with the paper-clip exercise, ideas tend to arrive in fairly homogeneous clusters. In fact this is a signal that 'freewheeling' has taken place and that the participants respond to each other with associative ideas. When this happens every member knows that the rules of brainstorming are being adhered to and that creative 'synergy' among the members is being achieved.

Even when the team manages to produce 150 ideas it is rare for all these ideas to span more than a maximum of 15 clusters. Human creativity is not able or willing to exceed such a number. This is all to the good, as it is possible to screen and evaluate ideas in their natural clusters rather than as individual ideas in isolation.

An observer of an effective brainstorming group can trace the flow of ideas and the almost logical strand that runs through them in spite of the ostensibly chaotic way in which the group operates. The group's activity is reminiscent of a spider spinning its web. To the casual observer the spider appears to be spinning its web in an haphazard fashion, yet the end result is the most perfect and beautiful lacework. The analogy between brainstorming and a spider spinning its web is somewhat spurious, but it was sufficient for the expression 'spider diagram' to be coined to describe the way ideas emerge in fairly homogeneous and logically-linked clusters.

Figure 41 describes the way a spider diagram is constructed. It is based on the paper-clip example given earlier and has been filled in only in order to demonstrate the use of this simple technique. It has not been completed because only a partial list of the ideas generated has been provided. The main use of this tool is to highlight the natural groupings of the ideas generated during the brainstorming sessions. These are the main benefits.

(a) It provides an opportunity to discuss each cluster in its totality, eg the 'jewellery' cluster or the 'executive toy' cluster, thus supplementing the list with a number of additions in that area which the group may have missed.

(b) It is much easier to screen and evaluate ideas in clusters than as 150 individual ideas.

(c)   It helps the group to assess the quality of their idea-generation
work. When ideas flow in an associative fashion and can be
inserted in the various 'enclosures' of the spider diagram the
members of the group know that their session was a successful
one.

Skilful scribes can complete a spider diagram as the brainstorming session progresses. Instead of recording ideas sequentially on a
list in the conventional way they surround every cluster in a border
and then move to the next cluster. Should the group meander back

Figure 41.   Spider diagram.

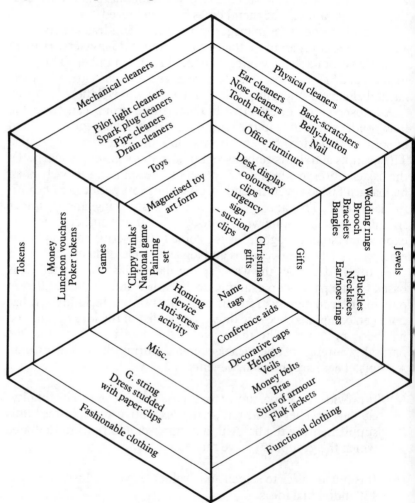

to one of the clusters that were explored earlier the scribe inserts those ideas in the appropriate border. By the time the session is finished all the ideas are recorded in their proper 'homes' and a good portion of the screening is thus completed.

The 'spider diagram' is an extremely contrived title for a simple but useful method. It provides a most valuable and natural link between creativity and innovation, namely between the idea-generation routine and the subsequent screening, evaluation and implementation of the best ideas.

8 Morphological analysis

Morphological analysis or 'morphological method' is one of the most valuable techniques for generating a large number of ideas in a short time. Of all the techniques I have studied or used over the years, I find that this method is not only a prolific source of ideas but is a most stimulating aid to broadening people's horizons and forcing them to think more laterally. Although this technique was mentioned briefly in connection with problem-solving activities (see Chapter 5) its main application is in 'exploratory creativity' where the main task is to generate ideas with the aim of surveying as many future opportunities as possible.

Morphological analysis was developed by a Swiss astronomer by the name of Fritz Zwicky, who worked at the Mount Wilson and Mount Palomar Observatories in California, during the forties. His method was developed in the context of complex technological and scientific research in astrophysics and rocket research. Zwicky became the champion of the morphological method and in 1961 became the President of the Society for Morphological Research in California. Unfortunately, the complex nature of his method coupled with poor communication has obscured the true value of his approach. The name 'Zwicky' became famous, especially in the field of technological research, but his method was somewhat lost in the depths of pure research establishments. In his 'Applied Imagination' Osborn mentioned morphological analysis briefly. It is only in the last few years that Zwicky's ideas have found their way into general management and, more specifically, into the area of creative thinking and innovation.

The method of morphological analysis

The complicated-sounding term morphological analysis belies a very simple method. In its most basic form it is not more complex than an ordinary matrix. If one takes a matrix of two axes with, say, ten items on each axis, one finishes with $10 \times 10 = 100$ combinations.

Figure 42. **Idea-generation through a two dimensional matrix. The task: 'How to add utilities to a walking stick or an umbrella'.**

	Radio	Tape recorder	Telephone	Telescope	Snuff box	Flask	Filofax time keeper	Camera	Swiss army pen knife	Dymo
Cricket Grounds										
Tennis Matches										
Ascot										
Glyndbourne										
Henley Regatta										
Stock Exchange										
Climbing holidays										
Skiing holidays										
Air shows										
Hunting										

If this is done as part of an idea-generation exercise one can produce 100 ideas with the greatest of ease. Let us take a simple example.

'A manufacturer of walking sticks and umbrellas is known for his highly specialised and unusual products. His sticks and umbrellas have added utilities such as hidden swords, seats, etc. The company now wishes to explore new products for development and is searching for ideas.'

One can undertake brainstorming or trigger sessions. However, morphological analysis is probably a more fruitful method in such circumstances. It is an exploratory exercise—after all what the company wants is a list of ideas for further exploration and quantification. It is an attempt at identifying opportunities rather than solving specific problems.

As a starting point a matrix can be structured with two axes: on the first axis one inserts the various 'utilities' that customers may value such as radio, telephone, flask, telescope, camera, 'dymo', etc. On the other axis one lists useful 'venues' such as cricket grounds, Ascot, Wimbledon, Henley, Stock Exchange, etc. If one manages to find ten items on each axis one finishes with 100 ideas!

Figure 42 illustrates the outcome of such a simple exercise. It shows ten items on the 'utility' axis and ten items on the 'venue' axis, making 100 ideas. Hopefully, one or two of the 100 ideas will prove good ones!

The novel concept that Zwicky propagated was that by adding a third dimension it was possible to multiply the output of the idea-generation process by the number of items on that dimension. Therefore, if one can think of a useful third dimension and place on it ten items one will finish with as many as $10 \times 10 \times 10 = 1,000$ ideas. This is a larger output than any brainstorming session could ever hope to produce. A three-dimensional 'morphology' can still be shown in pictorial form.

Figure 43 shows a morphological analysis of a situation which I had to grapple with a few years ago. The case in point related to a packaging company that wanted to develop a new packaging concept which was different from everything that had been available in the market at that point. Three dimensions were selected for exploration: (a) the shape of the pack; (b) the material that could be used; and (c) the content of the pack. In that particular instance the team that worked on the project finished with $7 \times 7 \times 9 = 441$ cells. Each cell represented an idea and a potential opportunity to be evaluated and quantified. If the theoretical statistics of conversion between ideas and innovation are right there should be around six or seven good ideas in the list.

Figure 43. The application of morphological analysis to the exploration of new packaging ideas.

* Simon Majaro, 'International Marketing – A Strategic Approach to World Markets' George Allen & Unwin London 1986.

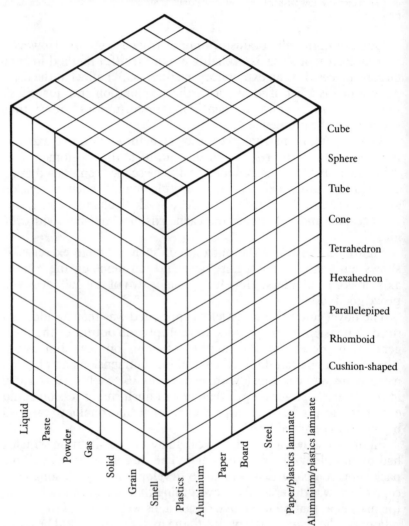

Figure 44 shows another example of morphological analysis at work. It describes an attempt at innovation in the field of air fresheners. Once again three dimensions have been chosen: (*a*) the kind of smell; (*b*) the configuration of the package; and (*c*) the location where it can be used or is needed.

So far we have looked at matrices based on two axes or morphologies consisting of three dimensions. The great advantage of both is that one can depict them in a diagrammatic and visual way. By doing that one can attain maximum interest and participation from the group members.

If one is prepared to develop a non-pictorial morphology, namely one that cannot be shown in a diagrammatic form, one can add as many dimensions as one wishes. Thus if we take a three-dimensional morphology and add a fourth dimension we can multiply the number of cells by the number of items inserted upon that fourth dimension. If the first three dimensions represent $10 \times 10 \times 10 = 1,000$ cells the addition of the fourth, invisible dimension with another 10 items will mean that we now have $10 \times 10 \times 10 \times 10 = 10,000$ cells. This represents, literally, a mass-production unit for ideas. This is why I often refer to this technique as an 'idea factory'.

Clearly, screening and evaluating ideas on such a scale cannot be done in one session. One of my clients uses these prolific lists as part of the weekly 'morning prayers'. A four-dimensional morphology was prepared some time ago. All the permutations were worked out by a computer into printed lists, all numbered sequentially so that it is easy to refer to each cell by its number. The idea is to pick up a number of ideas from the list and chew them over with the view of establishing how far they can be turned into practical propositions. During each session around ten ideas are looked at, discussed and screened and given a mark to indicate whether it is a 'high', 'medium' or 'low' idea. The 'highs' will be evaluated more fully at a subsequent session, but meanwhile the enormous list is reduced to more manageable proportions. In truth, the boss of that firm feels that these sessions help to stimulate the kind of climate which facilitates creativity. Obviously, he also hopes to identify a few winning ideas during these sessions, but claims that his first priority is the effect that these sessions have on the firm's climate. It is interesting to note that the boss participates in all these sessions and prefers other members of the organisation to act as leaders.

Below is illustrated a four-dimensional morphology in response to the following project: 'A manufacturer of disposable containers is looking for new and unusual products for segments which hitherto have not been exploited by other competitors.' Four dimensions have been selected: (*a*) shapes or configurations; (*b*) materials;

Figure 44. **A three dimensional morphology.**
The task: 'Develop a new concept in air fresheners'.

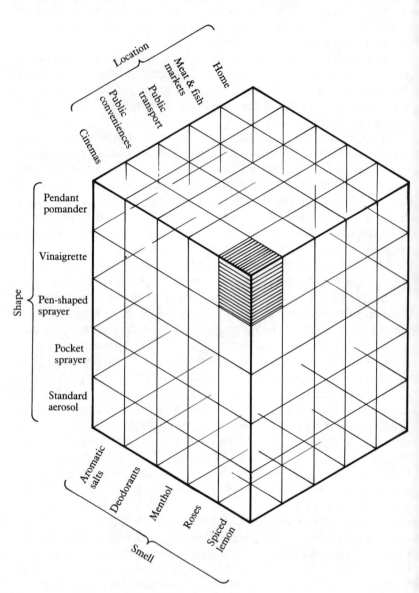

(*c*) contents; (*d*) locations of use. Four separate lists of ideas have been generated in response to each dimension. For convenience the numbers on each dimension are shown as ten. In practice the number can be either smaller or larger than ten. The outcome is that we have 10,000 combinations at our disposal. The likelihood that among this avalanche of ideas not even one is a superb idea is remote. The one I would love to have for myself is: 'inflatable belt with drinking straw,' made of 'high barrier plastics laminate', containing 'whisky' for 'golf courses'.

A four dimensional morphology for new products in the disposable containers business

Materials	Shapes	Content	Where
Paper	Beakers	Coffee	Home
Waxed paper	Cups	Tea	Canteens
Polystyrene	Plates	Juices	Coal mines
Polyethylene	Multi-compartment	Meals	Army
Aluminium foil	Grenade shape	Whisky	Climbing
Rubber	Condom	Glucose water	Cycling
High barrier plastics	Balloon	Syrup	Golf courses
Aluminium/paper Laminates	Sachets	Pain killers	Space
PVC	Hip flask	Energy producers	Gliding
PET	Inflatable belt with straw	Juices	Cross-country skiing

Unfortunately, the minute one adds dimensions beyond the first three one cannot display the whole output in an elegant diagram. It is necessary to list all the combinations on many pages of printout. In order to give the reader the flavour of the enormity of the task a few combinations derived from the above four columns are listed hereunder:

1. Paper-beakers-coffee-at home
2. Paper-beakers-coffee-canteens

3. Paper-beakers-coffee-coal mines
4. Paper-beakers-coffee-army
5. Paper-beakers-coffee-climbing
6. Paper-beakers-coffee-cycling
7. Paper-beakers-coffee-golf courses
8. Paper-beakers-coffee-space
9. Paper-beakers-coffee-gliding
10. Paper-beakers-coffee-cross country skiing

We have just scratched the surface—ten ideas only were listed and the morphology encompasses 10,000 ideas! This is sufficient to highlight the enormity of the task.

There are two methods which can be used to simplify the task of screening such a mountain of ideas.

Evaluating ideas in clusters

Instead of discussing each idea individually one can analyse the relevance and validity of a number of ideas in clusters. Thus one can explore the 'attractiveness' of 'Paper Beakers for Coffee' in relation to the ten 'where' items as a total group. This immediately reduces the dimension of the task.

Moreover, the discussion can encompass a broader range of combinations such as 'Paper-beakers for coffee/tea and other hot drinks' for the 'where?' items listed. This can help to accept or reject a much larger cluster of combinations emerging from the list thus simplifying the task.

It is important that during these explorations the participants do not consider the morphology as a constraint or a strait-jacket. In other words they must be ready to supplement the list in front of them by additional insights that were missed during the exercise. For instance, whilst looking at a total cluster of 'Paper beakers for hot drinks' they should not limit themselves to the ten 'where?' items if it occurs to them that schools, hospitals, prisons and universities are potentially even more interesting segments to explore at the same time. The whole method is designed to stimulate and help to generate ideas and must not be treated as an end in itself.

To some extent what is being suggested here is a logical extension of the spider diagram method that was discussed in the previous chapter. Masses of ideas do come in fairly homogeneous clusters.

Multi-phase screening

The idea here is to attempt to look at the output of the morphological analysis in two stages. If one ignores at first the fourth dimension one can analyse the first dimensions on a visual diagram like the ones we saw earlier. Somehow, a group of people functioning as a creative group normally find the screening of cells that appear on a neatly presented diagrammatic structure an easier task than just scrutinising cold phrases or an amalgam of words.

Once the first three-dimensional diagram has been screened and the number of variables reduced to more manageable proportions, the fourth (or even fifth) dimension can be added. During the second tranche of the analysis one puts aside one of the other three dimensions and thus once again the exercise can be supported by a visual aid to which the members can relate. It is an iterative process which facilitates the screening and evaluation sub-routines and helps to maintain group interest and stimulation.

Basically, every leader must evolve his own style and modus operandi for handling this important technique. It must be remembered that the method as outlined here was not specifically designed for the idea-generation process and therefore the user should approach it with minimum inhibitions and fear of breaking sacred principles. When Zwicky developed this method he intended it to be used as a multi-level aid to technological forecasting and to complex technology-transfer systems. The method that emerged from his work is almost incomprehensible to ordinary mortals. The way I describe and use the method is my own simplified version of the work of a brilliant man. In fact by referring to this method as morphological analysis I attempt to pay homage to Zwicky, who provided me with the inspiration to resort to this multi-dimensional way of looking at problems and opportunity-seeking activities.

Nonetheless, as in the case of brainstorming, a few valuable rules should be borne in mind when using the morphological approach. They should help the leader and the team to derive maximum benefit from the use of this technique.

Composition of the groups

The recommendations made in connection with brainstorming apply to the use of the morphological analysis approach almost fully. In fact, the technique is often used by the same groups either (*a*) as an attempt to provide a change of pace or variety in the proceedings, or (*b*) because the nature of the subject under discussion calls for an open-ended exploratory idea-generation exercise.

However, a number of observations ought to be made.

(*a*) In order to be able to use morphological analysis effectively one needs a leader/facilitator who is fully familiar with this method. Otherwise the group tends to fumble with its use and this can lead to considerable frustration at the end of the session.

(*b*) It is not necessary to have a 'scribe' during such exercises. The leader fulfils the dual role of a facilitator and collator of ideas. In fact each participant acts as his own scribe.

(*c*) The introduction of 'inexperienced' guests to the sessions is a more difficult task and must be backed by careful briefing and a number of succinct and convincing exercises. Otherwise the 'guests' can stifle the smooth running of the sessions.

I have found, over the years, that morphological analysis can be conducted with smaller groups than brainstorming. A group of six or seven members, plus an active leader, can function very effectively in most situations.

Topics for morphological analysis

Overall, morphological analysis is a most valuable technique not only for generating a large number of ideas but also for helping participants to get out of the cerebral 'squirrel cage', which is so easy to drift into in an organisational environment. Experience has taught me that a few well-prepared exercises in morphological analysis can stimulate groups to a high level of creative output.

Nevertheless, it is useful to recognise that there are certain situations in which the technique is more suitable than others. An experienced leader/facilitator would normally identify fairly quickly what kind of cases justify the use of morphological analysis and which do not. A few simple guidelines in this regard may be helpful.

Suitable topics

Morphological analysis is an ideal technique for generating a large number of ideas in respect of exploratory and opportunity-seeking

requirements. The need to define a problem in detail is less stringent than in the case of ordinary normative problem-solving situations. Thus the method is particularly valuable when one is being
invited to undertake any of the following activities.

New product development

A few of the exercises described earlier (see Figures 42 and 43) are
relevant examples in this regard. Any company that wishes to
escape from an existing, boring and extremely competitive product
range can derive a considerable injection of fresh perspectives and
ideas by using this method. If nothing else, it helps the firm's management to escape from the mental trap that imposes upon them the
thought that the products of the future will be no different from the
past and the present.

Use of new materials

Coupled with the previous point, morphological analysis can be
used when one wants to explore the use of different raw materials.
For instance, if a manufacturer of multi-product sports equipment
wants to consider how far the vast number of new raw materials can
be applied to the various products the company manufactures, a
multi-dimensional matrix can be used with helpful results.

Similarly, a pharmaceutical company can develop a 'morphology'
depicting the various 'cocktails' which its scientists are working on
together with one or two other axes such as 'diseases' and 'age of
patients' with the view of identifying as many areas for further
screening and eventual research as possible.

New segments and/or applications

This is an important area where morphological analysis can be of
great assistance. It can be used by top management of the firm in
searching for a new mission or by marketing management in exploring promising new market segments for exploitation. The aim is to
identify as many segments as possible for subsequent analysis,
evaluation and quantification.'

Thus, for instance, a chemical manufacturer who currently produces six different compounds which are being used in eight different application areas and sold to four types of fabricators can

broaden his search zone by looking at, say, 15 application areas and ten types of fabricators whilst exploring ten compounds, instead of the existing six. The firm's current marketing structure consists of $6 \times 8 \times 4 = 192$ cells. The new morphology to be explored will consist of $15 \times 10 \times 10 = 1,500$ cells. If after all this effort one does not find even one creative cell for development one is entitled to feel disappointed. Nevertheless, the firm's creative vistas will have been widened in spite of such a disappointment.

Developing a competitive advantage

It is universally accepted nowadays that in the competitive arena the most successful companies are the ones that have managed to identify and develop a sustainable competitive advantage. The theory in this regard is obvious and few people would challenge its compelling validity. However, identifying such a competitive advantage is not always an easy task. One needs to galvanise the firm's creative talent in order to explore as many avenues for achieving such an objective as possible. The morphological analysis route can be a most fertile tool for helping in this direction.

Novel ways to promote products

Companies wishing to explore new, better and/or cheaper ways to promote their products can benefit from an occasional morphological excursion. By placing products on one dimension, available media (above and below the line) on a second and a variety of possible target segments on the third, one can generate a myriad of ideas for subsequent evaluation.

Search for location opportunities

Firms that have a significant presence in the High Street who wish to explore new locations or alternative venues for marketing their products or services can derive fresh insights from the morphological approach. For example, a firm of opticians can build a morphology consisting of the following dimensions: types of services and products offered by opticians; locations (eg supermarkets, railway stations, airports, aeroplanes, schools, public conveniences etc) and types of patients.

Unsuitable topics

There is no harm in trying to use this exciting method whenever the mood of the creative group calls for some diversion. However, experience shows that there are some cases where it is best left alone as it is unlikely to be particularly helpful or yield valuable results, for example:

(a) any situation for which there can only be one solution and where the group's attention ought to focus on a narrow rather than on a broad field of search;

(b) creative sessions organised with a limited remit such as the development of a new trademark or brand name;

(c) any problem which is known to have only one dimension to it. Thus there is no point in attempting to create a morphological structure where one is looking for an alternative way to pack a given beer. It is difficult to visualise the development of a matrix and/or a three-dimensional morphology in such a situation. Brainstorming or the trigger method are probably much more useful in such cases.

With experience one learns which cases are suitable for the application of the morphological approach and which are not. The important thing is not to be afraid of trying the method when it is felt that it can be of some assistance, but also to be prepared to drop it if group proceedings are bogged down by its use in a given situation. The essential part of any creative work must be the smooth flow of ideas. Any activity which stifles this flow ought to be discontinued fairly quickly before it causes the group to lose interest and enthusiasm.

Preparatory procedures

Explaining the method

Whenever the method is being used for the first time the leader must explain its use with some care. The technique itself as described here is not very complicated. However, groups often struggle with its application for the simple reason that they have not been properly briefed. The main problem which they encounter is the ability to identify the dimensions into which a given problem or situation can be divided. Once the two, three or more dimensions have been agreed upon the exercises normally flow smoothly. There are a few basic principles which should be mentioned during the briefing session.

(*a*) The dimensions into which a situation is divided must have some logical interrelationship. The starting-point for structuring a morphology must be relatively logical. Thus in designing a morphological structure aimed at identifying new types of vehicular transport systems there is a logic in selecting the travelling *posture* of the driver and/or passengers; the *mode of propulsion* and the *medium* through which or upon which the vehicle can travel. On the other hand, if one chooses the *posture, mode of propulsion* and the six or seven *most popular cheeses made in France*, needless to say one will get garbage. Similarly, in developing a new concept in packaging *shape, content* and *material* are interrelated. At the same time *shape, content* and *country* are far less meaningful in the circumstances and the result of such an exercise is less likely to be satisfying.

(*b*) Whilst the dimensions themselves must bear some semblance of reality one can brainstorm to one's heart's content in respect of the items to feature in each dimension.

If a bank is seeking to identify potential new products or services to be rendered to its customers within the definition of 'financial services' the following dimensions would be realistic: *type of services, venue of use, type of customers*. Once these three dimensions have been agreed upon, the group can start thinking in terms of wild ideas to be placed on each dimension. On the first dimension it is perfectly legitimate to place such items as dating service, 'exchange and mart', mortgages, drain-cleaning, disposal of old furniture, insurance against casino losses, policies for funeral fees, etc. The absurd ideas will either trigger a few sensible ones or be rejected during the screening process.

Warming-up exercises

Warming-up exercises are even more important with morphological analysis than they are with brainstorming. The participants must have an opportunity of trying their hand at a number of simple cases. They must attempt to determine the nature of the dimensions into which the situation under discussion can be divided, and then they must try to break each dimension into as many items as possible. After they have completed this analysis they must look at the results and identify a number of ideas that look attractive and novel.

The most difficult part of the task is the identification of the axes, but once this is done the participants usually find the listing of the items on each axis an enjoyable mental exercise. During the warm-up phase I start by distributing one or two blank diagram forms like the one shown in Figures 45 and 46 on pages 189 and 190 and ask the members of the team, individually, to list their choice of dimensions in relation to a given case-study. Once this is done I ask for every member's decision in this regard and try to reach a consensus among the whole group. I have learnt from experience that quite often one or even two of the dimensions are repeated many times by the various members. It is normally the third dimension that generates a debate. However, with patience one can get the whole group to agree on the third dimension as well. I believe that concurrence in this area is an essential part of effective group work. Once agreement on all the dimensions has been reached one can start, as a group, to generate a list of ideas to go on each axis of the 'morphology'.

When the exercise is completed I discuss the outcome with the group for about 20 minutes in order to identify the lessons learnt. I then distribute a second diagram with a larger number of 'cells' and ask the group to agree again on the three dimensions pertaining to a slightly more complex situation. Once again the group is invited to complete the morphology.

The following are the kind of cases which I find evoke considerable group interest and keen involvement: 'A bank's management are inviting you to suggest as many ideas as possible for new services which they ought to consider developing'; 'Develop a new type of vehicle—different from a motor car'; 'A telephone company wants you to submit new ideas for a telephone service. No holds barred!'.

Defining the task

Before starting to use morphological analysis in relation to real tasks it is important that the group agrees on the precise terms of reference. In many cases this is provided to the group in advance, but if there is any ambiguity it ought to be clarified. It is useful to place the defined task in a conspicuous place in the room in which the group is operating—it acts as a continuous reminder to the 'creative brains at work'.

A statement like 'identify new applications for milk' is clear. On the other hand an invitation to develop a morphology on the lines: 'Submit ideas as to what else we can do with our obsolescent plant' would be a difficult task for a multi-dimensional morphology structuring. The aims and scope of the task must be such that it is capable of being broken down into a number of interrelated functions or dimensions.

Morphological analysis is a technique that combines rationality, when selecting the dimensions, with the freewheeling of ideas when placing individual items on each axis. If one allows oneself to think wildly at both levels the outcome can be quite unhelpful.

Morphological analysis at work

The group can now commence working on the task in hand. Having carried out one or two warm-up exercises they should be able to approach the real project with confidence and ease. The first step is to agree on the various dimensions into which the task can be divided. If the group identifies more than three dimensions they should try to determine their relative importance and priority. Initially it is better to experiment with a three-dimensional morphology rather than drive straight away into a larger number. Through iteration the group can at a later stage play around with different third dimensions and ultimately develop, if necessary, a fourth dimension. I find that the four-dimensional approach, which can only be presented as a long list of combinations, is far less congenial to handle in group work.

Seating arrangements

Similar comments to those given in the previous chapter can be made. A round table is always to be preferred to any other sitting configuration. If a round table is not available the participants can sit in a circle without a table. It removes any vestige of hierarchical hang-ups and inhibitions associated with functional politics. In common with all creative techniques the ability to generate an egalitarian atmosphere is conducive to the effective flow of ideas. It is therefore important to remove the barriers that the presence of people from different levels of management and functional areas can bring about.

Blank diagrams

If the leader of the group feels that the morphological analysis approach is likely to be used during the planned session he should have a number of blank diagrams prepared and duplicated. Each participant will be given a blank form to complete either individually or in group discussion. I normally start with individual work and subsequently open the exercise for general debate and concurrence.

Clearly, it is not possible to assess in advance the number of items that the participants will insert into each dimension, and therefore one does not know how many 'cells' the pre-printed diagrams should consist of. I normally bring along batches of around four or five blank forms with a variety of cell numbers similar to those described in Figures 45 and 46. We start with the smaller morphologies and, if I discover that the team is able to complete them easily, I hand over a larger blank diagram and ask them to start again whilst re-thinking some of the items already inserted in the previous diagram. This has the merit of introducing a partial evaluation of their initial creativity. Unlike brainstorming, a touch of self-judgement is not harmful.

Figure 45.   Blank form for a morphological analysis warm-up exercise.

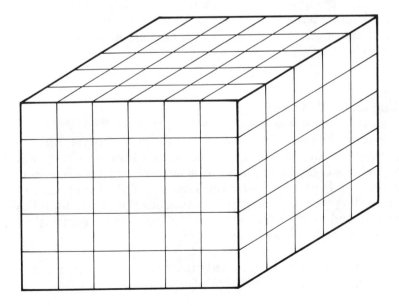

Figure 46. **Blank form for a morphological analysis excercise (second phase).**

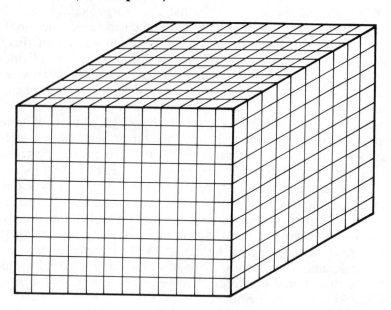

I also bring to the meetings blank transparencies of the various diagrams for an overhead projector. When the time comes to coalesce the group's collective creativity into one presentation I find that the completion of a blank transparency on an overhead projector is a most effective way for maintaining group interest and participation.

The method at work

The team should have gained the feel for the technique during the previous briefing and warm-up exercise(s). They are now raring to go and tackle the task at hand. It is important that the momentum is kept at a fairly steady pace and a minimum number of lulls in the proceedings occur. Non-active intervals, except breaks for refreshments, tend to interrupt what I call the 'magic of the occasion'. The session should take the following format.

(*a*) The task at hand is unveiled (unless previously communicated) and placed in a conspicuous place in the meeting room.

(*b*)   Each participant is asked to reflect upon the task and identify the three most important and interrelated dimensions into which the problem in question can be broken down.

(*c*)   All the participants are now asked to read aloud their thoughts about the various dimensions. A few of these dimensions will have unanimous support. Others will be somewhat more controversial.

(*d*)   An open discussion should take place with the view of reaching an agreement on all the dimensions. The leader should attempt to steer the discussion towards a high level of concurrence in this regard. Should some of the participants insist on having one or two other dimensions the leader can suggest that they will be worked upon during a second interaction.

(*e*)   Each participant is now given a number of blank diagrams (to start with, the smaller version, say $5 \times 6 \times 5$), and is asked to complete the 'cells'. After about 10–15 minutes the participants are invited to read their conclusions aloud and a general debate ensues.

(*f*)   At this point the leader may decide to repeat the exercise with a much larger diagram, say $10 \times 10 \times 10$ format. The second round will benefit from:
   (i)   the fact that the participants have had an opportunity to reflect upon the whole subject in greater depth;
   (ii) the general discussions will have provided them with some cross-fertilisation of ideas with the other participants;
   (iii) they should feel altogether more comfortable with the whole method.

(*g*)   The leader now tries to coalesce the individual analyses into a single and agreed diagram on an overhead projector transparency. This is the most difficult part of the leader's role and calls for skill, patience and diplomacy.

(*h*)   Once the unified diagram has been completed and agreed upon the leader can ask the group to undertake one or more of the following activities:
   (i)   to run through the myriad of 'cells' and list the five 'most exciting' ideas among them;

Figure 47.   Timetable for a morphological analysis session.
Assumptions: 1 The session is devoted to this method only
2 Participants are newcomers to this method

Activity	Timing	Remarks
I Preparatory procedures A Explaining the method, its value and limitations	 30 minutes	Support briefing with illustrations of successful assignments based on this method
B Warm-up exercises	45 minutes	
1 2 exercises 2 De-briefing	 15 minutes	Bring along blank diagrams
II Define task at hand	15 minutes	Display agreed text in a conspicuous manner
III Develop the morphological diagram		
1 Identify the dimensions and discuss	20 minutes	Leader to collate group output on a master diagram on overhead projector
2 Fill 'cells' on first Diagram	20 minutes	
Discuss	15 minutes	
3 Fill 'cells' in second Diagram	20 minutes	
Discuss	15 minutes	
IV Finalise list of ideas agreed and supplement if necessary	45 minutes	Leader to complete work and have short- list of best ideas typed and circulated

(ii) to identify the five most absurd 'intermediate impossibles' and attempt to salvage them;
(iii) to pick up a few of the more sensible ideas and develop a
'scenario day-dreaming', attempting to visualise the destiny of the idea in practice over the next few years;
(iv) to undertake a screening procedure with the view of
identifying the 'high'/'high's'; see Figure 11 in page 44.

Undoubtedly the group has an enormous quantity of raw
material at its disposal. The way all this output is capitalised upon
depends to a great extent on the experience and skill of the leader
coupled with the enthusiasm and motivation of the members of the
group. Where both these forces are at work the team can create the
world.

Figure 47 summarises a typical timetable for a session in which
morphological analysis is the main thrust of the proceedings. It
must be appreciated that it is only being provided as a guideline to
whoever is responsible for planning such sessions. It should not be
construed as an immediate routine. In common with all other
methods associated with creativity and innovation flexibility is a
vital ingredient.

9 Scenario-writing and scenario-daydreaming

'The future is hidden even from the men who made it.'

Anatole France

'Scenario-writing' is a technique which emerged from the recognition that the need to anticipate the future is an essential component in national and/or corporate planning. Planners have come to realise that planning is not simply an exercise at extrapolating the past into the future but a systematic attempt at developing a 'vision of the future' and targeting one's strategies, resources and effort at such a future.

Unfortunately (or perhaps fortunately), nobody can anticipate future events with any level of certainty. As a wise futurologist once retorted: 'the one certain thing about the future is its uncertainty'. The best one can do is explore the likelihood of future events on the lines of highest probability level and encompass contingency safeguards in the event that the future, as anticipated, takes a somewhat different direction. Scenario-writing was developed as a technique aimed at exploring a step-by-step sequence of events likely to occur between now and some given point in the future.

Scenario-writing was initially applied to the exploration of potential military and geo-political events. Clearly it was vitally important for military strategists and world politicians to gaze into the distant and unknown future before committing national resources to specific strategies. One of the early leaders in the field, the late Herman Kahn, applied the scenario technique to a much broader context by embracing cultural, social, political, economic and technological patterns of possible futures. In the context of the Hudson Institute, which he headed, he published a comprehensive future scenario document under the title: '*On Alternative World Futures*: *Issues and Themes*'. Subsequently he published a book (jointly with Anthony J Weiner), 'The Year 2000' predicting the world's environment in the year 2000. Whilst many of the conclusions and assumptions made in the book will probably not survive the test of

195

time, the idea that one can attempt to assemble a scenario of a probable future has gained ground among strategists.

The main attraction of the scenario-writing technique is the fact that many aspects surrounding the future environment of a given problem are being looked at more or less simultaneously. Thus if one attempts to prepare a scenario for the future of the fertiliser industry one would expect to focus one's attention on a myriad of interrelated factors such as technological forecasts, economic trends, political and social patterns, income distribution, buying patterns of products that depend on fertilisers at source, ecological pressures, etc. Obviously, if an anticipated increase in the population's standard of living means a change in dietary habits causing a shift in crop patterns, it is useful to incorporate such an insight into one's corporate plans.

The scenario-writing document has been referred to as the 'History of the Future'. The expression may sound like a contradiction in terms—nonetheless this is precisely what the technique is all about. Herman Kahn once suggested that the following were the main benefits of the technique.

(*a*) An attempt at lessening the 'carry-over' thinking of the past. Scenarios force one 'to plunge into the unfamiliar and rapidly changing world of the present and of the future by dramatising and illustrating the possibilities they focus on'.

(*b*) It forces the analyst 'to deal with details and dynamics which he might easily avoid treating if he restricted himself to abstract considerations'.

Why is scenario-writing receiving so much attention in the context of a book on creativity and innovation? The whole development of this method was in relation to long-term planning and technological forecasting activities. It is true that such activities require a high level of creativity, but at first glance it is difficult to see how scenario-writing and its verbal counterpart, scenario daydreaming, justify a whole chapter in a book on the subject of creativity. If one accepts the concept that one of the major roles of an effective manager is to 'invent the future' any doubts in this regard will be dispelled. Over the years, in my capacity as a consultant and as an academic, I have discovered that the two techniques have an enormous value in three areas: (*a*) corporate planning; (*b*) management development; and (*c*) creativity and innovation. I wish to say a few words about the first two before concentrating upon the third aspect.

Scenario-writing and corporate planning

Planning was defined as the process of matching a company's strengths with future opportunities. This means that one of the main tasks of the planning process is the need to compile an appreciation of the future environment in which the company will be likely to operate. Invariably a large number of factors impact upon a firm's environment. The most significant among them have to be identified and their future direction anticipated.

In a competitive world the company that manages to forecast the future more accurately is more likely to develop strategies that are germane to the needs of the future. This is the hard truth which many managers often prefer to ignore inasmuch as, intellectually, 'inventing the future' is too challenging a task for most of them. Yet, when one recognises that many corporate disasters stem either from a failure to attempt to anticipate events or from a wrong assessment of the data assembled, one should ascribe a higher priority to such an activity.

A few well-known examples may strengthen the point

Life style and the food industry

The food and beverages industries are being affected by the trend towards healthier foods. The number of consumers who keep an eye on the nature of preservatives, additives, calories, etc is on the increase. This trend has been with us for a while, but its intensity has certainly grown in the last few years.

The more 'proactive' and creative members of the food and beverages manufacturing fraternity were able to spot the trend and anticipate its development. These were the companies that responded to this market niche and capitalised on a rich opportunity. The less 'proactive' companies were left behind. Clearly a scenario-writing exercise would have helped to highlight trends in this regard and assist company strategists to focus on potential innovations.

Opticians and the law

The optical trade in the UK was cocooned, for many years, by laws which prohibited it from advertising and promoting its services to the public. Opticians were prevented from communicating with their customers by normal promotional means. The result was that the skills of advertising, sales promotion and publicity were completely lacking among members of the profession.

The Government decided to change the law in this regard and removed the various legal constraints that had existed. The profession got itself into a turmoil because the majority of them, especially a few of the multiples, were incapable of adjusting their marketing strategies to a more liberal environment. On the other hand, a number of organisations in this field responded to the challenge created, and developed suitable and extremely successful strategies. The former are struggling now, the latter are thriving.

Was it impossible for people in the industry to forecast such an event? This is almost a naive question, as the Government's intentions in this respect were known for some time and full consultations with the industry took place. The industry resisted the change and was unwilling to plan for the new marketing situation which was on the way. Suggesting that the industry was not being 'proactive' is almost a compliment to some of them. Yet a few operators understood the potential marketing 'scenario' and exploited the opportunities creatively and effectively.

Ferries and the Channel Tunnel

One does not have to be a prophetic genius to recognise the threat that the advent of the Tunnel will have upon the channel ferry business. The national plans in this regard are fairly clear and a scenario of future events can be assembled without the need to gaze too deeply into a crystal ball. Yet among ferry operators there are a number who appear to work on the assumption that all will be well.

The smarter strategists in the business will assemble a scenario of the chain of events to come and the probable impact that the Tunnel will have and develop creative strategies in response. With a clearer understanding of the social, psychological, political, technological, economic environments of the post-Tunnel-building era more innovative responses can be developed. I have no doubt that a few creative operators will continue to thrive in spite of the Tunnel.

Many other examples from different industries can be listed to illustrate how important the scenario-writing concept is to the development of creative strategy search activities. In fact my assertion is that a carefully prepared scenario-writing exercise must be an essential and integral part of every company's planning cycle. It is the most valuable safeguard against complacency and the refusal to acknowledge the force of dynamism in the firm's environment.

Scenario-writing and management development

Here is an idea for personnel and management development bosses! Many companies recruit young graduates at a steady rate. The 'milk round' is a recognised routine for identifying budding talent and for inducing the selected few to join the recruiting companies. Most graduates join with the expectation that the recruiting organisations will provide them with a structured and effective 'graduate training' programme. Unfortunately such training is still a minority practice. I meet dozens of very frustrated graduates who have joined industry and commerce almost under a false description of the reality. Graduates are often thrown into a company without any exposure to the rudiments of management principles and theory. They simply move around from department to department in an unstructured way on the understanding that this is the 'best way to learn'. Obviously the more enterprising graduates cope with the challenge, and through a determined process of observation coupled with self-development overcome the lack of a truly effective management development programme.

A scenario-writing assignment is a wonderful opportunity for (*a*) harnessing the fresh minds that young graduates bring along to the business; (*b*) utilising to the full the newly recruited manpower; and (*c*) providing them with a first-class platform from which to learn about every aspect of the business and at all levels. A period of six months to one year working on a scenario-writing exercise in small groups of newly-recruited graduates is a God-sent opportunity for turning graduates into well-informed managers!

The idea is to invite four or five graduates, under the supervision of an experienced and enlightened manager, to undertake a comprehensive scenario-writing project pertaining to the company they have joined in an explicit time-frame, say ten years. This entails a full analysis of both internal and external data relating to the company and its environment. It also means that the team will have to identify and study all published information about the industry, technology development, economic matters, competitive trends, customers and their anticipated life-style, etc. The team will need to apply statistical and quantitative methods in attempting to forecast future events in the company and its external environment.

The end result will be a document setting out the operational scene for the company ten years hence. This is a most demanding but exciting project for young recruits. For the company such an assignment will provide a futuristic scenario of possible things to come and at the same time a group of all-round future-orientated young managers. What more can a company hope to gain from its management development system?

I have managed to convince a number of enlightened organisations of the creative nature of such an approach. However, I hasten to add that this is not an approach suitable for the faint-hearted or those at the lower level of the 'excellence' spectrum.

Scenario-writing and creativity

Hopefully, the previous two sections have by now paved the way towards the main thrust of my message. Scenario-writing is a sophisticated technique for stimulating the firm's management to identify creative ideas for development and implementation. The sheer momentum of talking, thinking and dreaming about the future opens vistas which hitherto were closed to the organisation owing to the narrow horizons and frame of reference in which its members have been constrained. This applies both to organisations and to individuals. An individual who can forecast that at some point in the future a derelict part of London will undergo urban rejuvenation is more likely to benefit from such an insight. By the same token, an electronics company that develops a 'vision' of a future in which every consumer will wish to have an integrated audio/video/telecom/security network in his home stands a better chance of attaining innovation than the firm that sees the future purely through present-day eyes.

Let us imagine a group of managers getting together in order to reflect upon events that are likely to take place in some distant future and consider the impact, favourable or otherwise, which such events will have on the firm. Let us also assume that the group consists of experts in a variety of functional areas such as marketing, technology, economics, research, finance and personnel. Each individual is asked to consider the world environment five or ten years hence with particular reference to his area of specialisation. Members of the group will be expected to support their predictions through the submission of some evidence from such sources as speeches made by well-informed people, published articles, documents issued by trade associations or national and international forecasting bodies, etc. The group tries to immerse itself in the future and compile a stage-set depicting the world in which the firm will be functioning at a future point in time. Clearly, the whole scenario may prove wrong either through the group's misreading of the way events are progressing or through an unexpected event that may deflect the world from the predicted course. Nonetheless, the sheer process of 'gazing over the fence' of present-day reality into the unknown can have a most salutary effect upon management's creative vistas.

The main point I wish to make is that the accuracy of the scenario is almost secondary. The most important element in the whole exercise is the fact that the whole process opens the team's mind to new perspectives and potential opportunities. To that extent my assertion is that scenario-writing is not only a valuable input to company planning and management development but also to the whole process of corporate creativity and innovation.

Scenario-writing usually ends with a document which forms an input to a firm's strategic thought process. It is an attempt to set up a logical sequence of events in order to show how, starting from the present (or any other given moment of time), a future state might evolve step by step. From the vantage point of creativity scenario-writing is particularly helpful to the strategic level of the firm, to those who have to search for new directions and strategies for the organisation. It alerts them to ideas and opportunities which do not come to people's minds in the context of a routine and relatively static operational scene. Well-conceived and all-embracing scenario-writing documents can help the motor car industry to develop product innovations for the future. Without such an input it is a lot more difficult to conceive and develop creative new strategies. Similar projects can assist the pharmaceutical industry to identify the best way to channel its R & D funds for more marketing-orientated developments and innovations.

From the point of view of creativity and innovation, these are the main weaknesses of scenario-writing projects.

(a) Their complex nature means that they are normally undertaken, if at all, at infrequent intervals. This in turn means that their credibility inside the organisation is fairly low and people do not ascribe much value to their content.

(b) The tendency is to commission such assignments from outside firms of consultants or forecasting establishments. This derogates from the catalytic effect upon the firm's own creative processes. I personally believe that scenario-writing projects should be undertaken by members of the organisation itself even if the outcome is less polished or convincing. From the point of view of creativity the benefits could be enormously greater.

(c) The fact that such projects are normally undertaken at top management level imparts an aura of remote superiority to their existence. This in turn reduces interest among middle and operational management in their conclusions. Once people dissociate themselves from such an important project, its contributory role in stimulating creative ideas is greatly diminished. Companies that indulge in scenario-writing projects must ensure that a general involvement in their preparation and interpretation is promulgated. It must not be seen as an elitist exercise for the people at the top only.

Scenario-daydreaming and creativity

Scenario-daydreaming seeks to undertake the same task but over a shorter period and without the same depth of information and intelligence that the former technique normally demands. The method can be used over a period of one or two days and the final output is seldom expressed in a published report. The only items which are likely to be published at the end of the session are the various ideas which may emerge during the deliberations. As the word 'daydreaming' implies, the participants are invited to gaze laterally and futuristically into events to come. The dreaming must be in relation to the company and the people who work in it. As we shall see later, a touch of brainstorming is allowed but it must be relevant to the business under discussion. The participants are invited to explore a synoptic view of as many developments as they can simulate in a realistic fashion.

Of the two variations on the theme I find that scenario-daydreaming is the easier one to manage in the context of a short creativity session. Inevitably, it is seldom supported by the same amount of corroboration from quantifiable sources as scenario-writing projects are. It is probably less valuable for planning purposes as it is often based on a fairly superficial analysis of facts and figures. On the other hand, it is a powerful aid to stimulating peoples' imaginations and forcing them to think in broader terms than they are normally accustomed to.

In the light of these remarks it is proposed to concentrate upon the scenario-daydreaming method rather than upon its complex counterpart.

Scenario-daydreaming in practice

As emphasised earlier, the technique is not designed to generate ideas. It is meant to be a futuristic scene-setting excursion during which creative ideas may emerge as a by-product. It aims to generate a discussion during which the participants can shed the mental constraints imposed upon them by present-day operational expediencies. It can be a most exciting activity and, if properly conceived and managed, can have a far-reaching effect on the creative thinking of those who take part in it.

Basically, scenario-daydreaming is a method whereby a group of people meet in order to reflect upon their business or activities in the context of the future. They seek to catapult their thinking into a distant point of time and conjecture how they will fare in that future which they are anticipating. Why do it in a group? Surely individuals can sit down and produce their own vision of the future and generate their own scenario-daydreaming on their own? In fact, many people do it without realising that they are using a method that enjoys such a fancy title. Indeed, many people often undertake such excursions whilst having a brief nap. It is probably true to say that many major success stories in the world of industry, business and commerce have probably stemmed from inadvertent 'daydreaming' flashes. However, there are considerable benefits in conducting structured scenario-daydreaming sessions in pre-selected teams. The main benefits from such an approach can be summarised as follows.

(*a*) As with most creative techniques it is a potent aid to stimulating a creative climate.

(*b*) If the members of the group are selected for their diverse functional or technical expertise the exercise may yield an integrated scenario encompassing multi-disciplinary insights.

(*c*) Daydreaming with colleagues, who have a variety of convictions regarding the future, can help to mitigate the risk of polarised and entrenched perceptions. One finishes with a 'jury of executive opinion' scenario rather than an egocentric viewpoint.

(*d*) Finally, undertaking such an exercise with colleagues is greater fun than attempting it on one's own. I normally find that it has the added benefit of creating a strong bond among the members of such teams. Undoubtedly, this is a most valuable bonus.

Composition of the team

This depends on the nature of the business and the main problems and threats that the company is facing. If the company is operating in an industry in which the technology is moving at a very rapid rate it is essential to incorporate people who understand the intricacies of the technology. Where the main threat is from overseas competitors who are determined to buy their way into market share dominance, it is advisable to invite people who are familiar with international marketing intelligence sources and methods. If a patent is under threat a lawyer must be co-opted.

It is also worth remembering that scenario-daydreaming is a more complex activity to mount than an ordinary brainstorming session. It normally entails a two-day event in an external venue. It removes people from their work routine for a couple of days and involves the additional expense of hotel or conference centre accommodation and facilities. It is therefore essential that the details are prepared in a painstaking way and that the participants know what to expect in advance. It is not the sort of exercise that one would normally recommend to mount at a very short notice as part of the Friday morning 'corporate prayers.' With these remarks in mind the following should be noted regarding the team.

The leader/facilitator

The use of an experienced external leader/facilitator is essential unless such a person can be found inside the company. The role of such a person is:

(*a*) To plan the exercise in detail. Under this heading he must carry out the following tasks:
   (i) prepare a briefing note encompassing details of the exercise and its objectives, the approach to the session and the role of the leader;
   (ii) list the areas at which the group will need to direct its futuristic gaze (the list need not be comprehensive but must incorporate the main issues which are likely to affect the firm's destiny);
   (iii) explain the main rules of creative group work and stress the barriers that can stifle a successful outcome.

(*b*) To lead the proceedings during the session. In this regard the leader must be prepared to stop the proceedings from time to time in order to recharge the 'mental batteries' with other exercises and/or techniques. He must motivate and stimulate the group at all times and prevent them from running out of steam.

(*c*)   To encourage idea generation in the context of the exercise and its objectives. To this extent, the leader must decide when to digress into ancillary idea-generation activities.

(*d*)   To help in summarising the results and the lessons derived from the exercise, and if appropriate, to list the ideas that emerged from the proceedings.

It is not normally necessary to have a scribe, but a member of the group should keep minutes of the proceedings and make a special note of all the ideas that were aired. Some creative gems may emerge during the proceedings, and it is important that they are not lost through the passage of time.

Members of the team

Properly organised and directed, a scenario-daydreaming session can yield valuable outputs and generate a host of novel ways of looking at the future direction of a business. This means that the participants should be people who are capable of looking at the business in a broad and objective way. Managers with egocentric and parochial attitudes should not be invited to attend the session. Neither should people who are renowned for their intolerant 'attitude spectrum' towards the ideas of others.

The following individuals are particularly useful for scenario-daydreaming meetings.

(*a*)   Managers with specific expertise in areas which can have a significant impact on the future of the company's business. Thus companies operating in the pharmaceutical business will probably need to invite one or two pharmacologists, an epidemiologist, a medical practitioner and, possibly, a patent lawyer specialising in the field of medicines—in addition to representatives from marketing, production, personnel, etc.

Similarly, if the exercise is undertaken by a transport company specialising in hanging garments it would be useful to invite experts in the retail trade, somebody who is familiar with the trends in urban transport development and a specialist in urban logistics.

In most situations it is useful to have an economist or someone who was trained in the subject.

(*b*) Individuals whose job in the company has given them an opportunity to work closely, in a managerial role, with functions other than their own, must be preferred to those who have not had such an opportunity. In other words representatives of a department which seldom 'interfaces' with the rest of the organisation are less likely to be useful participants in such a session. For instance, if the company has an architectural department dealing with the design and maintenance of buildings, their contribution to such sessions is not likely to be high.

(*c*) Ideally one or two members of top management should participate in order to impart legitimacy and credibility to the whole project. In fact a scenario-daydreaming exercise is a most useful activity for the board of a company or the chief executive officer of a firm and his top team. It can give them an opportunity to consider the future mission and direction of the firm against the backcloth of a scenario that the team as a whole has explored, debated and agreed to adopt. I have participated in many such sessions and have encountered a few that stand in my memory as dramatic examples of events that helped the companies to forge ahead into the future in a more creative and purposeful way than they ever felt that they could.

How large should the group be? There is no hard and fast rule here. As with other creative group activities the team should not be so large that the sessions get easily deflected from their main task through mob indiscipline. In this connection a good leader/facilitator should be able to cope with such a hazard. Nevertheless, it is seldom advisable to have more than ten participants, plus the leader.

At the same time it is unlikely that small groups could cover the ground effectively in a short session of two days. Bearing in mind that the group needs to explore a plethora of external dimensions like technological, economic, social, political, cultural, ecological developments and many others, a fair number of intelligent people with as many areas of expert knowledge must be roped in.

In summary, it is recommended that one strives to assemble a group consisting of between eight and ten participants with as wide a range of specialisations as possible and, in particular, with experts in fields that are likely to impact on the future environment of the firm.

Venue

Scenario-daydreaming should not be held on company's premises. It is important that the group moves to a quiet and well-appointed location. It can be a hotel or a conference centre or an academic establishment during vacation. The atmosphere must be relaxed and the amenities comfortable, but not necessarily luxurious. Excessive luxury and opulence can distract the participants from the demanding cerebral task ahead of them.

It is essential that the participants keep away from the telephone and desist from contacting their respective offices. For two days or so they will be living in the future and therefore the problems of the present should be left behind them. This is a condition that I always insist upon most vigorously.

The meeting room should be bright and airy and possess a round table, an overhead projector with a roll of acetate, a couple of flip-charts and a few spare pads with a number of coloured pens. More-over, in the event that the leader decides to break the team into smaller sub-groups there should be two or three syndicate rooms or quiet corners in which the smaller groups could meet and deliberate. The essential ingredient throughout is a pleasant and relaxed location where the participants can feel at ease and be comfortable.

Suitable topics

It is evident from everything that has been said that scenario-day-dreaming sessions are particularly helpful in situations demanding a creative input relating to a longer-term perspective. It is ideal for stimulating a company's management to detach themselves from day-to-day operational matters and gaze into a more future-orien-tated world and, in the process of doing so, identify a number of creative ideas for development.

The following are suitable projects for scenario-daydreaming exercises:

(*a*) defining the firm's 'mission statement';

(*b*) searching for strategies to maintain one's market position and/ or developing a competitive advantage for the future;

(*c*) identifying companies to acquire and/or to merge with;

(*d*) developing new products or markets;

(*e*) identifying locations and/or countries in which the company's products could be manufactured more productively in the future.

This is not a comprehensive list. It is simply provided in order to give the flavour of the type of assignments that can benefit from this technique. Any project that requires imagination and foresight relating to a future point of time can be a suitable topic for a scenario-daydreaming session.

Scenario-daydreaming at work

Sessions based on this method must be prepared in detail and with some care. Participants must know what to expect when they arrive at the session and must be mentally prepared for the nature of the proceedings. Moreover, members of the team who are invited for their specific expertise may want to bring along with them documents supporting their specialised contribution.

Preparatory procedures

A briefing document setting out the objectives of the session and details of the way the session will be conducted must be sent to all the participants in advance. The briefing note must also explain the role of the leader and the hoped-for outcome of the meeting.

Participants must be reminded of the importance of maintaining a positive and tolerant 'attitude spectrum' throughout the proceedings. It is best to alert them to this requirement in advance rather than having to reprimand them in public during the session.

During the session, and before commencing the actual proceedings, it is useful to 'soften' the ground by 'playing' one or two scenario-daydreaming warm-up exercises in relation to situations which are unrelated to the company's affairs. For instance: 'Consider a scenario for tourism in year 2000, bearing in mind your prediction of social, attitudinal, political, economic, ecological, infrastructural developments between now and year 2000'.

Obviously the participants will not have intimate knowledge of the industry. On the other hand most people are familiar with the growth of tourism, either by having been tourists themselves or by having observed the hordes of tourists that flood most major cities of the world. It is not difficult to simulate the chain of events that is likely to take place in the next few years and consider the kind of innovations that tour operators could develop in response to such a scenario.

One or two such exercises can be extremely helpful in setting the scene for the real assignment. It is advisable to spend around half an hour on the first exercise and around 20 minutes on the next (if appropriate).

Determining the main factors

Once the warm-up exercise(s) are out of the way the group is ready to tackle the task in hand. At this point the group should discuss and consider the various factors which are likely to impinge on the future success of the company. As was suggested earlier, this is likely to vary from company to company and from industry to industry. Some companies may consider that ecological and environmental pressure groups are likely to be the most significant threat on the horizon, whilst other companies may consider the control of raw material supply by an irresponsible nation as the potential problem. It is therefore useful to consider all the significant factors which are likely to impact upon the firm's future and list them in some order of priority—the most important ones at the top of the list.

In seeking to identify the main areas that ought to be explored during the scenario-daydreaming session the following list may be of some help. It is not a complete list, but should provide the session organiser with some idea as to the areas which may be relevant in this regard. Other important factors may be added to the list depending on the nature of the company and its business.

Factor for exploration	*Possible impact on future*
Economic trends.	Inflation and impact upon purchasing power of future customers; fiscal policy and its impact upon Government public spending; expenditure on infrastructure; exchange rates.

Factor for exploration	*Possible impact on future*
Cost of commodities and raw materials (including the emergence of trans-national cartels like OPEC).	Impact upon company's cost of production; opening for substitute raw materials; marketplace pressure for reduced consumption of the more expensive materials.
National and international politics (including change in traditional alliances, geopolitical unrest).	Emergence of good new markets and disappearance of traditional markets.
Military developments and general security matters (eg disarmament, SDI, new weapons, nuclear threat from small and irresponsible nations).	Impact upon arms and allied industries; Government expenditure on defence; demand for research engineers.
Para-military developments (including need to combat specific national paranoias and terrorism).	Better personal security system; more efficient mobile communication methods; increased cost of travel and/or executive international mobility.
Demographics.	Changes in birth-rate, life expectancy, age breakdown of society can have a significant impact upon marketing strategies of many organisations.
Changes in legal and quasi-legal regulations.	Impact on marketing strategy can be important. Implications have to be predicted and evaluated.
Consumer life-style.	Such changes can have considerable impact upon product development, promotional strategies and channels of distribution.

Factor for exploration	*Possible impact on future*
Technological changes.	An important area for 'scenario' exploration. The impact upon the firm's manufacturing processes can be immense and must be evaluated.
Institutional developments.	This covers a myriad of possible scenarios: change in existing channels of distribution; the location where the consumer of the future will wish to shop; media and communication systems that are likely to emerge; the probability that the consumer of the future will be buying products via an interactive television network system.
Social structure.	Changes in the fabric of our social environment can have a major impact upon the firm's marketing strategies and must be evaluated carefully during a scenario development exercise.
Ecological/environmental lobbies and pressure groups.	Can affect a company's manufacturing processes; use of raw materials; location of factories and, altogether, product acceptance by customers.
Information technology.	Every facet of the firm will be affected by the use of electronics—fund transfer; data communication; office automation; stock control, re-ordering procedures and logistics.

Factor for exploration	*Possible impact on future*
Infrastructural developments (eg channel tunnel; new airports; closure of railway lines; new port terminals; new motorways like the M25 etc).	Effect on firm's logistics must be considered; impact on local labour availability; change in marketplace catchment areas due to new population concentration.
Change in consumer attitudes towards contents of products (eg fats, additives, colourants in food products).	Major impact upon consumption levels of various commodities and products. Need to consider changes in product and packaging strategies.
Change in consumer habits (eg more sport and leisure; greater awareness of the value of outdoor activities etc).	Important to forecast and assess by firms operating in the leisure business or allied industries.
Biotechnology.	Impact upon pharmaceutical industry can be significant.
Consumer's attitudes towards savings and/or capital formation.	Of importance to insurance companies, banks, building societies and house-builders.

These are just a few factors likely to affect the destiny of companies. The role of the session leader is to stimulate the group to immerse itself in a wide-ranging exploration of as many such factors as possible. With the right guidance the number of factors that can emerge from a touch of brainstorming can become a flood. The next step is to try to pinpoint the truly important ones. These are the ones that will receive particular attention during the detailed syndicate work.

The aims of the 'main factors' analysis are two-fold: (*a*) to identify the areas which are likely to impact upon the firm's future direction and destiny; and (*b*) to stimulate a 'futuristic mode' among the participants.

The latter is extremely valuable to the quality of the discussions and to the final outcome of the proceedings. It is important that for the duration of the exercise the participants almost simulate the sensation that they have catapulted themselves into some future point in the life of their organisation. The ability to reach such a mental transformation can make the session into a most powerful tool in generating creative ideas and strategies based on 'proactive' perceptions of an unknown future.

Syndicate and plenary discussions

At the end of the previous plenary session the team should have yielded a fairly comprehensive list of factors that ought to be aired and their impact upon the firm predicted. Moreover, the relative importance of these factors must be evaluated and placed on a priority list with the most significant ones at the top. This should determine the amount of the time and the level of detailed work that should be devoted to each item thus listed.

The group should now be broken into sub-groups or syndicates. Each syndicate is given a number of factors to consider in some depth and produce a scenario pertaining to each of them. Each syndicate should get no more than three or four topics for discussion. In allocating factors to the sub-groups the leader should bear in mind the specific expertise which is available to each group. In fact, when dividing the participants into syndicates the leader should bear in mind the distribution of expertise that exists among the members. Clearly if the factor under consideration is 'UK and EEC legislation relating to the use of nitrates in the future', participants with some knowledge of the legal system, both in the UK and the EEC, and also an expert in chemistry, should be attached to the group charged with that topic.

If the number of factors is large and the number of participants relatively small the syndicate discussions can be repeated a number of times in order to cover all the topics. The leader may consider re-arranging the groupings in order to provide the participants with a change of intellectual 'scenery' and to maximise the opportunity for cross-fertilisation of ideas among all members.

Syndicate sessions should last about two to three hours. The overall aim is to provide the members with an opportunity to discuss every listed main factor for around half-an-hour. Thus if they have to cover four factors, two hours is the minimum time that they ought to be allocated for such a task. At the end of the syndicate work the members should plan to present their scenarios to a plenary session. If there are four members in a syndicate and four factors it would be useful if each member is responsible for one presentation. It is a more efficient use of resources, and more interesting for the audience during the plenary meeting.

Following each presentation a brief discussion takes place in order (*a*) to reach consensus about the various hypotheses submitted; and (*b*) to identify and eliminate contradictions among the various sub-scenarios. The group is now ready for the very important task of integrating the various sub-scenarios into a single all-embracing statement of the group's vision of the future. The leader's role in this regard is to steer the group into a unanimous perception of things to come.

The final part of the exercise is carried out again in syndicates: each group is invited to consider the final scenario completed in the earlier sessions and submit ideas as to how the opportunities and challenges that have coalesced could be responded to by the organisation. At this stage the sub-groups can resort to the various techniques which are available to creative groups at work such as brainstorming, morphological analysis, metaphorical analysis, etc. This is an idea-generation session directed towards responding to a future world which the group believes is ahead. The outcome of the various creativity sessions can now be collated and summarised and a brief vision document prepared by the session's leader. However, it is important to emphasise that preparing a written record of the group's conclusions is not mandatory. In fact some companies feel that the exercise itself is the valuable part of the proceedings and that an attempt to reduce the 'magic' of the moment into a written format can detract from the enriching effect of the whole session. Clearly this is a matter to be left to the discretion of the organisers of the session and the leader of the proceedings.

Whether the group will have 'hit the jackpot' or not at the end of the two days is immaterial. What is important is that they have broadened their strategic perspectives and gazed into the future with a powerful telescope. Anybody who cannot see the value of such an activity in a firm's attempt to improve its innovation in a future-orientated way is undoubtedly suffering from managerial myopia.

Figure 48 describes a typical programme and timetable for a scenario-daydreaming workshop. If the detailed description of the technique provided in this chapter is adhered to and if the members of the team join the proceedings in the right frame of mind, this method can have an enormously valuable impact upon the firm's direction and clarity of purpose. Readers belonging to the strategic level of the organisation are strongly advised to try it from time to time.

Figure 48.   Timetable for a scenario-daydreaming workshop.
(example only)

Evening	Participants assemble at selected venue and over an informal dinner in order to get to know each other and their leader. Main aim is to generate a relaxed atmosphere. All participants will have received a briefing note in advance and should be familiar with the objectives of the session and general orientation.		
Day I	**Theme**	**Timing**	**Contributors**
		(Approximate)	
9.00–10.30	**Introduction to session; preparatory procedures**		Leader/facilitator
	A Review of session objectives and modus operandi	20 minutes	,,
	B Warm-up exercise(s)	30 minutes + 20 minutes (optional)	Plenary session
	C Discuss and consider main factors likely to affect future events	30 minutes (to be continued after break)	Plenary session
10.30–11.00	**Break**		
11.00–12.45	**Main factors analysis** (continued)	45/60 minutes	Plenary session
	Discuss, agree and summarise	45 minutes	Leader/ facilitator
12.45–14.00	**Buffet lunch**		
14.00–15.30	**Scenario-daydreaming**	$1\frac{1}{2}$ hours	Syndicates
15.30–16.00	**Break**		

(continued)

Evening	**Syndicates prepare their presentations with help of leader**		
16.00–17.30	**Scenario-daydreaming**	$1\frac{1}{2}$ hours	Syndicates
Day II 9.00–10.30	**Syndicates presentations and discussion of each presentation**	$1\frac{1}{2}$ hours	All syndicates in a plenary session
10.30–11.00	**Break**		
11.00–12.45	**Integrating sub-scenarios** —Removing contradictions —Identifying main threats and opportunities	$1\frac{1}{2}$–$1\frac{3}{4}$ hours	Plenary session
12.45–14.00	**Buffet lunch**		
14.00–15.30	**Idea-generation in response to agreed vision**	$1\frac{1}{2}$ hours	Creativity sessions in syndicates
15.30–16.00	**Break**		
16.00–17.30	**Moving towards the vision**	1 hour	Plenary session
	—Exploration of ideas for exploiting the vision	1 hour	(syndicate presentation)
	—Summary of proceedings and the 'way ahead'	$\frac{1}{2}$ hour	Leader

NB Leader (with the help of one or two members of the team) may be invited to summarise the proceedings, especially the main ideas that resulted therefrom, for future reference.

10 'Think Tanks' and innovation

'Think Tanks' have become a popular concept in the last few years. Both companies and governments appear to have taken the view that a group of 'thinking' people, working close to the nerve centre and reflecting upon major issues, can enrich the organisation's strategic vitality and ability to innovate. A number of governments, especially among the western industrialised nations, have established permanent units charged with the task of reflecting upon future strategic ideas and recommending courses of action for further consideration by the top decision-makers. More recently, the concept has been adopted by a number of companies operating in a variety of industries and markets. The underlying rationale is that a group of relatively independent, intelligent and well-informed people working as a group can generate creative responses to challenges on which they are being invited to work. This is particularly true where these challenges are outside the normal work routine and direct responsibility of the members of the team. The theory is that people who come fresh to a challenge are often capable of generating novel ways of tackling it. This can easily elude those who are constantly in touch with the situation and its details. It is a question of being able to 'see the wood for the trees'.

Whether one refers to such a body as a 'Think Tank' or calls it by some other title, the concept is not new. The idea that problems can be solved, strategies developed and innovations identified through the 'synergy' of a group of people 'thinking' together in some depth, about issues of major importance to the organisation, is as old as Jethro's Council of Biblical days. It may be recalled that Jethro, probably the first consultant ever, was the person who advised Moses about organisational matters which culminated in a structure which made the challenge of crossing the desert more manageable. In fact it was thanks to Jethro that the task was ever completed. Is it possible that Moses could have completed the whole journey in one year instead of 40 years if he had held his 'Think Tank' earlier?

There is little doubt that given the right conditions and adequate planning, a Think Tank can provide an organisation with a valuable

217

cutting edge. On the other hand if such conditions do not exist the same body can be a waste of time and resources. It must be remembered at the very outset that a Think Tank is never an end in itself—it is purely an aid to the collective thinking process and designed to meet a set of objectives. A collective thinking process undertaken without clear objectives is less likely to be of benefit to the organisation. It may be recalled from Chapter 2 that one of the valuable ingredients that companies must possess in order to improve their chances of being innovative is the availability of organisational 'slack'. Viewed in this light it might be suggested that a properly constituted Think Tank is the way the organisation attempts to institutionalise its creative 'slack'. However, the establishment of a Think Tank *per se* does not guarantee innovation and does not necessarily provide the firm with a competitive edge or enhanced success. It is the way Think Tanks are structured, managed, led and stimulated that *can* yield the desired outputs.

The aim of this chapter is to review the role of so-called Think Tanks and help those responsible for designing them to take the appropriate steps to ensure that they are properly constituted and directed.

Conditions for successful Think Tanks

Clearly defined roles and objectives

I never tire of reminding clients that a 'Think Tank' must have a clearly-defined role and objectives, and must be constituted in response to defined needs and not as a panacea for all ills. Even a remit as limited as 'a desire to improve the overall climate in which the firm's creativity can flourish' is valid if it is established in response to the recognition that the company's climate is obstructive and unempathetic to ideas.

What is far less satisfactory is the design of a unit with vague objectives and ill-defined modus operandi. Think Tanks established to deal with 'problems and challenges to be presented to them by top management from time to time' are less likely to produce credible outputs. Sooner or later doubts about their continued existence are likely to be expressed.

A Think Tank can be a powerful weapon in a company's quest for innovation, but its success depends on the clarity of purpose which is ascribed to it. The sponsors of such a body must reflect very carefully on the role and objectives they wish to attach to the whole concept and the pay-offs they expect to derive therefrom. As stated earlier, Think Tanks are not an end product. They are a means to some end and if that end is not clearly defined it is difficult to evaluate the benefits that may emanate from their existence. It is therefore essential that sufficient thought and attention are invested in formulating the goals and designing the structure of the group. Moreover, the precise membership of the group will ultimately depend on the sought-after benefits. Thus, if the main role of the Think Tank is in the area of technological innovation, an emphasis on scientific and technical specialists would be appropriate. If, on the other hand, the Think Tank's main role is to identify innovative marketing strategies it would be more relevant to select marketing-orientated participants. The one thing that one must not expect is that by assembling a random group of well-meaning and intelligent individuals, innovations will emerge by themselves. The choice of members must be compatible with the terms of reference given to the unit.

Obviously, the role and objectives of a Think Tank will depend on the circumstances of each organisation and the business it is in. Furthermore it is perfectly legitimate to review the objectives from time to time and adapt them to the changing needs of the organisation. It is important that such bodies are not allowed to become totally isolated from the dynamism of the core business.

The following is a list of objectives which I have extracted from the 'mission statements' of a number of Think Tanks with which I have been associated over the years. The list is not meant to be comprehensive. It is simply provided in order to give the reader the feel for the kind of goals that well-constituted Think Tanks should seek to achieve.

Company 1: 'To provide the company with a mechanism for exploring and evaluating strategies aimed at reducing present-day dependence on products that require raw materials derived from parts of the world which are likely to become hostile.'

This description of the role of the Think Tank is brief but clear. Members of the unit know what is expected of them and the quality of their output can be evaluated at regular intervals.

Company 2: 'The current success of the company hinges upon the fact that its "Star" product is enjoying a defendable patent. However, this patent will expire in three years.

The role of the Think Tank can be summarised thus:

(*a*) To search for strategies which will help the company to overcome problems associated with the expiration of the patent. The main aim is to find a new source of revenue and profit to replace the inevitable decline of profits resulting from the end of the patent protection.

(*b*) To evaluate strategies thus identified and recommend a programme of implementation.

(*c*) To explore patentable product improvements that may help the company to obtain an additional patent coverage for the improved product.'

The terms of reference described above are succinct and little room for doubt exists as to what the group is invited to do. The tasks are demanding but at the same time they are unequivocal. Moreover the nature of the terms of reference is such that little difficulty should be encountered in determining what kind of individuals ought to be attached to the team. Moreover, the performance of the unit can be evaluated from time to time and its general effectiveness monitored.

Company 3: 'An audit of the firm's creativity and innovation during the last five years has unfortunately shown that little creative output has emerged from the company's management. Few ideas are ever generated by the company's personnel. Very few ideas are ever screened and considered for implementation. The result is that the firm's innovation is at a very low ebb. Steps are being taken to correct this weakness. One of the strategies selected in this direction is the establishment of a Think Tank.
   The objectives of the Think Tank are:

(*a*) To provide a mechanism for generating ideas, screening them and identifying the best among them for exploitation. The activities of the Think Tank in this regard will always be in response to tasks and problems given to it by top management.
   It is understood that the task of implementing ideas chosen for exploitation will be the sole responsibility of those in charge of the operating units whose problems the Think Tank is invited to solve.

(*b*) To act as a catalyst of change in the climate of the organisation and with the aim of stimulating an overall improvement in the firm's creativity and innovation.'

These represent perfectly legitimate objectives, but it is easy to see a myriad of problems:

(*a*)   The Think Tank has to respond to 'tasks and problems given to it by top management'.

     Whilst this represents a legitimate constraint upon the unit's freedom of action the constant danger is that the Think Tank's activities may atrophy through a dearth of instructions from the top. Should top management lose interest in the Think Tank's activities or simply forget about its existence the unit will be starved of projects and its future threatened through lack of projects to work on. This in turn imposes upon the Think Tank the need to 'market' its existence to those who set it up in the first place.

(*b*)   The terms of reference are fraught with political undertones which can undermine the credibility of the unit. 'Top management' are the only people who can instruct the Think Tank as to what projects they should work on.

     On the other hand, the implementation of recommended strategies is the prerogative of 'those in charge of the operating units whose problems the Think Tank is invited to solve'. This is a political minefield, and any quasi-independent group of creative people which has to tread such a delicate path is likely to find life pretty difficult. In designing what is intended to be an effective Think Tank and ascribing to it a meaningful role one must be careful not to bestow upon it a set of objectives which entail ambiguous roles fraught with potential conflicts. To be charged by top management to develop ideas which can only be implemented by members of middle management is an invitation for an unhappy 'piggy in the middle' role.

     In governmental or semi-governmental environments similar problems can occur when a Prime Minister or an organisational head asks a central Think Tank to explore creative solutions to problems that should normally be tackled by Ministers or departmental heads. If a Think Tank is going to be effective and valuable it ought not to be exposed to such political overtones. It must be able to function openly, cleanly and without a need to please too many 'masters' at the same time.

(*c*)   One of the terms of reference listed above included an overriding instruction 'to act as a catalyst of change in the climate of the organisation'. Once again, this is a legitimate objective and shows a recognition, on the part of top management, of the need to improve the firm's overall creativity as a preamble for enhanced innovation. This is fine, but it must be remembered that the task of stimulating creativity must stem from the top. Top management must be seen, at all times, as the promulgators of the firm's climate. They must be seen to believe fervently in what they expect others to carry out. It is not reasonable for them to delegate the task of changing a firm's attitudes, 'shared values' or 'superordinate goals' to a group of people who possess no hierarchical authority. If one wants to stimulate a change in a firm's climate the bosses must take a leading role in bringing such a change about. If one instructs a somewhat peripheral body called a 'Think Tank' to undertake such a task, top management must be seen to be the main initiators of such a strategy. They must be seen to support the proceedings in an unequivocal way, possibly through active participation. Alternatively, they must provide the unit with some 'developmental teeth'.

In summary, the three sets of 'terms of reference' provided above are aimed at reminding management that the process of establishing Think Tanks must be accompanied with clearly-defined and unambiguous objectives. Furthermore great care must be taken to ensure that such objectives are capable of being achieved without scope for hierarchical and organisational conflict. Think Tanks surrounded by overt or covert antipathy from the rest of the organisation cannot function effectively.

Other conditions for success

Great emphasis has been placed on the need to define terms of reference clearly. However long it may take to deliberate and agree on a viable set of objectives, the unit must not start functioning until this task has been completed and a high level of concurrence has been reached. Moreover, such terms of reference must be communicated throughout the organisation so that a general appreciation of what the unit is commissioned to do is reached. The unit itself is well advised to refer to its terms of reference or 'mission' from time to time in order to ensure that its activities are compatible with its prescribed remit. The nature of a Think Tank's activities is such that it is very easy to deviate from its defined role into esoteric and irrelevant distractions. By referring back to the prescribed objectives of the unit one can avoid falling into such a trap.

Other conditions should be borne in mind if one wants to extract maximum benefit from the establishment of a Think Tank-type unit in the organisation. The following points should be of some help to those responsible for such projects:

Commitment

This represents a very important ingredient for success. Total commitment to the effectiveness of the unit is required from its sponsors, from the members of the unit and from the organisation as a whole.

'Commitment' is not a feature that can be accurately measured or quantified. Nonetheless, when it does not exist one soon discovers its absence. The following norms of behaviour by the various 'stakeholders' are incompatible with the existence of a wholehearted level of commitment:

(a) Commitment by the unit's sponsors. Sponsors of the unit who do not show continuous interest in the activities of the team are guilty of a lack of commitment. Similarly, those who fail to respond to requests for help, guidance or advice are equally guilty of harmful apathy. It is difficult to expect a group of well-intentioned individuals actively pursuing creative avenues on behalf of the organisation to maintain their enthusiasm and dedication if the people at the top who created and sponsored the unit manifest a certain amount of indifference to the proceedings of their own brainchild.

The following is a strong warning to anybody thinking of establishing a Think Tank: do not create such units unless you are prepared to demonstrate a total personal commitment to their success.

(b) Commitment by members of the unit. The activities of the Think Tank must be considered as so valuable that the timing of meetings must be treated as of overriding importance. Members who are not willing to accept these activities in such a spirit are obviously not sufficiently committed to their long-term welfare and should be given the opportunity to quit.

Membership of a Think Tank must be regarded by those invited to join it not only as an accolade but also as a worthwhile activity which justifies a total personal commitment. If members do not share such a sentiment the quality of the group's work will soon deteriorate.

(c) Commitment by the firm as a whole. This is another important area for attention. It is often overlooked by the sponsors of Think Tanks. A commitment of the total organisation to the activities of the unit must be sought. Where such a commitment exists the Think Tank can operate in an empathetic environment which can act as a powerful spur to creative output and innovation. On the other hand, where the unit has to function in cynical and possibly even hostile surroundings the chance of the group managing to come out with useful results is greatly diminished.

In other words both the sponsors and the members of a Think Tank must take steps to ensure that the unit is properly 'marketed' among the total organisation at an early stage of its establishment.

Effective communication with colleagues

Experience has shown that membership of a Think Tank is often construed by casual observers as a signal of elitism and potential candidature for rapid promotion. This erroneous image must not be allowed to develop and persist because it may reduce the general acceptance of the value of such units to the welfare of the company and willingness by non-members to support their work. The success of central 'thinking' units does depend on the members of the unit being able to draw advice and support from the rank and file of the organisation. The only way to achieve such cooperation is through relaxed and open communication between the unit and the rest of the organisation. The unit's leader must recognise this point and ensure that a system of regular communication is established at an early stage. It may take the form of a short newsletter or periodic briefing sessions with department heads seeking to communicate information about the unit's work and progress. A well-designed communication system can be of considerable value in removing doubts and/or suspicion of the unit's role and activities.

Lack of communication with the rest of the organisation can nullify a lot of the benefit that bodies like Think Tanks can impart to a company. Some groups have found that inviting other senior colleagues, from time to time, to attend as observers has helped to cement a fruitful and supportive relationship between the Think Tank and the rest of the organisation.

An additional hazard in the life of a Think Tank-type unit may occur when the company's personnel develop high expectations from the establishment of such units. The news that top management has decided to sponsor such an activity is often interpreted as a signal from above that exciting new events are about to happen. People are waiting for something of importance to take place and complete silence can easily cause a general feeling of anti-climax. Judicious and fairly frequent communication can alleviate this danger.

Need for tangible and visible results

Think Tanks are established for a purpose and ideally the ability of the unit to attain such a purpose must be capable of being measured from time to time. Psychologically it is important that such units manage to 'chalk up' some tangible outputs at a fairly early stage of their existence. Such successes, however small, can be of tremendous help in convincing the most cynical observers of the value of the whole concept and can encourage a more committed support from the rest of the organisation. It is perfectly normal for members of any organisation to reserve their judgement and withhold support from a novel type of activity in their midst which appears to absorb considerable resources and attention from top management. To that extent a few visible results can remove any residual doubt about the unit's real worth. An experienced leader would recognise such a need and would search with the members of the newly-formed team for suitable projects which are capable of a fairly rapid breakthrough.

Composition of a Think Tank

Unlike creativity sessions conducted on an ad hoc basis, a Think Tank represents a permanent or semi-permanent unit designed to meet and work at regular intervals. It is therefore important that the members are selected carefully with an eye to their ability to maintain a continuous level of attendance and enthusiasm for the unit's activities.

Furthermore, in the business world it is rare to find Think Tanks which are manned by full-time members. It is therefore important to identify individuals who are so well-organised that they can hold a full-time job and, at the same time, participate actively in proceedings which can be extremely different from their normal routine jobs. This in itself calls for a mental agility associated with creative people. It is worth spending sufficient time to interview potential candidates and take informal soundings, from their past and present superiors, in order to ensure that no mistakes are made before the unit commences functioning. Selecting unsuitable members can be harmful as it can create unnecessary problems for the smooth running of the unit and this, in turn, can tarnish the public image of the Think Tank among other members of the organisation.

The following points may help organisers of a Think Tank group to avoid some of the pitfalls associated with such a venture.

Choosing a suitable leader

The person to head such a unit must be selected with particular care. He or she must be conversant with the mechanics of organising such activities and familiar with the various techniques associated with the idea-generation process and the management of innovation. If it is difficult to identify such a person inside the firm it may be a wise strategy to use an external resource, such as a consultant, with the appropriate experience. However, if it is decided to use the services of such a resource it must be as a temporary measure and for a long enough period to enable an internal resource to pick up the threads and assume the leadership of the group as soon as practicable. Leadership in this context means not only possessing the capability of managing groups at work, but also the semi-technical skills associated with creative problem-solving and the management of ideas.

It is appropriate to repeat what was said earlier in connection with other creative techniques—'leadership' does not entail a hierarchical seniority within the overall context of the firm. In other words, the leader must be a person capable of directing a group of diverse individuals without having the hierarchical authority that one associates with normal organisations. It is perfectly possible for a less senior person to assume the mantle of leadership of a Think Tank for the simple reason that he is more conversant with the creative process and its associated procedures. Nevertheless, it is probably prudent not to expose too junior a person to such a responsibility, especially if he has to rub shoulders with people with whom he may be working during the rest of the year. A judicious balance between experience, personality and position in the company must be struck.

The following are the ideal characteristics of a suitable leader:

(*a*) emotional maturity;

(*b*) excellent 'attitude spectrum' (see Chapter 3);

(*c*) good communicator (both as a verbal presenter, as a listener and in the quality of his report writing);

(*d*) excellent motivator;

(*e*) breadth of experience, both inside and outside the company (eg through hobbies or general interests);

(*f*)   ability to think laterally and encourage others to do so;

(*g*)   good track record in the area of creative thinking and innovation;

(*h*)   hard working.

The role of the leader can be summarised as follows:

(*a*)   To plan the meetings and prepare agendas for a few meetings in advance. In this connection he must ensure that agendas are properly circulated among the members of the Think Tank in good time before the unit meets.

(*b*)   To maintain contact with the members between meetings and take steps to ensure that they are all highly motivated and enthusiastic about the unit's activities.

(*c*)   To lead the meetings and if appropriate allocate specific tasks to individual members or to groups of members.

(*d*)   To act as the spokesman of the unit in discussions with the sponsoring bosses or when asking for additional resources.

(*e*)   To summarise the proceedings and circulate minutes whenever appropriate.

(*f*)   To report about the unit's output to the relevant authorities.

All these tasks may sound onerous for one individual, especially when they are duties additional to a person's normal work. It is therefore advisable to rotate the leadership of the unit every six months or thereabouts. The first leader/chairman should normally be the one who is the most experienced in this kind of activity, but after a while other members should be capable of assuming this role. Furthermore, the leader's duties can be eased if other members of the unit could act as scribes or minute-takers thus, at least, relieving him of the administrative chores associated with the team's leadership.

The important point to remember is that the choice of the right person who can lead, stimulate and motivate the unit is the most vital decision in the life of an effective Think Tank. If the unit can start on the right foot the quality of the work and output emanating therefrom is almost guaranteed. The opposite is, unfortunately, also true.

Other members

The choice of the other members of the team is equally important. No effort should be spared in identifying the right participants and ensuring that only suitable and highly-motivated members are invited to join. During detailed interviews and briefing discussions they must be alerted to the demanding nature of the unit's activities and the kind of contribution that they would be expected to make. It is essential that nobody joins a Think Tank without full cognisance of what it entails. The worst event is when participants start complaining shortly after a unit commences its activities that they have not been warned of the frequency of meetings and the demands imposed upon their time, in addition to their normal work responsibilities. A clear description of the unit's routine, the pressures as well as the mental stimulation, must be expressed in a firm and detailed manner.

It is sometimes appropriate to invite 'outsiders', namely non-permanent members, to join the proceedings. Again, it is very important that they are fully briefed about the nature of the unit's activities and the behavioural do's and don'ts associated with the group's proceedings.

Number of members

I am often asked to recommend a number of members that should be invited to join a Think Tank-type activity. It is difficult to answer this question in abstract terms as it depends on the following factors:

(*a*) The terms of reference of the unit. Clearly, if the terms of reference are wide and are likely to affect the future of a large organisation there is a strong case for a somewhat larger number of members. Thus if the unit's remit encompasses the search for future direction and strategies it would be wise to incorporate as much talent in the discussions as possible. Think Tanks established by Governments or semi-governmental bodies tend to be larger than one would expect to find in industry.

(*b*) The size of the organisation. In large companies one would expect to find larger units than in small companies. This is often simply a matter of resource availability and quantum of 'slack' that can be harnessed in the organisation. Yet unless a

firm can 'field' at least six permanent members the whole idea
of setting up a Think Tank is probably unwarranted.

Multinational organisations with ambitious terms of reference are well advised to target for the largest manageable unit,
namely around 12 members. This should provide the unit's
organisers with the opportunity of inviting a group of executives with multi-national experience as well as multi-disciplinary backgrounds. In this connection the largest unit I have
come across consisted of 24 members of a very diverse international company. However, the unit functioned in three separate sub-units of eight with each having a different set of
terms of reference: the first was orientated towards technological issues, the second was charged with international marketing strategies and the third with the development and quest for
licensing arrangements.

(c) The available resources and willingness to deploy them on
such projects. In order to be a successful unit capable of generating valuable outputs it is essential that the appropriate
resources are placed at its disposal. A firm may find it
extremely difficult to release such people from their full-time
commitments or it may simply not have the kind of talent
envisaged by the terms of reference ascribed to the unit. The
terms of reference, for example, may expect the unit to work
on a project of considerable technological sophistication
requiring skills and resources that the firm is unable to field
from within and unwilling to recruit from outside. Such a constraint must be acknowledged, and would of course affect the
size of the unit. In fact the size of the unit and the terms of
reference are interrelated: if one cannot raise the appropriate
resources one must be prepared to lower the level of aspirations from the Think Tank and its activities.

Qualifications for membership

Care must be taken in matching the personal characteristics, the
experiences and skills of the members to the needs of the unit and
its terms of reference. One of the dangers that promoters of a Think
Tank often have to face is that one is tempted to appoint people
who are known not to be very busy at a certain point of time and
invite them to join the unit in order to keep them fully occupied.
Such a temptation must be resisted at all costs. Members must be

identified for their qualifications and suitability and not because they happen to be available and not fully extended at the time.

Once again, the suitability of members would depend on the nature of the unit and its objectives. If the unit's remit has a strategic focus the most attractive participants would be individuals with experience in the area of corporate strategy, marketing, business policy and finance. If, on the other hand, the main task of the unit is to strive towards technical innovations the emphasis must be placed upon individuals with a stronger bias towards technology, scientific research and engineering. 'Horses for courses' is the name of the game. Nevertheless, there are a number of personal characteristics which must be considered and favoured during the selection stage.

(*a*) Like the leader himself, members with a tolerant 'attitude spectrum' towards other people's ideas must be preferred.

(*b*) Individuals known for their general negative outlook and response to ideas must be avoided: they can have a dampening effect on the other members during the unit's activities.

(*c*) Optimists are better members than pessimists.

(*d*) Individuals who have demonstrated an ability to change direction during their career in the firm (or in other firms) are normally more suitable than those who have spent all their career in one function.

This last remark must not be interpreted as a criticism of their track record—what is meant is that people with a variety of successful changes in functional responsibilities very often have a broader range of experience. In the context of a Think Tank-type activity such people are of particular value.

(*e*) People with some proven record of an ability to think laterally and the ability to generate creative ideas are useful members to have around.

(*f*) A balance between numerate and literate persons must be sought. The numerate members can bring along a certain level of quantitative analysis; the more literate participants can contribute a more artistic flavour and fluency in communication. It is therefore important that in selecting members this factor is borne in mind. A unit consisting of one type only can be greatly handicapped.

(g) People with many interests outside their work environment
     normally make good members. Individuals who play musical
     instruments, draw or paint, take part in a variety of sports,
     enjoy cooking and so on are useful participants because they
     are capable of 'changing gears' during group work and are able
     to impart some colour to the sessions. The most successful unit
     which I helped to structure consisted of eight members who
     represented between them around 25 hobbies and fields of
     interest ranging from a passion for observing and drawing
     mushrooms to one person who re-furbished war-time fighter
     aircraft.

(h) Diligent and hard-working members are usually most valuable
     for such groups. A Think Tank's activities can be demanding
     both in terms of intellectual grasp of a subject under discussion
     and the need to absorb a vast amount of new bits of knowl-
     edge. A person who finds the assimilation of a plethora of facts
     and figures a tiresome activity would soon find participation in
     the unit an unpleasant chore. It is best to identify such a
     characteristic in advance and remove that person from the list
     of potential candidates.

It is appropriate to mention again that mistakes in selecting the
wrong members must be avoided. In some respects it is even more
serious than selecting the wrong person for a normal job. In this
instance one has to cope with the added problem of explaining to a
faithful and successful manager the reasons for removing him from
the unit. Moreover, such a step can create apprehension and ten-
sion among those staying behind. It is therefore essential to check
the credentials of potential members again and again and evaluate
their suitability with the utmost care. Figure 49 provides a simple
selection matrix based on the portfolio management concept. On
one axis one seeks to identify the credentials of each candidate
against objective criteria and, on the other axis, one attempts to
match each individual against a list of specific needs pertaining to
the successful operation of the Think Tank. Those who score 'high'
on both dimensions are the most suitable candidates.

The effective management of Think Tanks

A Think Tank is much more than just a problem-solving unit or an
ad hoc brainstorming session. It is a unit designed to provide a
more ambitious service to the organisation. It represents a collective

Figure 49. Selection matrix for suitable members for a Think Tank.

Member attractiveness

	High	Medium	Low
High	Ideal members	Second best	Avoid
Medium	Second best	Keep in reserve	Avoid
Low	Avoid	Avoid	Avoid

Compatibility of each member with unit's aims

Criteria of member attractiveness (examples only)	**Criteria of compatibility with Think Tank needs** (examples only)
Past experience Age/maturity Tolerant 'attitude spectrum' Breadth of career pattern Enthusiasm Track record in creativity work Good communicator Outside interests	Specific knowledge in area covered by terms of reference Available 'slack' in work routine Personal motivation for Think Tank success Willing to devote time beyond call of duty Optimism Good relationship with other members of the Think Tank

'thinking' process charged with the task of reflecting on major strategies or the development of alternative ways to run the business. An effective unit can impart considerable strength to the organisation and provide it with a valuable competitive advantage. Clearly, a poorly-managed unit would fail in achieving such an important role. The quality of the unit's leadership and the members was highlighted in the previous sections. It is now useful to consider the way procedural and operational effectiveness can impart a cutting edge to the unit.

Frequency of meetings

There are no definite rules as to how often a Think Tank should meet. However, what is important is that the meetings are held sufficiently frequently for continuity of reflection to take place. Long intervals normally interrupt the mental involvement of the participants. If the members have to recapture the main thrust of the earlier discussions too much precious time is wasted in getting everybody back 'on line'. It is essential that the main themes of the previous meeting are still fresh in the mind of the various participants. To that extent having meetings about once a month can obviate this danger. In this connection it is useful to remind the unit's leader that one of his roles is to maintain a level of continuity in the group's work. Through an effective and succinct summary of each meeting's deliberations and conclusions the process of 're-entry' into the spirit of the earlier discussions can be greatly facilitated. In the absence of such a simple precaution the group may experience some difficulty in regaining the momentum of the previous meeting and this, in turn, can generate considerable frustration and loss of precious time.

Unless a Think Tank has been designed to function as a full-time activity, a monthly meeting is normally adequate. Obviously, it depends on the circumstances and the urgency of the issue upon which the group is expected to focus its attention. Less frequent meetings can affect the continuity of thought and lower the personal commitment of the individual members which is so essential for the effectiveness of the unit. On the other hand, more frequent meetings can interfere with the members' normal responsibilities and work. Thus it is recommended that a monthly meeting represents a safe norm of frequency, but the leader and the participants must feel free to review the situation in the light of the tasks ahead of them and the rate of progress achieved.

In general, it is quite important that dates for meetings are fixed well in advance in order to ensure that all the members are aware of such dates and can make arrangements to attend. In the absence of such a timetable, say for six months, one finds that trying to fix a date for the next meeting at short notice can present the problem of individual members not being available, and difficulties are encountered in finding dates that suit everybody. At that point members start missing meetings and the general effectiveness of the unit starts slipping.

Length of meetings

Experience has taught me that each meeting should last longer than one day. It takes a couple of hours for all the members to revert to 'creative thinking mode'. It is therefore wise to start the meeting the previous evening with an informal 'get-together', possibly over dinner. The first session takes place either immediately before or immediately after dinner. Its main aim is to review the content of the previous meeting and a summary of the tasks which the group intends to cover during the next day's work. This approach can help to ensure that the next day is spent on effective and productive proceedings. It is important that the ground is 'softened' before the group starts working on the published agenda and that the normal day-to-day anxieties and preoccupations are shed.

Location

Meetings should be held away from the normal work environment of the members. It is vital that the participants are not disturbed by their respective offices or called to the telephone except in the event of major calamities. The leader must ensure that this rule is adhered to at all times. A slight relaxation of this condition can easily drift into a constant stream of interruptions which can destroy the concentration of the group and the quality of its output.

The ideal venue is either a quiet boardroom, a lecture room inside the firm's training facilities, or in the event that such facilities do not exist, in some quiet hotel or training centre. The venue must be comfortable, quiet but not necessarily opulent or extravagant. The main criterion of choice in this regard is an environment which is conducive to work and reflection and not too tempting from the point of view of leisure activities or holiday atmosphere.

Comments made in previous chapters regarding room facilities apply here as well. The room for plenary sessions must, if possible, contain a round table with the normal visual aids such as flip charts, overhead projector and possibly a blackboard.

Agendas

Agendas must be prepared for every meeting in advance. Agendas are important for every type of meeting, but in the case of Think Tank activities are particularly important inasmuch as the nature of the unit's sessions can be somewhat imprecise and an agenda can help to provide a structured framework for the proceedings. Ideally, it is desirable to prepare rudimentary agendas for a period of six months with a detailed agenda for each forthcoming session. It is always better to have a fuller programme mapped out than the available time. What is less satisfactory is to arrive at the unit's meetings without a clear idea as to how the team proposes to spend its time together. Some flexibility must be retained for unexpected time-consuming discussions and/or the use of creative techniques. However, it is essential that a fairly clear framework for each meeting is maintained.

A typical agenda is illustrated in Figure 50 below.

Figure 50.   Agenda for a Think Tank meeting.

(Illustration only)

The illustration is based on the assumption that the Think Tank's main task is to develop a vision for the firm's long-term strategic direction

	Theme	Detailed activities
Day I 17.30–19.00	**Assembly of members** **Summary of previous meeting** —Progress made and lessons learnt	Leader to provide a brief summary of previous meeting in order to help members 're-enter' into the spirit of the unit's work. Achievements and failures must be spelt out
	Objectives of current meeting —Discuss, review and agree upon next day's agenda and approach	Objectives for the next day's proceedings must be clearly stated

	Theme	Detailed activities
19.00–21.00	**Working dinner**	Main aims of the dinner are —To help the members to shed anxieties and preoccupation relating to their respective routine work —To stimulate a re-entry to a 'Creative Mode'
Day II 09.00–10.30	**The future environment for our type of business** The impact of changes in: —Demographics —Anticipated life style.	Previous meeting explored scenarios based on changes likely to take place in 'life style', technology and demography. Today Mr S J, economist/statistician, will take the chair and report on the outcome of his own analysis based on the literature he scanned
10.30–11.00	**Break**	
11.00–12.45	**The future environment** (continued) Group summary of potential threats and opportunities 5–10 years hence	Group to explore, debate and agree on trends based on scenario-daydreaming method
12.45–14.00	**Working lunch**	Continue discussion regarding group's final view of future environment
14.00–15.30	**Our response to these challenges** Screen and evaluate proactive strategies	Group to consider alternative strategies aimed at meeting the challenges and opportunities presented by the future environment as stated by the team

	Theme	Detailed activities
		Use: Brainstorming 　　Morphological 　　　analysis 　　Scenario- 　　　daydreaming Allocate time to screening ideas
15.30–16.00	**Break**	
16.00–17.30	**Strategy search** (continued) Identify most suitable strategies for further exploration and development	Screen and evaluate every idea against pre- determined criteria of 'attractiveness' and against criteria of 'compatibility'

Use of techniques

Depending on the nature of the task and the point reached during the group's deliberations the leader may suggest using any of the methods which are appropriate in the circumstances. Thus if the group needs to explore a future scenario for the organisation they can undertake a scenario-daydreaming exercise. If, on the other hand, they need to explore fresh avenues for the firm's identified talent they can allocate some time to morphological analysis and/or brainstorming. All the tools of the game are available to the team and should be resorted to as and when required by a given situation. To that extent it is important that both the leader of the unit and all the members are fully conversant with the details of most of the techniques that help to generate creative ideas or solve problems.

Sub-group work

The activities of Think Tanks often require the allocation of certain tasks to sub-groups. This is particularly appropriate when the programme of work calls for specialised tasks involving details of a technical or professional nature. Let us explore a brief case study by way of illustration.

'A Think Tank unit has been established by a large insurance company in order to explore strategies for a future world in which a comprehensive and integrated "financial services" package will be required by the marketplace. The anticipated scenario consists of a vision that customers will want to "buy" all their financial requirements from one well-integrated source. The unit is charged with the task of reviewing the scenario, validating its conclusions and developing a strategic blueprint for implementation.

After lengthy deliberations the team comes to the conclusion that a number of major and interrelated projects must be explored simultaneously.

(*a*)   An identification of the most attractive segment of the market at which to target the service. Clearly, this requires an in-depth marketing understanding and knowledge and creative thinking in this function.

(*b*)   The contribution that modern electronic technology can offer to such a project. This would need the harnessing of all the expertise that the group may possess in the field of information technology and office automation. If such knowledge in the team is inadequate additional resources may have to be identified and recruited.

(*c*)   An analysis of the financial implications to the company. Pro-forma balance sheets and profit-and-loss statements have to be considered and prepared. Accountants, investment specialists and possibly actuaries need to be allotted to such a task.'

An effective leader would attempt to break the project into a number of discrete parts and divide the available resources in such a way that each sub-group would have the appropriate skills at its disposal. The aim must be that every sub-group can devote its attention to that tranche of the work for which it is best suited. Plenary sessions should be postponed until the sub-groups are ready to report about their findings and ideas and the total material is capable of being collated into a meaningful whole.

This brief illustration helps to highlight another area in which the skills of the leader can be put to a very stringent test. A poor division of labour in running sub-groups of a Think Tank can easily lower the overall effectiveness of the unit's output.

Minutes of meetings

The assembly of clear and succinct minutes of each meeting of the Think Tank can be a useful instrument in ensuring continuity in the thinking process of the group. The role and value of such minutes must be explained to the members—otherwise it may be regarded as a bureaucratic bit of paperwork. The minutes must be detailed enough to provide the gist of the items discussed and also attempt to convey the atmosphere of the meeting but they must not be so long as to become turgid and boring.

The leader, after consultation with the team, can delegate the task of preparing the minutes to a member of the group. This role can be rotated among members of the group at intervals of around four to six meetings. Such an arrangement is to be preferred to the use of an external resource, such as a secretary, as it avoids using a person who is not part of the team and its culture.

Review of progress

The continued success of a Think Tank-type activity can be maintained through periodic and systematic de-briefing sessions. During such sessions the members of the unit, either alone or together with the founding-sponsors of the whole concept, attempt to audit the general effectiveness of the team and review the progress that might have been achieved. It is important that such a session is held at least once every six meetings. The main aim is to ensure that the unit is performing its tasks as originally envisaged by the unit's terms of reference and also to assess whether the creative juices are still flowing at a suitable rate. If such an 'audit' is not undertaken at regular intervals, the risk is that the unit may drift into a routine existence and lose some of its initial creative fervour. With a judicious turn of the flywheel the team can regain its creative excitement.

A summary

Think Tanks can be a valuable tool in the management of innovation in most organisations. However, a number of basic conditions should be borne in mind before pursuing such an activity.

(a) Clear and attainable objectives must be ascribed to such units during the formation stage.

(b) Such units must be able to operate in an atmosphere free of hierarchical policies and conflicts.

(c) If invited to help in stimulating attitudinal changes top management must be seen to provide the authority and wholehearted support for such a role.

Figure 51 describes the steps that need to be considered in the form of a flow diagram. Those who follow the various steps thus shown are likely to avoid many of the pitfalls that the establishment of Think Tanks often entails.

Figure 51.   Planning and developing a 'Think Tank'.

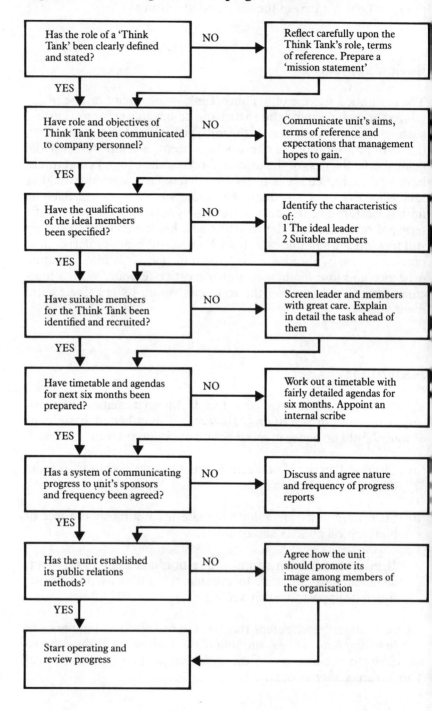

11 Effective suggestion schemes

In a fit of enthusiasm for creativity many firms establish suggestion schemes of one form or another. The recognition that members of the firm or even customers or visitors to the firm's premises are capable of submitting valuable suggestions and ideas has prompted a large number of companies to set up a system for catching such ideas. One encounters a myriad of systems on one's travels: suggestion boxes conspicuously placed in airports and railway stations; 'comment forms' in retail shops; complaint and/or eulogy forms in hotels, aircraft and ships; other types of receptacles for suggestions in factories and/or offices. All these can be very valuable if properly conceived and managed. Such schemes can produce for the organisation a useful flow of ideas and raw materials for innovation. However, such schemes encompass a lot more than just the placing of colourful little boxes in a prominent corner with the magic expression 'suggestion box' printed on them. Considerable thought must be invested in the whole scheme, and the amount of planning which ought to go into the establishment of an effective system entails many important and interrelated steps. The aim of this chapter is to explore the whole rationale of suggestion schemes and the way they can help the firm to become more innovative.

The rationale behind suggestion schemes

The main thinking underlying the various types of suggestion schemes is that a plethora of ideas is locked in people's minds and, if employees are not encouraged to present them to somebody in the organisation, such ideas simply wither away and get lost for ever. This applies to company personnel and also to other people who come in contact with the organisation such as suppliers, customers, sub-contractors and others. If the firm can harness all these invisible and unexpressed ideas it may find its creativity greatly enriched. In earlier chapters we saw that on average a firm requires an input of 60 ideas in order to attain one successful innovation—on that basis every source of ideas must be welcome and be encouraged

241

to communicate its output to somebody in the organisation. However, this can only be done if a definite communication system for catching all these ideas is in place. It is very unlikely that people would go out of their way to force ideas down the throat of a company which has not shown its desire or willingness to receive ideas from internal or external well-wishers. A message inviting and motivating people to submit their ideas must be loud and clear. To that extent suggestion boxes provide the banner that tells the audience: 'we welcome your creative ideas and in order to make life easier for you we have placed these boxes in convenient locations so that you can insert your ideas inside'. Some companies go even further in their endeavour to facilitate this communication process: they place special forms next to the box and sometimes even pencils or pens. The whole aim is to make the life of those who want to submit their suggestions to the firm as easy as possible. Yet my investigations over the years have shown that in spite of all these aids to the communication of ideas some companies complain that after a first flurry of enthusiasm, the boxes remain empty for months on end and nobody bothers to place ideas in them. Undoubtedly, in such situations the schemes have failed. The invitation, implied by the placing of the suggestion receptacles, has failed to attract members of the organisation and/or the public to think of ideas and submit them to the 'owners' of these boxes.

It is obvious that what is needed is more than just the installation of so-called suggestion boxes. What is needed is an integrated programme of work aimed at (*a*) alerting one's target audience to the importance the firm attaches to their ideas and suggestions; (*b*) motivating them to submit ideas; and (*c*) communicating with them in an interactive fashion so that the 'traffic' is not moving in one direction only. People who submit ideas are entitled to know what is happening to them. One-way-traffic in the idea communication game is a formula for stifling interest in any scheme.

The main role of any suggestion scheme is to harness the many ideas which are buzzing in people's minds and which, without a prod from the firm's environment, do not normally get communicated to the company's management. However, it must be remembered that such schemes often have ancillary objectives.

(*a*) To tell members of the organisation that the firm is truly keen on them becoming more creative and innovative.

(*b*) To communicate the message to all customers and/or other stakeholders that the firm cares about them.

When a hotel asks its customers to complete suggestion forms it not only wants to obtain ideas and comments, but it also wants its customers to know that the management of the hotel is eager to improve the hotel's service.

(c) An additional objective may be to improve personnel relations. The fact that the firm's management is interested in receiving personnel's ideas about how the business can be improved can be a valuable tool in improving the relationship between top management and the rest of the organisation.

(d) Associated with the above objective, it must be remembered that well-conceived schemes can help to establish a better system of communication and relationship with the firm's labour force.

(e) An indirect objective can be to enhance the image of the firm in the eyes of investors, the financial community and even the media.

In other words, suggestion schemes can have many more objectives than the obvious one of wanting to catch all the ideas that can be harnessed from members of the organisation. Such schemes can be much more powerful and wide-ranging in their scope and aims.

It is therefore recommended that before establishing a complex system of suggestion boxes or some other method of catching people's ideas, the organisers of such schemes reflect carefully upon the whole subject and collate all the appropriate objectives that should be ascribed to such schemes. Some of these objectives would be prime ones, others secondary. Nevertheless, they must all be spelled out and a system designed to meet them. It would be a great pity if a straightforward suggestion scheme is established for catching ideas without considering the ancillary and fringe objectives that the scheme can easily help to meet.

The following represents an example of a set of objectives which were recently defined for a suggestion scheme designed by a large multinational organisation in the fast-moving food business.

'We propose to establish a system for catching ideas generated by members of our organisation throughout the world and *also* by our many customers, seeking to fulfil the following objectives.

Primary objectives:

(a) to ensure that our reservoir of ideas available for screening and evaluation is always full;

(b) to stimulate in the firm a more responsive climate for ideas and innovation;

(*c*) to encourage our customers to consider our company as their partners.

Secondary objectives:

(*a*) to break down some of the barriers that appear to exist between senior management and the other levels of the organisation;

(*b*) to improve the flow of ideas from the various markets of the company and head office;

(*c*) to find out, indirectly, more about competitive practices and their attempts at innovation;

(*d*) to improve the overall "observing skill" of company personnel. It is felt that with improved observation one can become more vigilant for unexpected ideas;

(*e*) to assist in improving the firm's image as a company that attempts to "do things better, cheaper and in a different way", namely a firm that is trying to become more innovative.'

The above example helps to illustrate how one can have a multi-faceted range of objectives as the basis upon which to structure a programme of work of which a suggestion scheme is one element only. The full text of the objectives ascribed to the scheme is being provided in order to show how many additional benefits a firm can aspire to extract from a well-conceived idea-catching scheme. Over the years I have discovered that whenever I ask managers for the rationale for having established suggestion schemes I receive, on the whole, vague and woolly answers. Managers who can spell out a full set of interrelated objectives are normally the ones who have given the whole subject careful thought and have understood the role that an effective suggestion-catching programme can have in the organisation. Invariably the companies that can respond to my questioning with a carefully-worded set of clearly-defined objectives are the ones that derive true benefits from such schemes.

In summary therefore, it is important to emphasise once again the fact that a suggestion scheme ought to be designed in response to clear objectives and not simply be established because it is a fashionable thing to do. Moreover one must remember that the objectives thus defined can be much more far-reaching than just an attempt at catching ideas from people working for or associated with the firm.

Reasons for failure

Companies that have had suggestions schemes for any length of time and in which the quality and quantity of the ideas submitted have been disappointing normally tend to reject the value of such schemes out of hand. 'We have tried them before and they did not work' is the sort of reply which I hear with boring regularity. The thought that the system was ill-conceived and became discredited as a result of inadequate planning is rarely accepted by the sponsors of the scheme as the true reasons for such a failure.

Let us explore a few of the main causes of unsuccessful suggestion schemes.

Poor 'promotion' of the scheme

A scheme and its objectives must be communicated to all those people that the firm hopes will respond to it. One cannot simply place little coloured boxes with the title 'suggestion scheme' printed on their front and hope that the system will take off as a result of such a move.

The concept that management has taken a decision to initiate such a scheme must be communicated to the firm's personnel and/or customers with a brief explanation as to why such a scheme is being established and what the firm is hoping to achieve from it. The basic rules of sound marketing must be applied to such an internal activity. People must be made 'aware' of the scheme, then they must be stimulated to 'like' its aims and only then can one hope that they will 'act' favourably. Awareness per se, as every competent marketer would know, does not necessarily constitute 'liking', and it is the latter frame of mind that makes customers 'buy' offered products. In the case of suggestion schemes it is the insertion of ideas in the 'box' that amounts to the 'buying' process. The amazing thing is that in many companies in which first rate brand management is in existence, the sponsors of suggestion schemes often fail to recognise the value of such talent in promoting the schemes inside the company. The resources which are needed to market any product or brand can be used with equal efficacy in marketing a suggestion scheme. Yet many companies fail to recognise the similarity.

Lack of motivation

'What is there in it for me?' represents a dangerous but not an unusual attitude that exists in many organisations. It is the kind of attitude which indicates that people in the firm do not share the same goals that members of the more senior levels pursue. Clearly this attitude does not present a problem in firms in which every individual working in the company believes wholeheartedly in the fact that success of the organisation is good for all its personnel. The old maxim that used to circulate among General Motors personnel a score or so years ago that 'What is good for General Motors is good for the United States' was the complete antithesis of such an attitude. People working for General Motors used to believe that what was good for the firm was equally good for them as individuals. In such a climate the chance is quite high that people would respond to an invitation from the top to submit ideas and suggestions.

It is often erroneously assumed that 'motivation' in this regard means a financial reward. Obviously a financial reward is always a welcome incentive. However, the question immediately arises as to the quantum of the award and the basis upon which ideas earn such a reward. Anybody who understands the basic principles of motivation knows that people do not always consider monetary incentives as the only basis for motivation. The most successful suggestion scheme which I have ever come across does not have any financial rewards. Motivation is provided by earning a mention in the 'Creative Corner' of the company's house magazine. The best ideas submitted and accepted receive a certificate in which the president of the company acknowledges that the person who submitted the idea is the winner of the year's 'Best Idea' accolade, and in recognition a well-designed and framed certificate is handed over to him which he can place on the wall of his office. It is almost like an Oscar. Moreover, at the entrance to the firm's headquarters there is a list of all the winners of the scheme since its inception. No money ever changes hands as part of the motivation system, yet everybody in the firm is extremely keen to be placed on the roll of honour which was established for the scheme.

Another scheme ensures that the winners of the 'good suggestions scheme', namely those who have had their ideas accepted by the screening committee, earn points. These 'points' do not provide monetary rewards, but are brought into consideration during the personnel appraisal system. Earners of a large number of points stand a good chance of being awarded higher salary adjustments during the review period. Clearly this does have a financial angle, but it is more remote than cash or a cheque for a specific amount given as a direct reward for good suggestions.

The points worth emphasising in this connection are:

(*a*) Suggestions schemes often fail because of the absence of the motivational stimulus to contribute towards their success.

Lack of motivation is not necessarily the absence of a financial reward—it is much more a matter of attitudinal malaise endemic to the firm's culture and climate. Fundamental heart-searching of personnel policies ought to be undertaken before one can hope that people will respond to suggestion schemes in a generous and dedicated way. Failure of suggestion schemes is often a symptom of a more serious shortcoming in the firm's environment.

(*b*) The whole gamut of 'motivational hygiene' factors must be explored and one cannot simply assume that the only language that people understand is monetary awards. The latter often cause more trouble than benefit.

(*c*) The greatest motivation in this regard is the general climatic attitude that what is good for the firm is good for its individuals. The ability to attain such a system of shared values is the most creative preamble to a successful and fertile suggestion scheme.

Lack of feedback

Lack of feedback is a wonderful killer of suggestion schemes. Individuals submit their ideas to the 'communication system' either in a prescribed format or in an ordinary note and never hear anything from the organisers of the scheme. The idea simply gets lost in what appears to be a bottomless pit. People expect some acknowledgement, some response, even if it entails a rejection. They want to know that the suggestion has been received by those responsible for its screening and evaluation and that, in due course, they will receive some feedback as the outcome of such procedures. One cannot expect company personnel to maintain their enthusiasm for a scheme in the face of complete silence. Moreover, one must remember the power of internal mass-communication and grapevine: if people get no response to their suggestions it does not take long for them to communicate their disappointment and frustration to their colleagues in the firm and the system gets into disrepute.

The message is that in establishing a suggestion scheme some system of effective acknowledgement and/or response must be designed at the very outset. Participants in the scheme must never be kept in the dark as to what has happened to their suggestions. It must be remembered that every person normally believes that his or her ideas are the best. Lack of feedback is tantamount to an unacceptable insult.

Whilst on the subject of feedback it is also appropriate to mention that one must be careful not to fall into the opposite trap of being over-effusive when acknowledging the receipt of ideas. I recently came across a firm that understood the need for a feedback system. However, the sponsors of the suggestion scheme indulged in a series of computer-processed letters acknowledging receipt of each suggestion in a way which caused a lot of merriment. These letters were exaggerated in their expression of thanks for 'having submitted such promising ideas which, in due course, may prove to be so valuable to the future of the firm', etc, etc. Moreover, when people compared these letters they soon realised that similar letters were sent indiscriminately to anybody who had submitted a suggestion. It was over-the-top, and went far beyond what a normal feedback system should consist of. A happy medium between the two extremes should be struck.

Poor screening system

This is probably the most hazardous obstacle to a successful and effective suggestion .scheme. Participants in any scheme of this nature want to know that a judicious and competent system of evaluation exists. The minute members of the organisation start feeling that the screening is carried out in a capricious or haphazard manner, general interest in the whole scheme wanes rapidly. During the initial design of the scheme a system for screening and evaluating suggestions must be formulated and, ideally, communicated to all members of the organisation. If company personnel know how the system functions and who is responsible for the actual process of screening ideas, evaluating them and identifying the best among them, they are more likely to respond to it with enthusiasm. If, on the other hand, the general feeling gained is that screening is carried out in an amateurish and unsystematic manner, the whole scheme is soon discredited. We shall see later what kind of steps should be taken in order to ensure that the screening procedures are both effective and acceptable to those who are expected to contribute to the scheme.

Lack of tangible payoffs

In an organisation that operates a suggestion scheme it is perfectly normal for the personnel of that company to expect to hear, from time to time, of some tangible results, irrespective of how significant they may be. Tangible innovations resulting from a suggestion scheme are the best incentive for fuller co-operation and participation in the scheme. When months, and sometimes years, pass by without any visible signs of creative ideas being implemented, the tendency is to ignore the existence of the scheme and cease to bother to submit suggestions in the prescribed manner.

Organisers of suggestion schemes must pay particular attention to this point. It is essential that a few suggestions get implemented at regular intervals, especially during the early stages of the scheme. This is the only way in which the credibility and acceptability of the scheme can be gained. It may sound like a semi-political manipulation of people's commitment to a system. Nevertheless, human beings need some real evidence of value and relevance of a system before they are prepared to take part in its activities.

Furthermore, the implementation of successful innovations must receive some prominence and be communicated to the whole organisation as part of the scheme's mass promotion.

General negativity towards the ideas of others

In some companies the scheme suffers from the general negative attitude of those responsible for screening and evaluating the ideas submitted. The following examples illustrate the sort of comments that display this kind of negativity.

'Many thanks for your suggestion. We looked at a similar idea five years ago and decided to reject it then'.
'Your idea is interesting but (note the 'but') we cannot accept it because it is not compatible with our company policy.'
'The idea will be too expensive to implement.'
'We cannot pursue this idea further because the Stock Exchange may frown upon such a step on our part.'

Many similar responses can be construed as negative and unsupportive and can help to demolish the continued interest of company personnel in the whole scheme. All the responses given above may be legitimate and valid. Yet it must be remembered that a message of rejection and its wording are always discussed among colleagues and the damage to people's creativity resulting from pernicious negativity can be far-reaching. Striking a balance between being fair and supportive and, at the same time, being able to reject ideas that fail to meet certain criteria of acceptability is one of the keys to a successful suggestion scheme. People realise that not every idea can be accepted, but they are not willing to submit ideas to a scheme which says 'no', as a matter of routine, to every suggestion.

As we shall see later, one of the solutions to this particular obstacle lies with the individuals that are selected to man the screening committee. The choice of members of such a team can often make the difference between a successful scheme and one which becomes an empty shell.

The 'not invented here' syndrome

This point is closely associated with the previous one inasmuch as it manifests a certain level of negativity. It often happens that those responsible for screening suggestions take the view that ideas emanating from external sources are always bad and those originating from inside the firm are, almost by definition, better. This means that whenever somebody comes along with an idea gleaned from other countries, other industries, and from competitors, the natural reaction is to find fault with such an idea. The emotion which is being communicated, invariably in non-verbal fashion, is: 'It was not invented here and therefore it cannot be good.' Such an attitude can have a devastating impact on the flow of suggestions and starves the firm of all those ideas that originate from observing the external environment. Unfortunately this often happens without the culprits realising that they have been instrumental in such a syndrome. However, the members of the organisation soon recognise its existence and ensure that only internally-generated ideas are submitted.

An integrated approach

In an earlier context it was stated that well-designed schemes should encompass as many elements as possible aimed at integrating them with the overall objective of making the firm more creative and more innovative. A scheme which forms part of such a wide-ranging process is more likely to be of benefit to the firm than a narrow and limited suggestion-catching programme.

In other words a scheme that represents one brick in a far-reaching and ambitious management development programme, designed to move the whole organisation towards a more innovative era, is where the company can attain maximum rewards.

These are examples of a multi-faceted programme of work which can provide the suggestion scheme with a true value.

(*a*) A training programme for all the company's personnel with the aim of making them aware of the importance of creativity as the forerunner of innovation.

   If the firm is large and its employees scattered in many locations, the management development function ought to consider the assembly of 'distant learning' packages, specifically designed for the company and its many offshoots. If the firm is small and operating in a single location a face-to-face training programme can be planned and conducted by an experienced consultant/facilitator.

(*b*) The development of a climate in which ideas can flourish and in which people are eager to think of ideas and communicate them to their peers.

   This could be partially achieved through the training programme mentioned above, but must be buttressed by an imaginative use of the following supportive tools:

   (i) creativity circles;
   (ii) 'Creativity' house magazines or 'Creativity' page in the firm's house magazine;
   (iii) regular creativity sessions utilising the various techniques learnt;
   (iv) suggestion schemes.

In such circumstances suggestion schemes become part of an integrated programme. The chance that such schemes will achieve their objectives is greatly enhanced. They become an integral part of the firm's overall move towards a more fertile creative environment and their success is more likely to become real and permanent.

(*c*) The establishment of a communication system for ideas to flow. It may be recalled from an earlier chapter that one of the major conditions for the successful enhancement of innovation in an organisation is the existence of an effective communication system. A well-conceived suggestion scheme is nothing more than the establishment of an additional channel in the communication infrastructure of the firm. However, people must recognise it as such and only then may they respond to the invitation to submit ideas in the prescribed format.

(*d*) A system for screening ideas, evaluating them and identifying the best among them for implementation. The quality of the screening system and the people who man such an activity will be discussed in greater detail later. However, in this connection it is important to emphasise that in designing a suggestion scheme the procedures for 'managing innovation' must be carefully considered at the design stage and not left for a future date. It must all be integrated with the overall mission that the scheme is designed to attain.

(e) Finally, a system for announcing and communicating details of successful innovations (unless commercial prudence demands that they are kept secret) must be put in place.

The various communication tools selected for educating the company personnel (eg house magazines, posters, tapes, etc) can also be used for communicating success stories, coupled with details of those who were instrumental in submitting the original idea.

On the subject of an integrated approach to the whole subject, I have come across a company that used all these methods but in addition introduced the following steps:

(a) Large boards were placed in a few prominent locations showing, in a diagrammatic form (i) the number of ideas submitted on month-by-month basis, since the beginning of the year, and (ii) the number of ideas which were found useful and were chosen for implementation.

Some companies show how many days' work were lost through accidents. Others show the output per worker. This company has chosen to show its performance in the area of ideas versus innovations. Interestingly enough the ratio between ideas submitted and ideas implemented was around the 60 : 1 mark! The reassuring part of this system was that both the number of ideas submitted through the various schemes in existence increased every month, and also the implemented innovations grew, more or less at the same ratio.

(b) Once a month a poster showing the pictures and names of the winners was placed in a number of conspicuous positions in the company's head office and various factories.

(c) One of the aims of the whole scheme was to improve the flow of ideas from the large work force. In order to give this objective a fillip, a screening committee was established consisting of (i) two members of the senior management; (ii) two members of middle management; and (iii) two representatives of the work force. The system prescribed that the whole screening team would be changed every nine months, thus widening the screening experience of as many people in the firm as possible.

This brief description provides an illustration of a company that understood the true value of a suggestion scheme as part of a much wider objective relating to the firm's innovation. Their approach was integrated and single-minded. Clearly it is possible to think of a few additional items to be incorporated in the integrated programme of work in this regard. The significant message is that the more one dovetails the introduction of a suggestion scheme with other aspects of management development and personnel policies, relating to creativity and innovation, the more successful the whole scheme is likely to be.

Top management commitment

A suggestion scheme should never be introduced without the involvement and expressed commitment of top management. A scheme which is established without such an overt and stated commitment is less likely to be a successful one.

This means that the actual presentation of the scheme, its rationale, and the potential value to the firm must always be issued in the name of top management and a number of promotional statements must be seen to emanate from that quarter.

Venturesome top executives, who believe wholeheartedly in the need for creative ideas in the organisation, should be prepared to try their hand at submitting ideas to the scheme. This can represent the most powerful statement of commitment to the whole project.

Periodic audit of progress

This is another useful strategy for breathing new life into schemes that might have lost momentum. A yearly analysis of what has been achieved, both in terms of ideas submitted and the innovations that transpired, can provide a valuable lesson as to how the scheme is faring and how it can be improved. This kind of analysis should be discussed with departmental heads and other senior personnel in order to earn their full support and provide them with an opportunity to claim some 'ownership' of the amendments to the procedures. The most successful schemes are the ones that have many people who are able to claim part-ownership thereof. Thus the more people who contribute ideas as to how the scheme can be improved and enhanced the better.

The ability to show that since the scheme was launched the level of innovation has increased is always a useful aid to promoting the scheme and giving it a new lease of life.

The various Audits at the end of this book can form the basis for an organisational assessment of the way the firm's innovation has progressed over a period. If one can demonstrate, at the end of each year, that improvements in the total score have taken place, there is fair reason to assume that the suggestion schemes have played a role in achieving such a result.

A venturesome posture

Finally, it is appropriate to mention that those who expect others to put forward creative suggestions and ideas must themselves be able to demonstrate the ability to be creative and, at times, to possess a venturesome attitude of mind. Being creative needs a manifestation of courage, of some risk-taking, of 'guts'. If one wants others to be creative one needs to show that one is prepared to go along with 'gutsy' ideas. People are more willing to put forward unusual suggestions if they know that at the top of the organisation or the department there is a person who is capable of departing from the conventional trodden path.

One of the schemes which I helped to mount was for a company manufacturing confectionery products. The scheme sought to involve all customers in the process of submitting suggestions and ideas. The first task was to communicate the details of the scheme to all customers. Somebody suggested that the easiest and best idea was to print the details of the scheme on the outer wrapper of every item sold. I felt that the idea was superb, but top management concluded that it was too radical a departure from the acceptable standards in the trade and refused to authorise such a strategy. What harm would it do a firm marketing toothpaste if they decided to incorporate a suggestion programme in the outer packaging of the toothpaste? Similarly, why should not a whisky company invite its customers to take part in a scheme soliciting ideas for new cocktails based on whisky and communicate the details of the scheme through the label on the bottle? In reality, there is no reason why such schemes cannot be planned and launched. The truth is that the people responsible for these products are seldom prepared to embark on schemes which are so different from what the company has been accustomed to in the past. Most managers are reluctant to deviate from a trodden path. To be able to pursue a creative departure from a conventional routine requires a certain amount of courage, or what is best described by the word 'guts'. Some courage in the application of good ideas can provide a suggestion scheme with a cutting edge which otherwise it is not likely to enjoy. The fact that management is prepared to entertain and implement 'way-out' ideas can give members of the organisation considerable courage in submitting imaginative and sometimes unusual ideas and suggestions.

Screening and evaluating suggestions

The reader may recall that in Chapter 2 it was emphasised that one of the conditions of effectiveness in the field of creativity is the availability of procedures for converting ideas into innovations. The conversion of ideas into reality does not happen by itself. It requires a systematic method for looking at ideas, analysing their virtues, identifying the obstacles to implementation and, finally, selecting the attractive few for implementation. The main thrust of this book is based on the notion that creativity is an essential element for successful innovation and that innovation can only stem from a methodical process of converting ideas into reality. The symbiotic relationship between these two elements has been emphasised sufficiently in previous chapters. In the context of suggestion schemes it is useful to remember this fundamental principle—suggestion schemes are perfectly useless if they are not accompanied by a set of procedures for screening and evaluating suggestions, or, if such procedures do exist, they are not very well-conceived.

In Chapter 2, a number of procedures for screening ideas were explored. All the comments made in that chapter apply fully to the process of screening of suggestions submitted under the aegis of suggestion schemes. Nevertheless, a few special points should be made in respect of the establishment of an effective screening system for suggestion schemes.

Members of the screening committee

Membership of the committee charged with the task of screening and evaluating ideas must be in general empathy with the objectives of the scheme and personnel expectations. It is a delicate task and any member who is known among his colleagues as a hard and somewhat intolerant person may not be compatible with the nature of the screening process. Moreover, the presence of such people on the screening committee can act as a disincentive among company personnel to co-operate with the scheme. In other words, it is important that the membership of the screening team is chosen with an eye on the internal public relations value of such appointments.

In particular, the following points ought to be borne in mind when seeking to identify suitable members for the committee.

(*a*) The committee should consist of a heterogeneous range of skills and experience. Committees that only represent one or two departments or functions are less likely to be able to evaluate ideas relating to other areas of the firm.

(*b*) Having representatives of different levels is valuable inasmuch as (i) it provides the committee with a wider range of viewpoints and perspectives, and (ii) it ensures a wider appeal among members of the organisation as a whole.

We saw earlier how some companies take steps to incorporate representatives from every level of the organisation including one or two members of the labour force on the screening committee.

(*c*) People with a recognised positive 'attitude spectrum' must be preferred to those known for their negative response to ideas.

(*d*) Members of the committee must be individuals known for their fairness and objectivity. Individuals who have the tendency to favour ideas emanating from their own department can cause a lot of harm to the whole aim which the suggestion scheme is seeking to achieve.

(*e*) Persons known for their ability to think laterally and who possess a certain amount of entrepreneurial leaning are useful members. It needs creative people to recognise creative ideas.

(*f*) Only people who feel totally committed to the whole concept of 'mass-catching' of suggestions and ideas ought to be invited to sit on the screening committee. Those who feel that the whole scheme is a passing fad ought to be excluded. Such individuals can easily help to kill the whole venture by what they say, or through their body language.

(*g*) Volunteers who possess all the qualities implied in the last few
sections are the ideal candidates. Screening a plethora of
suggestions can be a pretty tedious job. Those who volunteer
to undertake this task are clearly highly motivated and should
be accepted with open arms provided, of course, they possess
some or most of the other characteristics.

Finally it ought to be remembered that membership of the
screening committee must not be a permanent appointment. Periodic changes in membership can help to maintain freshness of mind
and enthusiasm among the members of the screening team.

Screening procedures

Over the years I have had occasion to observe a number of committees charged with the task of screening suggestions. They varied
between those which simply read the suggestions, debated them for
a few minutes and then decided to accept or reject them, to those
which had developed clear procedures with definite criteria of
acceptability. The latter always managed to cope with the avalanche
of ideas in a systematic and relaxed fashion. The former normally
found themselves sinking in a morass of indecision and confusion.
The value of having well-defined procedures for screening, evaluating and identifying winning suggestions cannot be over-emphasised.

In this respect it is helpful to compile a number of procedures
similar to those described in Chapter 2 to include:

(*a*) the criteria of attractive suggestions (see Figure 12)

(*b*) the criteria of acceptability to the firm (see Figure 12)

(*c*) a matrix seeking to match the previous two dimensions (see
Figures 11, 13)

(*d*) a screening table (see Figure 15)

(*e*) a screening algorithm (see Figure 14).

Any combination of these simple procedures can aid the screening process. In all instances the team should work on the basis that
wherever a consensus cannot be reached the procedure can help to
reach an average score so as to attain a decision based on a 'jury of

executive opinion' approach. This helps to reduce arguments and is the fairest way to conclude a debate.

The most tedious part of the task is the establishment of procedures. When these are at hand the screening exercise becomes a matter of routine and every suggestion receives its fair share of adjudication and analysis.

Ideally, the basis upon which suggestions are screened and the main rationale for the screening criteria should be made known to company personnel. One does not have to communicate all the details, but the main gist ought to be explained. This normally helps to ensure that members of the organisation undertake a certain amount of pre-screening before they place their suggestions in the appropriate receptacle.

Frequency of screening

People are creatures of habit. If a suggestion scheme is to function effectively it is important that individuals who submit their ideas can expect to hear about the committee's verdict within a prescribed time. Whether this is done every month or every two months or even at longer intervals, it is the regularity of the process which matters. People who participate in football pools or other lotteries know when the results will be published. Similarly, a person who takes the suggestion scheme seriously wants to know that the idea submitted has been analysed seriously. Adhering to a regular timetable is one of the best ways to ensure that unnecessary suspense is removed from the whole exercise.

A well-known company in the retail field has laid down a rule that every suggestion placed in their suggestion boxes is screened within a week. Feedback, positive or negative, is sent to the individual who had submitted the suggestion within three days of the committee's verdict. Such a speedy routine acts as a real spur to people's creative juices.

Format of submissions

Should suggestions be submitted in a prescribed format or would any written note do? These are questions which sponsors to suggestion schemes often pose to themselves. This may appear a 'hair-splitting' topic, but in reality it represents an important practical issue. A number of advantages can be listed in support of having a standard format and procedures for submitting suggestions.

(*a*) It can facilitate the process of presenting the submission.

(*b*) By having a limited amount of space on a form one is forced to condense the suggestion to its bare essentials, thus reducing redundant verbosity.

(*c*) A standard format can help the screening committee during the analysis of the suggestion.

(*d*) Where standard formats exist it is possible to incorporate in the instructions a number of pre-determined criteria of desirability. This can help to attract suggestions which are germane to the firm's specific needs and aims.

Thus, for instance, if the promoters of the scheme feel that every suggestion submitted must incorporate financial savings to the company, the form may have special space in which the idea submitter can state in what way he expects savings to be attained. This has the dual effect of (i) forcing people to refrain from submitting suggestions that do not adhere to the 'savings objective,' and (ii) acting as an aid to the screening process undertaken by the committee.

(*e*) A standard suggestion format is generally helpful in creating better communication between the 'submitters' of the suggestions and the 'screeners'.

In summary, there is a strong case for designing a tailor-made form for the submission of suggestions. At the same time it is important to remember that a form which smacks of too much bureaucracy can act as a barrier to creativity. The answer to this dilemma is to design a form, but make it quite clear that it has been designed to assist the people who wish to submit suggestions and that any submission made in any other form will not suffer as a result of such non-compliance. The 'audience' must be made to appreciate that the format procedure is designed as an aid to effectiveness and not as a symbol of corporate bureaucracy.

Where the scheme is exclusively run for company personnel, the provision of multi-copy forms can be of additional benefit. A set of three copies can function as follows: two copies are placed in the suggestion box, one to be retained by the screening committee, one returned to the sender with details of the verdict inserted in an appropriate square; the third copy is retained by the suggestion 'submitter'. In companies that take the creative process seriously, individuals could be invited, during the personnel appraisal procedures, to bring along details of their respective contribution to the firm's creativity. The copies of the various suggestions submitted during the period under review can help to provide the appropriate evidence. Unfortunately, such a procedure sounds somewhat coercive in its implications. 'You must be creative, if you want to get on in the company!' is the kind of message which may come across to the firm's personnel. It is therefore suggested that companies that ask people to provide evidence of contribution made towards the firm's innovation, approach it in a fairly circumspect manner and do not elevate such procedures to the realm of unreasonable pedantry. One does not want people to submit suggestions in large numbers just because it may look good during the appraisal session.

Communicating results

The presentation of results can be a most powerful aid to maintaining the momentum and interest in the scheme. I have monitored the performance of many schemes in a variety of environments and am always saddened by the way the number of suggestions submitted sags over time. People who lose interest in the value of a scheme soon run out of ideas. One the other hand I have noticed that in those companies in which the outcome of the period's submissions is communicated in a structured way the momentum is maintained unabated. The lesson I have learnt from these observations has been of great value to me and the companies that I have been trying to help in this area.

The summary of a scheme's achievement during a given period can consist of the following elements:

(*a*) the listing of the numbers and types of suggestions received by the screening committee in the period under review;

(*b*) a synopsis of the five (or so) suggestions that were found to be the most valuable by the screening committee. A brief explanation of the reasons for finding them so valuable is of added benefit as part of the communication;

(*c*) in the event that the scheme has specific objectives (eg savings, increased productivity etc) the extent to which these objectives have been attained;

(*d*) some statistics providing details of the number of suggestions submitted since the beginning of the year on a moving average scale;

(*e*) other significant features pertaining to the period under review;

(*f*) details of the individuals who have contributed the winning suggestions and, in the event that specific rewards were won by anybody, details of such rewards.

In summary, suggestion schemes can be as effective as the amount of preparation and thought that have been invested in them. It is most unwise to think that by simply placing suggestion boxes around the company's premises the flow of creative ideas and innovations is assured. Without adequate thought and preparation such schemes are in most instances doomed before they have been launched. Finally, at the risk of repeating the obvious, it is absolutely essential that a system of feedback and interaction with all those people who have volunteered to submit suggestions is established.

Figure 52 summarises a checklist, in the form of a flow diagram, of the various steps that the sponsors of suggestion schemes ought to pursue. By following all these steps in a conscientious way the chances of having a successful scheme are greatly enhanced.

Figure 52.   Developing an effective suggestion scheme.

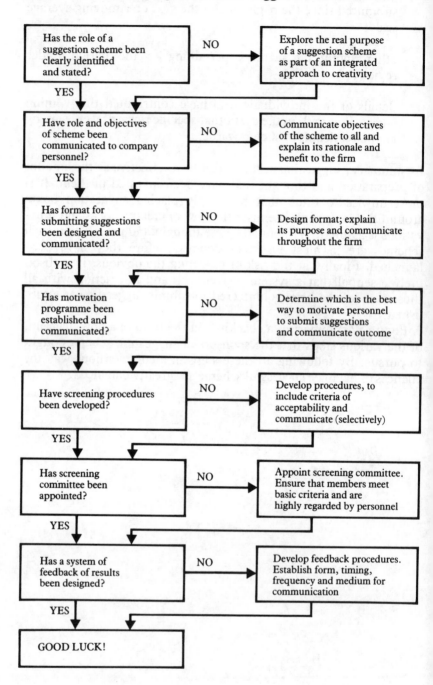

12 Managing innovation— a practical approach

In previous chapters we saw how important it is to have a large number of ideas in the creativity 'reservoir' before one begins the process of screening and evaluating such ideas. The rate of decay of ideas is so immense that if one starts with a small number of ideas, the probability is that very few of them will go beyond the first screening hurdles. This is the main purpose of the various idea-generation techniques which were explored earlier.

A large 'funnel' must be filled with as many ideas as the creative process of the organisation can muster. By the law of averages, one hopes that among the plethora of ideas in the funnel, at least a few might prove to be of immense value towards solving defined problems.

Moreover, as was emphasised earlier it is important that during the 'idea-generation' stage no judgement is passed on specific ideas. When filling the funnel one goes for quantity and not for quality. In theory at least, one should expect that out of every 50 to 60 ideas, one will prove a winner. Thus by exploring hundreds of ideas one could hope to increase one's chance of yielding a few useful ideas capable of successful implementation. Inevitably, the funnel would have in it a fairly large number of so-called 'intermediate impossibles'. This is all to the good, as such ideas often prove to be the catalysts for imaginative solutions to ticklish problems. The aim must be to provide the raw material which the subsequent innovation process can screen, evaluate and ultimately implement in selected cases.

The dilemma facing those responsible for managing innovation is the fact that during the 'idea-generation' stage it is imperative to suspend judgement and allow all ideas—the good, the bad and the indifferent—to get into the net. At the other end of the cycle, during the screening and evaluation, one must be prepared to be realistic, practical and results-orientated. Individuals who understand this split activity and can cope with its mental disciplines are the sort of persons that can help the firm to become more innovative.

The transition from idea to innovation can be rapid, a blinding flash, or a lengthy and, sometimes, a tortuous process. 'Innovation' is the moment of truth when the creators thereof know that they are 'hitting the jackpot' in the sense that something 'better or cheaper or more novel' is emerging from all the effort and is ready to be implemented. It is an exciting moment—people who have not experienced such excitement in their working lives have missed the joy of creation. Like seeds in nature, the speed at which ideas spawn into flowering innovations depends on a myriad of factors— the complexity of the problem or issue, the time devoted to the generation and development of ideas, the level of creativity that exists among the team charged with the whole task. In nature the quality of the earth, coupled with the appropriateness of the ferti- lisers used, determines the quality of the crop and its growth. Simi- larly, in a corporate environment it is the climate that helps speed up the crop of innovation.

To illustrate the way the process functions in practice two case histories will be traced in some detail. For obvious reasons the names of the companies are fictitious and the descriptions of people and events modified sufficiently to make recognition impossible. Any similarity to known firms is purely accidental. Nevertheless, all the stories originate from real situations and the lessons that are to be derived from them are valuable. The aim is to illustrate, through case studies, the way the cycle, from creative ideas to tan- gible and successful innovations, flows. Different lessons can be derived from each case. The main message that should emerge is that the conceptual framework described in the previous chapters does work in practice.

Case 1: Scales Industries Inc

Scales Industries is a large international company operating in about sixty countries in the field of electronics, business machinery, components for the telecommunication industry. The firm employs over 50,000 people throughout the world with about 6000 personnel in managerial and 'white collar' positions. A large number of these people are technicians, engineers, researchers, servicemen.

The firm is decentralised and most operating units function as self-contained profit centres. Most functional decisions such as marketing, production, management development and training are taken at local level. Some central services are avail- able at the centre to assist all subsidiaries, if required and requested to do so. Among such central services there is a cor- porate Management Development Adviser.

Top management came to recognise that a serious problem existed: all strategic decisions were taken in a radical 'production-orientated' fashion. Products and technologies were developed without any reference to the marketplace; research and development activities were undertaken without any commercial or marketing justification. The result was that all new developments were a game of 'Russian roulette'—success and failure were a matter of luck. Only one in six products proved to be a real success.

The president decided that the time had come to change the firm's corporate ethos from the traditional production orientation, which characterised the firm in the past, to a market-orientated philosophy. He and his Board of Directors fully realised the implications and the size of the task. They understood that changing a culture, a corporate attitude, an organisational ethos is a gargantuan task. Nonetheless instructions were given to the centrally located Management Development Adviser to take all the necessary steps to initiate a programme of work aimed at converting people's orientation from production to a market or customer orientated approach. 'This is our priority project for the next two years. I am willing to allocate substantial resources to this task but it must be effective and imaginative and I want to see results' was the president's unequivocal message.

Approach to the project

This case is being explored from the vantage point of the Management Development Adviser and his team. They were at a loss to know where and how to start with this project and finally decided to apply creative thinking and techniques towards developing solutions. As a first step and with the help of an outside facilitator the team decided to establish a 'task force' charged with the development of a suitable programme of work. Some time was devoted towards (i) defining the terms of reference of the task force, and (ii) defining the characteristics of the most suitable members of such a group. The president himself took a very active part in these discussions.

The terms of reference were finally defined as follows:

(*a*) to recommend an integrated and innovative programme of work designed to make everybody in the firm, regardless of functional affiliation, more customer-orientated;

(*b*)   to provide a blueprint for implementation;

(*c*)   to establish a mechanism for monitoring progress and providing a periodic impetus for further progress.

'Urgency' was stated to be an overriding factor in the task force's work and thinking process.

On the question of the ideal membership of the team it was agreed that one needed to strike a balance between three main elements: (*a*) individuals with a creative streak in them; (*b*) persons who, through authority and position, could help to 'make things happen'; and (*c*) people who could represent the interests of non-marketing functions. It was felt best to involve as many departments as possible in the exercise. This would remove unnecessary obstruction at the implementation stage and could also serve as an aid to management development as members of the task force could help to promulgate the new gospel among their respective colleagues. It was clearly understood that the ideal members would meet more than one criterion. With these thoughts in mind a task force of eight people was selected. It consisted of the Management Development Adviser, the Head of Central Marketing Services, two Country Managers (already convinced of the need for marketing orientation), a senior Product Manager (a staff role in one of the main markets), a member of the Research and Development co-ordinating team at Head Office (a creative, albeit somewhat cynical member, but a useful spokesman for the R & D function), the Corporate Planning Officer (a person close to the president) and a senior international trainer.

In addition the team co-opted an external facilitator to attend all the meetings and, initially, to act as the chairman. However, the idea was to rotate the chairmanship as and when it was felt that a fresh approach was needed.

It was understood throughout that the president of the company was the driving force behind the assignment. Whilst he had decided not to attend the meetings of the task force because he felt that he might dominate the proceedings, he expressed his wish to be fully informed of details at all times.

The team at work

The task force agreed, as a first step, to spend a long week-end (from Thursday morning to Monday lunchtime) in an outside venue to tackle the problem.

After a brief discussion they decided to apply the following agenda:

Phase 1
Diagnosing the true causes of the problem and defining the precise nature of what they needed to solve.

Phase 2
Generating ideas by whatever method was deemed appropriate.

Phase 3
Establishing screening criteria and commencing to screen and evaluate ideas.

Phase 4
Preparing a blueprint for implementation.

The task force met six times altogether over a period of four months and completed the assignment at the end of that period. In the next few sections their approach and activities are summarised briefly.

Phase 1—diagnosing the problem

The team sought to understand:

(*a*)   what precisely being 'customer-orientated' or 'market-orientated' or 'marketing-orientated' meant; and

(*b*)   the reasons for Scales not being thus 'orientated'.

It was agreed that a thorough discussion and understanding of these two elements would help to ensure that the task force addressed the real problem and did not just help to remove some of the symptoms.

On the first point, the group had read many papers on the subject and discussed the whole issue with a number of gurus in the field of marketing. Two members of the team who belonged to the marketing function made presentations on the subject, and after lengthy deliberations the group agreed that the various expressions relating to 'customer-orientation' boiled down to the following message:

'A company can be described as "customer-orientated" when every individual in the firm regardless of his or her level, functional affiliation or responsibilities seeks to respond to customer needs and expectations, at all times. It is a corporate attitude, an ethos, a culture that must be developed in a consistent and integrated fashion throughout the organisation. It is almost a religion.

The payoff is that such companies benefit from having satisfied and loyal customers. This in turn means better performance. It also reduces the risk of making costly mistakes in the way the company manages its affairs.'

The strongest message that emerged from these deliberations was that whatever the team decided to recommend it must be attitudinal and must apply to every individual working in the company. Moreover, it must be pursued with persistent and steadfast missionary work, almost like converting people to a new religion.

On the question of what were the 'reasons for Scales not being customer or market orientated' the team undertook a thorough 'cause-and-effect' analysis based on the 'Fishbone Method.' For the first time in the history of the company, somebody sought to identify why the company behaved in a certain way. Figure 53 summarises the way the discussions developed in this regard.

The main outcome of the Fishbone analysis was that the company was not 'customer-orientated' for the following reasons:

(a) the centre of gravity of the business demanded technologically orientated decisions;

(b) past recruitment policy favoured technical people;

(c) members of the top Board were mostly engineers and scientists who did not understand the meaning of 'marketing';

(d) the route to the 'top' was always through the technical functions;

(e) lack of management development and training in the area of marketing;

(f) lack of knowledge of what 'marketing' meant generated fear of the unknown.

Other causes were listed but these were the ones that the team felt were the main reasons for the firm's present climate and unempathetic attitude towards the 'marketing concept'. The use of the 'Fishbone Method' has helped the group to look at the problem in a very broad fashion and from a number of focal points. It was agreed that a multi-faceted programme of work aimed at neutralising all these causes was needed if the assignment was to bear long-term fruit.

Figure 53. **Fishbone Method of Scales Industries problem.**

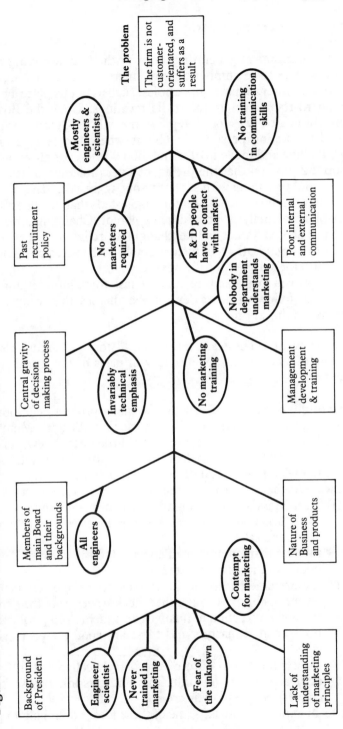

Phase 2—generating ideas

Various attempts at generating ideas by the brainstorming method were made. A large number of ideas emerged including a significant number of 'intermediate impossibles' such as 'let us place a bomb in the Board-room during one of its meetings. Once the Board has been eliminated we could replace the whole Board with hand-picked marketing personnel'. This is where the team decided to draw the line and move to other methods! Interestingly enough, the group did not feel that the president's very tolerant 'attitude spectrum' would go along with such way-out aggressive ideas!

At that point, the facilitator suggested that a synectics-type 'metaphorical analysis' should be explored. 'Changing a firm's culture and shared values is like changing a religion. Let us explore how other organisations in history coped with such a challenge' was the facilitator's trigger for the next session.

This proved most exciting, and the task force found it quite valuable. The following are a few of the themes that were aired in response to this approach:

(*a*) *Communism.* The team traced the history of Communism and the way this creed has penetrated vast parts of the world since its inception.

Long discussions centred around the main 'promotional tools' that were used by the Communist Party to achieve its aims. Members of the task force suddenly realised how little they knew about the Communist Party. Nevertheless, they attempted to crystalise their bits of knowledge and prejudices into some framework.

It was felt that the main strands of the movement's success were:
  (i) Karl Marx's 'Das Kapital' which provided some kind of a Bible upon which the party's 'missionaries' could base their creed and sales talk;
 (ii) the fact that Communism appealed to the oppressed and the poor and these represented the masses;
(iii) the extreme nature of the creed's neo-supporters generated public visibility through the 'shock waves' that they created;
 (iv) the hostile reaction of many Governments and public institutions created martyrs and these are good for propagating a creed;
  (v) the clandestine nature of the party's cell structure created dedicated teams of infiltrators and missionaries seeking to convert people to their creed.

The team explored how far some of these ideas could help to propagate the 'Marketing Creed' in Scales. They liked the use of a 'Book', the 'Cell' system and the notion that a saleable creed should appear to help the oppressed and deprived.

(*b*) *Communism in China*. Once again the team discovered how little they knew about Chinese Communism and Mao's role in propagating his version of Communism. However, they did realise that Mao's 'Little Red Book' had an important role to play in the process.

(*c*) *Scientology*. A member of the group had read a few books on Hubbard and the way he developed his 'scientology'. The main lesson that the group derived from what they heard was the way converts needed to submit themselves to a complex hierarchy of 'question and answer' hurdles in order to progress through the creed's structure.

(*d*) *Christianity*. The team was fascinated by the similarities that existed between the way Christianity had promoted its creed and how other religions had promoted theirs. Their interpretation as to why Christianity progressed from such humble beginnings was:
   (i) the appeal to the oppressed and the deprived;
  (ii) the existence of martyrs ('Can we create one or more martyrs at Scales? Crucify somebody? Send one or two managers to fight lions?')
 (iii) the existence of dedicated Apostles ('Who can we appoint as Apostles at Scales?')
  (iv) once again a book—the New Testament;
   (v) fierce resistance from Governments of the day.

The team pursued this line of thought by comparing their task to other well-known creeds—the good, the bad and the evil. Their deliberations included the exploration of Nazism which achieved total adherence through fear of death, terror and concentration camps. Freemasonry was also discussed; so were the Mafia, Moslem fundamentalism, and many others. All these analogies were helpful inasmuch as the group derived a few valuable lessons.

(*a*) Unless you apply 'fear' as a tool of adherence a creed is more 'promotable' if its underlying principles have a popular appeal.
    To that extent, the group agreed that the wisdom of becoming more marketing-orientated, the payoffs and even the social benefits of such a 'creed', must be strongly highlighted throughout the whole programme.

(*b*) Propagating a creed is greatly facilitated if it has a single charismatic champion aided by a number of dedicated 'Apostle'-type assistants.

(*c*) The existence of a 'book', which summarises the main commandments of the creed and in a form which is both readable and popular, appears to provide a major prop to effective mass communication. Most creeds, the group discovered, had a 'book', in one form or another, designed to promote them among the masses.

(*d*) Finally the task force recognised that one of the 'tricks' used by the promoters of most creeds, religions or philosophies, has been the development of persistent, consistent and multifaceted programmes. If people are exposed to the same message day-in and day-out and wherever they happen to be the message finally sinks in.

These four points, coupled with the outcome of the Fishbone analysis, emerged as the main thrust of the team's thinking. The discussions centred around the way these four elements could be woven into an integrated package. At this point the team played around with the 'how-how?' method which helped them to crystallise their collective thinking and conclusions. The diagram that summarised their position is described in Figure 53.

During the third session the task force was of the opinion that they had chewed the subject-matter in great depth and that the 'funnel' was pretty full with a large number of ideas. They therefore decided that the time had come to start screening and evaluating these ideas.

Phase 3—screening and evaluating ideas

Prior to the commencement of the screening process a part of the session was devoted to selecting the most appropriate screening criteria. After some deliberation the following criteria of 'attractiveness' were established (not necessarily in the order shown).

(*a*) Ideas which can be used internationally are more attractive than those which have applicability in a few countries only.

(*b*) Ideas which can be dovetailed into an integrated approach should be preferred to 'stand-alone' strategies.

Figure 54.   Scales Industries—the 'How How?' diagram used during the idea-generation phase.

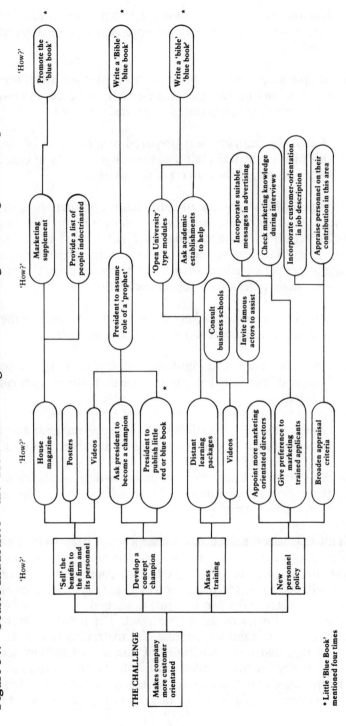

(c) Having established that people retain better what they 'see' than what they 'hear' visual approaches were deemed to be more attractive.

(d) Simple ideas likely to be understood by everybody, regardless of level and/or functional affiliation, were considered more attractive than complicated solutions.

(e) Whilst the company was prepared to spend a lot of money on this project the team felt that they ought to look at cost-effectiveness as one of the criteria of attractiveness.

In parallel with these discussions the group sought to identify the main elements of 'compatibility' of each idea with the company's specific requirements and style. In other words, it was felt that 'good ideas' which were inconsistent with the organisation's style, image or people's feelings should not be forced upon the firm. The following main points were considered in this regard.

(a) Drastic approaches, likely to create an upheaval in the firm's normal routine, were not deemed to be desirable.

(b) Anything likely to offend the cultural or religious susceptibilities of personnel in various parts of the world had to be avoided.

(c) Ideas had to be compatible with the firm's image as a first class, serious and caring company (albeit not marketing-orientated).

(d) Any strategy likely to humiliate existing managers or make them look a bit stupid had to be discarded as incompatible with the task's main aims.

This discussion helped to coalesce a set of rules against which to screen every idea in the 'funnel'. A screening matrix, not unlike those discussed in earlier chapters, but consisting of 16 cells was designed. All ideas (or parts thereof) were considered by the task force in relation to the two axes just described.

Figure 55 illustrates the matrix used. The numbers shown scattered, almost at random, around the matrix represent the many ideas which had been generated by the team and now screened. Clearly the ideas that landed nearest to the top left-hand corner were the ones that the task force selected for further exploration and development. At first, this task proved to be somewhat tedious

Figure 55.   Screening matrix for Scales Industries task force.

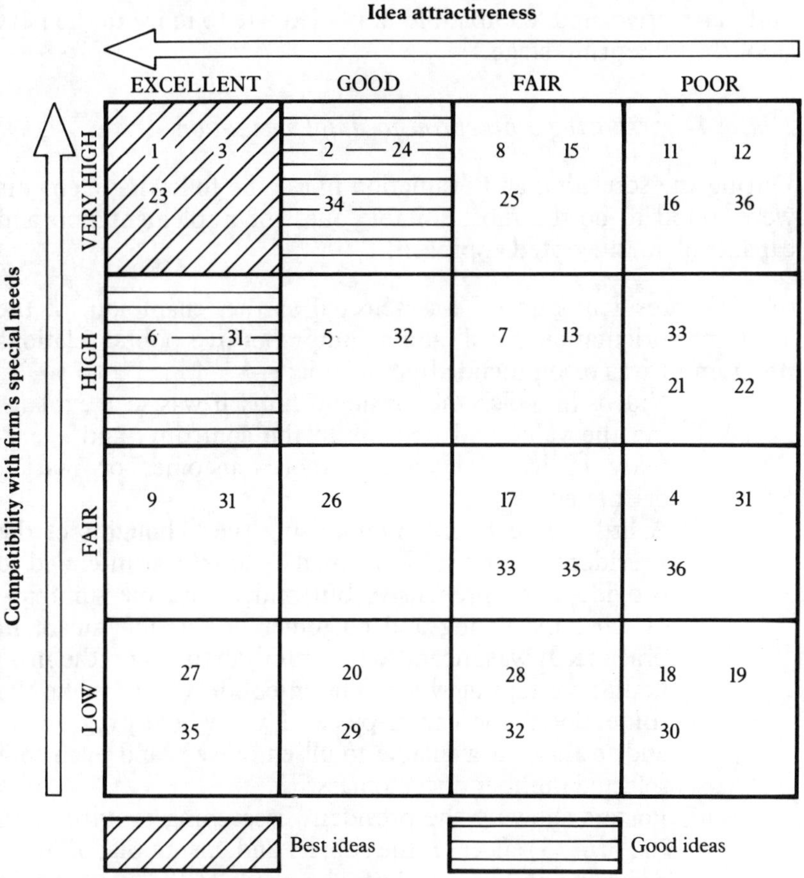

Ideas selected for further exploration

```
  * Idea 1  = A 'book'                                      * Best ideas
  * Idea 3  = Creed champion (à la Hubbard)               ** Good ideas
  * Idea 23 = Use of house magazine
 ** Idea 6  = Videos
 ** Idea 2  = Posters
 ** Idea 24 = Distant learning
 ** Idea 31 = Feedback to president following courses
 ** Idea 34 = 'Chapels'
```

Criteria of attractiveness	Criteria of compatibility

– International applicability
– Capable of integration
– Visual
– Simple
– Cost-effective
	– Minimum upheaval
	– Must not offend country
	   cultural susceptibilities
	– Compatible with firm's image
	– Must not make existing
	   managers feel incompetent

but once the group got into the spirit of it the members found it almost enjoyable. The final list of ideas which were found to be both 'attractive' and 'compatible' was adequate to move to the next step, the 'blueprint' stage.

Phase 4—preparing a blueprint for implementation

During the screening and evaluation phase the following elements were found to be the most suitable ones for implementation and capable of an integrated approach:

(*a*) The president himself was selected as the 'champion' of the 'customer-orientation creed' and a comprehensive public relations programme was recommended, to include:

> (i) Videos in which the president himself was seen explaining the value and benefits to the company, and everybody in it, of becoming more customer or market orientated.

> (ii) A little 'Blue Book' summarising the 'Thoughts of the President' on the subject. Such a 'book' was intended to provide a comprehensive but understandable summary of what marketing and customer orientation meant in practice. It was meant to be a mini-textbook on the marketing concept at work. The intention was to make the 'Blue Book' the centre-piece of the whole programme and to make it available to all employees and even to a selected number of customers.

> (iii) Posters showing the president beseeching everybody in the firm to reflect on the subject and ensure that all their decisions and actions bear the needs of the customer in mind, at all times. (The team felt that the poster should have a slightly Churchillian touch seeking to appeal to personnel's 'patriotism' to the firm. Coincidentally, the president's physique was slightly reminiscent of Churchill and therefore it was felt that the PR programme should exploit this similarity.)

> (iv) A supplement in the house magazine repeating all these messages.

> (v) A whole page in the house magazine providing news, on a regular basis, about examples of 'good responses to customer needs' and examples of 'bad response', everything to be described in clear and popular terms so that every reader could understand and relate to the message communicated.

(*b*) A comprehensive training programme to be designed for all company managers throughout the world.

The enormity of the task did not escape the members of the task force. They realised that the more traditional classroom courses or seminars would take years to carry out. It was therefore recommended that a computer-aided 'distant learning' approach be designed specifically for company personnel throughout the world. The little 'Blue Book' would be the centrepiece of the programme. The boss of each country, or operating unit, or department, was made responsible for ensuring that all the personnel undertook such training.

Each 'package' would start with the message from the president. At the end of each programme there would be a questionnaire, the gist of which was 'how do you feel that your behaviour will change as a result of the programme which you have just completed?', and 'do you have any other ideas as to how the message can be communicated and implemented throughout the firm?'. The completed questionnaire was directed to the president's office. The aim was to ensure maximum involvement and participation in the whole project among members of the company's personnel.

The house magazine would list every month all the people who had been 'briefed'.

(*c*) The total communication system of the firm, both internal and external, would bear the 'stamp' of the new philosophy.

Thus the firm's Annual Report would become a document meant to reflect the new ethos of the company. The product literature would do likewise. All pronouncements, both inside and outside the firm, had to give out the message that the company 'cares about its customers'. All pronouncements uttered by members of the organisation, from the president downwards, would be monitored by a member of the central PR department, and any deviation from the spirit of the new creed would form the basis for some feedback and counselling.

(*d*) The firm's personnel policy would be changed to encompass the following principles:

(i) During recruitment activities, the importance of being 'customer-orientated' would be shown as an important qualification for any job, regardless of the functional affiliation of the applicant.

(ii) People who can demonstrate evidence of a full understanding of marketing principles and ethos would be preferred.

(iii) Applicants who had worked in companies known for their 'marketing virtuosity' would be considered as attractive candidates even if their knowledge of the company's technology was found to be weak. 'We have enough experts in our technology' was the message.

(iv) The Board of Directors would be reinforced by the addition of people with a proven track record in the field of marketing. Due publicity would be given to such appointments.

(v) The role that people have played in helping the company become more customer-orientated would be explored during personnel appraisal sessions and commented upon favourably or otherwise.

(e) The task force came to the conclusion that some attention should be addressed to the Research and Development department and its activities. The task force felt that one of the major problems was the fact that projects were embarked upon without reference to the marketplace. Many of the product failures occurred because products had been developed at the whim of technical people who had no contact with the potential customers and did not understand their needs.

To that extent the following recommendations were made:

(i) In addition to the 'distant learning' package that all managers throughout the firm would be expected to pursue, members of the R & D department would be invited to attend marketing programmes in various academic establishments.

(ii) Each R & D centre would have a marketing person attached to it with the following duties:

help to develop a better understanding of marketing principles in the R & D organisation; provide an effective 'interface' between R & D and the marketing organisation; undertake market investigations, either alone or with the help of the marketing personnel, about projects that the R & D people are planning to undertake. The underlying aim was to stop R & D pursuing projects which have not received marketing validation.

(f) In order to involve the whole organisation in the new 'shared values' system called 'customer orientation' the following additional steps were recommended.

(i) The establishment of a Suggestion Scheme specifically

called 'The Customer is King'. Awards and Certificates of Merit were to be made available to winners.

(ii) The allocation of space in every location of the company in which members of the organisation could pick up copies of the little 'Blue Book', watch videos and obtain relevant information about the new 'creed'. The task force felt that these corners should resemble 'chapels'—a useful adjunct to propagating a new faith.

(iii) In every company in the group one individual should be charged as the person responsible for masterminding the implementation of the various recommendations (referred to, jokingly, as 'apostles' or 'missionaries' or 'commissars'). In selecting such individuals their acceptability and popularity should first be verified.

Twice a year these local co-ordinators would go on a 'pilgrimage' to Head Office to report to the President about progress achieved and to discuss additional steps to be undertaken.

Mechanism for monitoring progress

The task force recommended the following procedures for monitoring progress.

(a) A regular assessment of the success of new products against the following criteria of success:

(i) attainment of objectives in terms of sales, profits, and investment recovery;

(ii) market share achieved in relation to objective set;

(iii) maintenance of price pattern anticipated during planning stage.

(b) Comments expressed by customers either in response to questioning or spontaneously.

(c) Periodic formal market investigations to evaluate the marketplace view of the company, its image and quality of service.

The outcome of the task force's work and the recommended programme of work was summarised in a diagrammatic form (see Figure 56). The main message that the diagram sought to highlight was the multi-dimensional and integrated nature of the programme.

Figure 56.   Scales Industries—an integrated programme for developing a more customer-orientated organisation—task force recommendations.

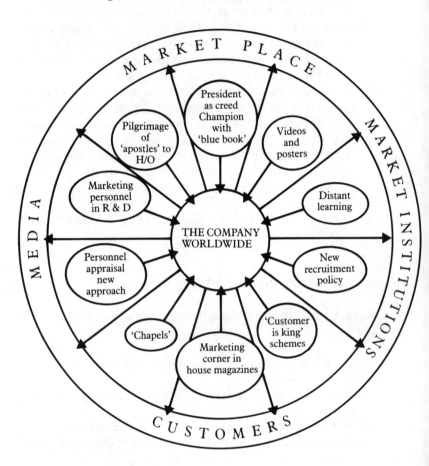

Within five years the firm became, in its industrial sector, one of the companies recognised for its ability to anticipate and respond to market needs in a dynamic and creative fashion. The strategy developed by the task force was thus truly innovative. The extent of the innovation only became apparent over time.

This case represents a fairly common situation whereby a firm is seeking to promulgate a drastic change in personnel's attitudes or 'superordinate goals'. Change in a corporate ethos is one of the most difficult tasks to undertake and requires an imaginative and steadfast programme. Creative thinking, coupled with a systematic analysis of ideas generated in response to the challenge, appears to have been used in this case in an effective way. The main purpose of this case is to illustrate the way a group of people approached the challenge, analysed its implications and developed a programme of work to meet it.

Case 2: Nogard Dredging Company

Nogard is a company operating in the field of international dredging. It operates a fleet of both mechanical and suction dredgers in various parts of the world. Dredging is normally needed during the building of docks and harbours. Its main purpose is to deepen harbours with the view of facilitating the entry, exit or mooring of ships in such locations. Furthermore harbours that are built on or near the estuary of rivers can suffer from gradual silting. The effect of such siltation is that ships of a certain draught cannot enter the harbour and have to drop anchor outside and unload into barges. Clearly, this is not a satisfactory and economic way to run a port. Dredging companies are invited from time to time to undertake dredging work with the view of deepening the harbour or to the entrance thereto.

The field of dredging is competitive and there are many international firms operating in this area. A few major problems afflict most of the operators in this business.

(a) Contracts are normally placed in response to tenders. As with most tender systems the contracts are gained on the basis of price. The result is that most dredging companies fight on price and that in turn means that margins are very tight indeed. The slightest error in costing can make a contractor lose a lot of money.

(b) The submission of a tender in itself is a costly exercise inasmuch as careful and labour-intensive estimates have to be undertaken. If the rate of exchange between the preparation and the submission of tenders is ten to one, in terms of the number of tenders submitted to one contract gained, the associated overheads of every successful tender are greatly increased.

(c) One has to compete against some countries that subsidise foreign projects in order to earn foreign currency.

(*d*) The cost of transporting dredgers and heavy equipment to distant countries can add substantial costs to the price quoted. This can make the company's price even less competitive if compared to somebody who happens to have dredgers in the neighbourhood of the job.

All these factors have made the life of Nogard rather difficult. The Managing Director invited a group of senior executives to join him on a Strategy Search weekend with the view of applying creative thinking to the development of a fresh approach to the whole business. The main aim of the meeting was to work out a strategy that could help to mitigate the obstacles created by the problems described above.

Approach to the project

The people who joined the Managing Director during the 'creativity' weekend were all senior people in the organisation but, with the exception of two, not directly involved in the dredging side of the business. In other words they were in the position of looking at the problem with a fresh perspective and an open mind. Altogether nine members participated in the meeting—eight managers plus an external facilitator who acted as the leader of the proceedings.

As a first step the team sought to reach some agreement on what problem they had been charged to solve. The situation seemed to encompass a large number of problems. All the problems were interrelated and appeared to stem from the fact that contracts were always gained through impersonal tenders and that decisions always hinged on the price upon which the tenders were based.

In order to understand the total situation more clearly the team tried to respond to a series of diagnostic questions similar to the one shown in Chapter 6, page 130. The team realised that responding to all these questions would not solve the problem but it might help to give them a better understanding of the background to the situation and the underlying causes that had brought it about.

As a second exercise in this regard they spent some time preparing a 'cause-and-effect' Fishbone Diagram like the one shown in Figure 54. The main conclusion that emerged from that exercise was the notion that the main problem that plagued the company was the lack of a 'sustainable competitive advantage'. The group felt that if Nogard could develop a distinctive and desirable 'competitive advantage' that would distinguish it from its many competi-

Figure 57. 'Fishbone' diagram used to understand Nogard's problem.

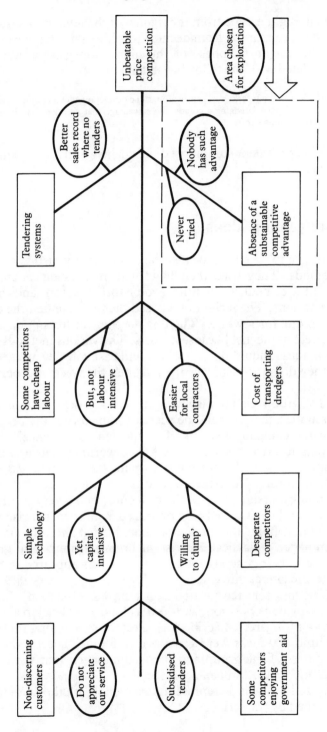

tors it might escape from the rigours of the tendering system. It was in this area that the team decided to address its creative efforts.

The diagnostic phase of the innovation process was therefore completed with the following statement:

'We believe that our task must centre around the development of a unique service that would impart to Nogard Dredging a competitive advantage that no other firm in the business is capable or willing to offer.'

This statement summarised the challenge that the team sought to solve.

Generating ideas

The group tried to tackle the problem by using a variety of methods. They tried their hand with morphological analysis, but found it difficult to identify two or three relevant and interrelated dimensions. The facilitator advised them to abandon the use of that technique for a while. 'There is no point in forcing oneself to use any technique just because it exists. The various methods for generating ideas should flow naturally and easily if they are to be useful. If they do not—just leave them alone', the voice of experience suggested.

The group tried to play with the scenario-daydreaming approach. 'Assuming that we shall be successful in solving the problem what will the company look like five and ten years hence?' They were hoping to extract valuable ideas from working their way backwards from a successful future. Once again, the outcome was somewhat disappointing. Nevertheless, the group discovered that the various mental excursions helped them to enter into a very fertile 'creative mode' and ideas were being produced at an ever-increasing rate.

At that point the facilitator thought that the time had come to commence a classical exercise of brainstorming. The group were relaxed, their general mood jovial, and they appeared to be capable of fertile lateral thinking.

The task selected for brainstorming was placed on a flipchart, in a conspicuous position, and read as follows: 'Develop a unique service for Nogard'. A scribe was selected from among those present. Around 100 ideas were generated in a quick succession. Both the members of the group and the facilitator felt that the session was extremely successful and constructive.

The following is a representative sample of the ideas that were recorded by the scribe:

1. Act as a bank and provide finance for dredging projects
2. Provide interest-free loans
3. Pay customers interest on money which they owe *us*
4. Charge an annual fee for keeping harbours in good condition
5. Take over the management of the harbours and charge for a total harbour management service
6. Join every harbour as partners—we invest in the harbour but they undertake to use our services
7. Develop a model harbour in our Headquarters showing what a perfect harbour should look like
8. Conduct courses in harbour management
9. Develop a consultancy service giving people advice about how to run their ports and harbours more effectively
10. Conduct an 'Audit' system for evaluating the productivity and quality of management of harbours—offer such a service free for customers only
11. Provide guarantees of workmanship for ten years
12. Provide an annual check-up of siltation
13. Provide a forecast service as to when further dredging would be required
14. Open a school for dredging and harbour engineers
15. Offer a new type of dredging service which will prevent any silting taking place in the future
16. Provide a much wider engineering service in addition to dredging
17. Offer a logistics service which may help the country use its harbours more effectively
18. Give up dredging and become logistics experts
19. Sell the dredgers to competitors and lease them back with crews for specific jobs
20. Get other people to do the dredging on our behalf as and when needed
21. Arrange with insurance companies that the premium for harbours dredged by us will be lower
22. In harbours dredged by us a very reasonable ship chandler service, owned and subsidised by us, will be installed as a service to shipowners
23. Put the President or Prime Minister of each country with whom we want to do business on our Board.

and so on—up to 100 ideas!

Screening and evaluating ideas

The team looked at the many ideas and discussed a few of them in some depth. At that point it was decided to use a modified version of the 'spider diagram' in order to build the ideas into cohesive clusters. The outcome of this analysis seemed to suggest that all the ideas fell into the following groupings:

(*a*) consultancy/advisory-type of service (about 15 ideas);

(*b*) financial support to customers (7 ideas);

(*c*) the 'joining' cluster, namely the provision of additional services in the harbour management business so that dredging becomes a small part of the total service (20 ideas);

(*d*) strategies unrelated to harbours (12 ideas);

(*e*) invest in customers' businesses (5 ideas);

(*f*) enter the airport business in addition to harbours (4 ideas);

(*g*) incentives to customers or members of their organisations, eg holidays, bribes, etc (about 20 ideas);

(*h*) miscellaneous ideas—the rest.

The ideas were screened in clusters against an algorithm like the one described in Figure 58. The cluster that the group found the most valuable and practical was the one which they described as the 'joining cluster'. The team discussed the 'joining' strategy for a considerable time. The more they talked about it the more they discovered interesting angles for development. They gradually moved towards the conclusion that 'joining' means knowing more about customers' needs than they know themselves. 'If we could create a situation whereby customers would get in touch with us, for help and advice about harbour management, before they actually need any dredging done, we would be their permanent friends. This is what we understand by "joining" . . . ' the group agreed during these deliberations.

At this point the group decided to brainstorm again on the 'joining' concept in harbour management. This fresh focus helped to generate very practical and realistic ideas which did not require specific screening procedures. The group suddenly realised that

Figure 58.   Algorithm used by the Nogard's team to screen clusters of ideas resulting from brainstorming.

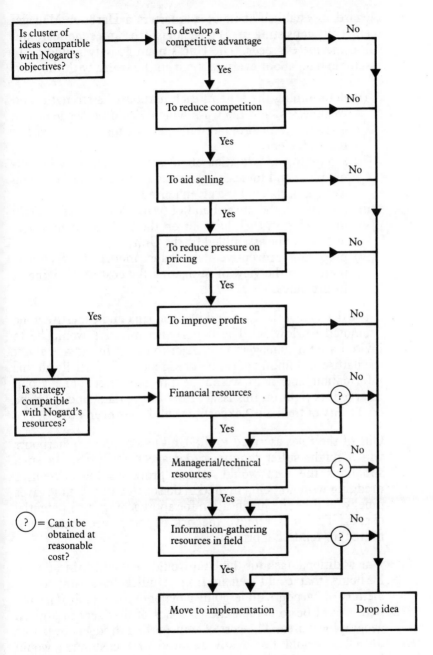

they were moving very fast towards an exciting strategy. The weekend finished on a high note with the following 'package'.

(*a*) Nogard to establish at its Headquarters a Harbour Management Unit consisting of (i) a geologist, (ii) an economist, and (iii) a marine engineer. The Unit's main activity would be to assemble data about every harbour in the world with the view of:

  (i) determining the state of each harbour, its strengths and weaknesses, and the work which would be needed to be carried out in order to enlarge its capacity or make it more efficient;

  (ii) assembling information about siltation that may be taking place and forecast what would happen if no dredging were undertaken for a given period;

  (iii) forecasting the inward and outward flow of traffic likely to develop in each harbour on the basis of econometric models, to be assembled by the Unit;

  (iv) preparing 'preventive maintenance models' for each harbour with the view of mitigating the cost of dredging at future dates.

(*b*) The existence of the Unit and its data bank and expertise to be promoted worldwide. The underlying objective would be to invite harbour managers to contact the Unit for advice about the nature and timing of future dredging work. Initially all this information and help would be provided free. The group reserved its right on this issue, for a future date, and once the credibility of the Unit's expertise would have been proved.

(*c*) One of the roles ascribed to the Unit was to identify harbours which might suffer long-term damage if neglected. In such situations the firm would submit proposals for preventive dredging without being invited to do so. 'A stitch in time saves nine' would be the justification for approaching such potential clients. This may remove the risk of the project being submitted for tendering procedures.

(*d*) One additional task for the Unit would be the identification of harbours that could benefit from a quick 'clean-up' in the vicinity of harbours undergoing a major dredging job. The aim here would be to exploit the presence of dredgers in a given geographical area. The cost of transporting dredgers over vast distances would be greatly reduced and customers would benefit.

Altogether, the idea was to create a Unit which through knowledge and expertise would provide the company with a cutting edge which none of its competitors had.

The purpose of this case was to illustrate how creativity can help a firm to develop innovations in all areas including the search for fresh strategies. The various principles, techniques and concepts developed in this book can be used by any organisation, in all functional areas and at all levels. They should not be regarded as the prerogative of an enlightened minority—they can be tried and utilised by anybody who wishes to search for excellence.

Appendix—Creativity and innovation— an organisational audit

The concept of auditing a firm's strengths and weaknesses as part of the planning process has gained ground during the last few years. Any company that has introduced a formal planning cycle undertakes such an analysis as part of the process. Copious 'audit' checklists are available to planners in order to assist them in identifying the areas in which the company is strong and in which it is suffering from some areas of weakness. Yet very few firms audit their effectiveness in the area of creativity and innovation. It is almost as if management has decided that the two topics are not relevant to the future success of the organisation. In practice it is difficult to visualise a successful organisation without a strong creative content to its operations. If one accepts the thesis that the combined force of creativity and innovation represents one of the most powerful elements in the achievement of excellence, it is incumbent on management to take stock of the firm's ability to generate creative ideas and translate them into innovation as an integral part of the planning cycle. In other words this must be done on as regular a basis as the planning cycle itself. If the company prepares its plans on an annual basis the audit of the company's creativity should be undertaken annually. It is the ability to compare the outcome of the audit from year to year which provides the relevant insight to management as to whether the firm's creativity has improved or has remained static (or even regressed, in some situations).

The remarkable thing is that many companies are creative without realising it and others are not creative but refuse to admit to themselves that they are not. This means that the need to audit the organisation's true standing in this regard is particularly important. The auditing checklists provided hereunder are meant to assist management to assess its true achievements and/or failures in this vital area. Seven checklists are provided—starting with creativity and innovation at the corporate level and continuing with the audit of these interrelated elements in the various functional areas of the average organisation. It is important to recognise, at the outset, that these audit sheets are not meant to be immutable. The users of these checklists should feel free to adapt them to their company's specific circumstances or requirements. On the other hand they represent a useful starting point for forcing managers to reflect upon issues which they do not normally consider during the SWOT analysis (strengths, weaknesses, opportunities and threats).

With experience the users will find that the checklists can be adapted to match the needs of their respective organisations more closely. Moreover as was suggested earlier the audit system becomes particularly valuable if one undertakes its completion at regular intervals. This is particularly appropriate if corrective measures have been taken between the two audits. At least this way the completion of the assessment form can highlight whether the attempt to promulgate improvements has been successful. This can be compared to a person who has undergone a medical check-up which highlighted a number of weaknesses. Regular subsequent check-ups are more meaningful than an isolated examination. It is the comparability of results that tells the doctor whether improvements have taken place. This is an important message to bear in mind inasmuch as I have encountered managers who were particularly depressed by the fact that the outcome of the first audit has yielded very low scores, placing the company in the 'poor' category. The optimist can view such a score as good news because one cannot get any worse! If managers would take the outcome of the audit seriously and undertake a programme of work designed to improve matters the next cycle of assessment will no doubt show a better score and this is precisely what the audit is aimed to do.

The following 'Audits' are provided:

Audit No. 1—Audit at Corporate Level
Audit No. 2—Audit of the Marketing Function
Audit No. 3—Audit of the Production Function
Audit No. 4—Audit of the Personnel Function
Audit No. 5—Audit of the R & D Function
Audit No. 6—Audit of the Finance/Accountancy Function
Audit No. 7—Audit of General Administration

The following notes should be read carefully before undertaking the completion of any of the audit checklists. They should help to ensure that maximum benefit is derived from the effort invested in completing them:

(*a*) In responding to the various questions or statements incorporated in the audit checklists it is important that one attempts to approach them with complete candour and integrity.

The audit document is not meant to be a test of individual quality or a public testimonial. It is designed for internal consumption and as a prod to reflection and action. If one is unable to respond to the various items with complete honesty it nullifies the true value of the exercise.

It must be remembered that it is the process of completing the questionnaires which is more valuable than the final score.

(b) The completion of the audit forms is best undertaken in groups. Each participant should be invited to consider each question and decide, individually, upon the appropriate score. The group should then compare notes and see if they can reach concurrence on a joint score. If this cannot be achieved an average between the various responses can be struck and placed on a master score sheet. The aim is to discuss every item of the audit list and reach a group score.

(c) The scoring system provides a broad spectrum varying between '1' and '10'. '1' is the lowest and means that the collective decision of the group is that the firm is particularly bad in that area. '10' is superb and should be reserved for exceptional performance levels. The choice between the two extremes is wide and should be chosen after due reflection. As was suggested earlier it is the relative score over time which is significant rather than the absolute figures inserted on the form. Thus if one places '4' against a specific question it does not sound too promising, but if in the next round one decides to score '5' or more it means that progress has been made.

A few of the questions are posed in such a way that one is tempted to respond by simply saying 'yes' or 'no'. For instance, in response to the question: 'Does a system for screening and evaluating ideas exist in the firm?'. Clearly if one says an unqualified 'yes' one feels inclined to record a score of 10. By the same token if one says 'no' one would feel that '0' is the appropriate score. In reality companies that have some kind of an idea-screening system should reflect upon its effectiveness and score accordingly. Firms that feel that they do not have any system may on reflection discover that in practice they have an informal method of screening ideas and therefore deserve to score a higher figure than just a '0'. In other words during the scoring the participants ought to reflect upon every question and attempt to score on the basis of more than just a 'yes'/'no' judgement unless such an answer is inevitable.

(d) The seven Audit questionnaires represent the main functional areas of most organisations. Should the company consider that there are areas which require specific attention, and are not covered by any of the checklists, a separate questionnaire can be designed for the purpose. Once again it is not the absolute scores that matter—it is the progress over time.

(e) The seven checklists were prepared with the aim of making them applicable to most companies. Inevitably some companies may find that important issues have been omitted which, in relation to their specific environments, are crucial. Thus, an airline may wish to add many items pertaining to the creativity level manifested by their ground staff, booking offices and cabin crews. A bank may wish to incorporate questions relating to the way branch personnel treat clients. Such items are implied in the checklists provided hereunder but the company may wish to add more explicit questions to the checklists. In other words readers who find that such omissions derogate from the completeness of the audit should feel free to add the missing items. The only point to remember is that the final score has to be amended on a pro-rata basis. If five additional questions are added the maximum total score that can be attained is increased by $5 \times 10 = 50$.

Scoring

On completing each Audit one ends with a total score. The maximum score that can be attained is 10 times the number of questions answered (plus 'Bonus' points in Audit No. 1). If one decides to increase or reduce the number of questions the total score, as explained above, should be adjusted.

If one remains with the existing Audit questionnaires the maximum scores achievable are:

Audit area		Questions	Maximum score
No 1	At corporate level	20	220 (with bonus)
	At corporate level (international firms)	21	240 (with bonus)
No 2	Marketing	40	400
No 3	Production	30	300
No 4	Personnel	36	360
No 5	Research & Development	28	280
No 6	Finance/Accountancy	28	280
No 7	General Administration	24	240

The final score should be then taken as a percentage of the maximum achievable. Thus if the score achieved on Audit No. 3 is '100' it represents 100 : 300 = 33% of excellence. The percentage scores can be interpreted as follows:

Quartile	*Interpretation*
75% and above	Excellent to superb. Keep going.
50%–75%	Good to very good—improvement possible. Try harder.
25%–50%	Fair. Improvements essential.
Less than 25%	Poor. Undertake a crash programme if you want to survive!

With these instructions the readers are invited to complete the most relevant Audit questionnaire, either alone or with colleagues. With some experience they should find the whole exercise a valuable 'food for thought' process. They may emerge with a feeling of confidence about their organisation's performance in the field of creativity or have their illusions shattered. Either way the firm's position in this area could be judged in a more realistic fashion.

Audit No 1   At corporate level

No	GENERAL	1	2	3	4	5	6	7	8	9	10	SCORE
1	Is the firm's climate supportive of the idea-generation process? Assess and score											
2	Does top management take an interest in the whole concept of idea-generation or does it simply expect to hear about ultimate successes? Assess and score											
3	Does the firm's 'mission statement' include a mention of either 'creativity' or 'innovation' or both, as part of the company's corporate ethos?											
4	Do people in the firm talk about 'creativity', 'ideas', 'innovation'? Assess and score											
5	Can one approach top management with ideas? Assess and score											
6	Do people in the firm know how and to whom to address their ideas? Assess and score											
7	Does the firm undertake periodic 'idea generation' exercises in order to stimulate the climate for creativity? Assess and score											

TOTAL SCORE CARRIED FORWARD

Audit No 1   At corporate level (*contd*)

No		1	2	3	4	5	6	7	8	9	10	B/F	SCORE
8	Does the firm undertake periodic 'idea-generation' exercises in order to solve problems and/or identify opportunities? Assess and score												
9	Does a communication system exist for 'marketing' the whole concept of creativity and innovation in the organisation?												
10	Does the firm attempt to communicate and cross-fertilise ideas a. Among functions?												B
	b. Among operating companies?												B
11 *11a	and, only if appropriate, c. Among international markets?												B
12	Does a system for screening and evaluating ideas exist in the firm?												
13	Is the number of innovations at corporate level considered satisfactory? Assess and score												
	'B' = BONUS POINTS—Double the figure shown in the Box when adding the total. * Leave blank if inappropriate. Final scoring system will adjust as necessary, see instructions												

<u>TOTAL SCORE CARRIED FORWARD</u>

Audit No 1 At corporate level (*contd*)

		1	2	3	4	5	6	7	8	9	10	SCORE
<u>No</u>												B/F ☐
	FUNCTIONS (GENERAL ASSESSMENT)											
14	A. MARKETING Assess the level of creativity and innovation in the marketing area. (N.B. For a specific audit checklist of the marketing function in detail see AUDIT No 2)											☐
15	B. PRODUCTION Assess the quality of creativity and innovation in the production area. (N.B. For a specific audit checklist of the production function in detail see AUDIT No 3)											☐
16	C. PERSONNEL Assess the quality of creativity and innovation in the personnel area. (N.B. For a specific audit checklist of the personnel function in detail see AUDIT No 4)											☐
17	D. RESEARCH & DEVELOPMENT Assess the quality of the creativity and innovation in the R & D area.											☐

<u>TOTAL SCORE CARRIED FORWARD</u> ☐

Audit No 1   At corporate level (*contd*)

No		1	2	3	4	5	6	7	8	9	10	SCORE B/F
18	Is it felt that the company's record in converting R & D projects into commercial innovations is satisfactory? (N.B. For specific audit checklist of the R & D function in detail see AUDIT No 5)											
19	E. FINANCE Assess the quality of the organisation's creativity & innovation in the finance area. (N.B. For specific audit checklist of the finance function see AUDIT No 6)											
20	F. CENTRAL ADMINISTRATION/ SERVICES Assess the quality of the firm's creativity and innovation in relation to this area. (N.B. For specific audit checklist of this area see AUDIT No 7)											
	TOTAL SCORE											

Audit No 2   Marketing

No	GENERAL	1	2	3	4	5	6	7	8	9	10	SCORE
1	Is the climate in the marketing organisation supportive of the idea-generation process? Assess and score											
2	Does the department's top management take an interest in the whole concept of idea-generation or does it simply expect to hear about ultimate successes? Assess and score											
3	Do the department's objectives include a mention of either 'creativity' or 'innovation' or both, as part of the department's climate and goals? Assess and score											
4	Do people in the marketing function talk about 'creativity', 'ideas', 'innovation'? Assess and score											
5	Can one approach the top people in the marketing organisation with ideas? Assess and score											
6	Do people in the department know how and to whom to address their ideas? Assess and score											
7	Does the department undertake periodic 'idea-generation' exercises in order to stimulate the climate for creativity? Assess and score											

TOTAL SCORE CARRIED FORWARD

Audit No 2   Marketing (*contd*)

No		1	2	3	4	5	6	7	8	9	10	SCORE B/F
8	Does the department undertake periodic 'idea-generation' exercises in order to solve problems and/or identify opportunities? Assess and score											
9	Does a communication system exist for 'marketing' the whole concept of Creativity and Innovation in the marketing function? Assess and score											
10	Does the marketing organisation attempt to communicate and cross-fertilise ideas among the various parts of the department (eg among regions, markets, offices etc)? Assess and score											
11	Does a system for screening and evaluating ideas exist in the marketing organisation? Assess and score											
12	Altogether, if marketing management is able to list the successful innovations that have been achieved during the last three years—has their number increased or decreased? (If their number has increased give a high score and vice versa.) Assess and score											
13	INFORMATION-GATHERING ACTIVITIES Has the company identified ways of collecting information which are cheaper and better than in the past? Assess and score											

TOTAL SCORE CARRIED FORWARD

Audit No 2   Marketing (*contd*)

No		1	2	3	4	5	6	7	8	9	10	SCORE B/F
14	Does the marketing management monitor the cost-benefit of input collected during the year and seek to improve its pay-off value? Assess and score											
15	Is an attempt being made to compare the relative cost of carrying marketing research activities in-house as against the commission of outside organisations? Assess and score											
16	PRODUCT POLICY AND PLANNING What is the firm's record in the area of new product development? Assess and score											
17	Assess the firm's record in the area of product improvements and/or modifications.											
18	Has the rate of conversion from ideas to implementation improved? Assess and score											
19	PRICING How many price ideas have been considered during the last few years and how many of them have been implemented? Assess and score											
20	Is the firm observing the price practices of other firms in order to solve difficult price problems? Assess and score											

TOTAL SCORE CARRIED FORWARD

Audit No 2   ## Marketing (*contd*)

No		1	2	3	4	5	6	7	8	9	10	B/F	SCORE
21	Has the marketing team solved pricing problems through creative non-price strategies? Assess and score												
22	Assess the firm's creativity in relation to the identification of customers' 'benefit-in-use' concept. Assess and score												
23	PROMOTIONAL MIX Assess the level of creativity demonstrated in the promotional area during the last few years.												
24	Has the cost-benefit of promotional campaigns improved or not? Assess and score												
25	Do people inside the firm participate in the development of creative ideas pertaining to promotional activities or do they rely on outside agencies to do the creative thinking for them? Assess and score												
26	Does the firm experiment with new communication ideas resulting from modern technology? Assess and score												
27	How effectively does marketing management scan the commercial horizon to identify good ideas from other enterprises operating in the same market or in other markets? Assess and score												

TOTAL SCORE CARRIED FORWARD

Audit No 2   **Marketing** (*contd*)

No		1	2	3	4	5	6	7	8	9	10	B/F
28	DISTRIBUTION Assess the firm's efforts in attempting to improve the quality and/or reduce the costs of logistics? Assess and score											
29	Has the company considered alternative channels of distribution in order to improve customer satisfaction? Assess and score											
30	How successfully has the firm managed to establish an interactive relationship with its channels of distribution in order to enhance their loyalty, support and improved service to customers? Assess and score											
31	Does the company involve its distribution channels in the process of generating ideas and/or planning innovative strategies? Assess and score											
32	Altogether try to assess the creativity of the distribution department.											
33	SELLING Assess the quality of creativity that emerges out of the sales force.											
34	Is there a procedure for cross-fertilising ideas among the various sales regions/areas? Assess and score											
35	Are members of the sales force ever invited to participate in idea-generation activities in response to problems existing in other departments? Assess and score											

SCORE

TOTAL SCORE CARRIED FORWARD

Audit No 2   Marketing *(contd)*

No		1	2	3	4	5	6	7	8	9	10	SCORE B/F	
36	Does the sales management attempt to identify what 'star' performers in the sales force do which is different from the rest of the team? Assess and score												
37	Are members of the sales team motivated to submit ideas for evaluation? Assess and score												
38	CONTROL PROCEDURES Assess the creativity that has been injected into the firm's control procedures eg controlled experiments, measuring sales effectiveness, advertising and sales promotion effectiveness etc. This is a fertile area for innovation. Reflect upon the whole issue and score.												
39	How quickly does the firm react to competitive threats? Assess and score												
40	Assess the speed at which the firm translates marketing strategies into reality.												
	TOTAL SCORE												

Audit No 3   Production

No	GENERAL	1	2	3	4	5	6	7	8	9	10	SCORE
1	Is the climate in the production organisation supportive of the idea-generation process? Assess and score											
2	Does the department's top management take an interest in the whole concept of idea-generation or does it simply expect to hear about ultimate successes? Assess and score											
3	Do the department's objectives include a mention of either 'creativity' or 'innovation' or both as part of the department's climate and goals? Assess and score											
4	Do people in the production area talk about 'creativity', 'ideas', 'innovation'? Assess and score											
5	Can one approach top managers in the production organisation with ideas? Assess and score											
6	Do people in the department know how and to whom to address their ideas? Assess and score											

TOTAL SCORE CARRIED FORWARD

Audit No 3   **Production** (*contd*)

No		1	2	3	4	5	6	7	8	9	10	SCORE
												B/F [ ]
7	Does the department undertake periodic 'idea-generation' exercises in order to stimulate the climate for creativity? Assess and score											[ ]
8	Does the department undertake periodic 'idea-generation' exercises in order to solve problems and/or identify opportunities? Assess and score											[ ]
9	Does a communication system exist for 'marketing' the whole concept of 'creativity and innovation' in the production function? Assess and score											[ ]
10	Does the production organisation attempt to communicate and cross-fertilise ideas among the various parts of the department and/or plants? Assess and score											[ ]
11	Does a system for screening and evaluating ideas exist in the production organisation? Assess and score											[ ]
12	Altogether, if production management is able to list the successful innovations that have been achieved during the last three years—has their number increased or decreased? If their number has increased give a high score; if their number has decreased give a low score.											[ ]

TOTAL SCORE CARRIED FORWARD   [ ]

Audit No 3   **Production** (*contd*)

No		1	2	3	4	5	6	7	8	9	10	B/F	SCORE
13	**QUALITY** Can the production organisation demonstrate examples of creative quality improvements? Assess and score												
14	Does the company use 'Quality Circles' as a way of solving quality problems? Assess and score												
15	Are members of the production team encouraged to observe and study the quality control practices of competitors? Assess and score												
16	Has the department carried out any investigations to find out whether customers appreciate the quality improvements implemented? In other words are these improvements customer-orientated? Assess and score												
17	**MATERIALS HANDLING/ LOGISTICS** Can the department demonstrate improved performance in the area of materials handling? Assess and score												
18	Have any ideas pertaining to the timely flow of materials and components been implemented (eg 'Just-in-Time' practices etc)? Assess and score												
19	Has the organisation improved the use of materials and/or reduced waste? Assess and score												

TOTAL SCORE CARRIED FORWARD

Audit No 3   Production (*contd*)

No		1	2	3	4	5	6	7	8	9	10	B/F	SCORE
20	Altogether has the production department introduced ideas for responding to customers' needs more effectively especially in terms of delivery? Assess and score												
21	Have creative steps been taken to improve the quality of physical distribution and reduce damage in transit? Assess and score												
22	PRODUCTIVITY Does the department explore ideas for improved productivity at all levels of the production process? Assess and score												
23	Have steps been taken to conserve energy in an innovative way? Assess and score												
24	Does the department undertake comparative studies in order to identify ideas for productivity improvements implemented by competitors? Assess and score												
25	MODERN TECHNOLOGY Assess the department's record in recommending and adopting methods associated with modern technology.												
26	Assess the department's ability to observe competitors' practices in regard to modern technology and derive lessons therefrom.												

TOTAL SCORE CARRIED FORWARD

Audit No 3   **Production** (*contd*)

No		1	2	3	4	5	6	7	8	9	10	SCORE B/F	
27	Assess the benefits that the firm has derived from the application of modern technology.												
28	PLANT AND FACILITIES Assess the level of innovation achieved in the area of plant maintenance (including preventive maintenance).												
29	Has the department demonstrated creativity in the choice of locations for its newer plants? Assess and score												
30	Assess the level of innovation achieved in the way the production organisation dealt with environmental regulations and pressure groups.												
	TOTAL SCORE												

Audit No 4   Personnel

		1	2	3	4	5	6	7	8	9	10	SCORE
No	GENERAL											
1	Is the climate in the personnel organisation supportive of the idea-generation process? Assess and score											☐
2	Does the department's top management take an interest in the whole concept of idea-generation or does it simply expect to hear about ultimate successes? Assess and score											☐
3	Do the department's objectives include a mention of either 'creativity' or 'innovation' or both, as part of the department's climate and goals? Assess and score											☐
4	Do people in the personnel department talk about 'creativity', 'ideas', 'innovation'? Assess and score											☐
5	Can one approach top people in the personnel or human resources organisation with ideas? Assess and score											☐
6	Do people in the department know how and to whom to address their ideas? Assess and score											☐

TOTAL SCORE CARRIED FORWARD ☐

Audit No 4   **Personnel** (*contd*)

No		1	2	3	4	5	6	7	8	9	10	B/F	SCORE
7	Does the department undertake periodic 'idea-generation' exercises in order to stimulate the climate for creativity? Assess and score												
8	Does the department undertake periodic 'idea-generation' exercises in order to solve problems and/or identify opportunities? Assess and score												
9	Does a communication system exist for promoting the whole concept of creativity and innovation in the personnel function? Assess and score												
10	Does the personnel organisation attempt to communicate and cross-fertilise ideas among the various parts of the department? Assess and score												
11	Does a system of screening and evaluating ideas exist in the personnel organisation? Assess and score												
12	Altogether, if personnel management is able to list the successful innovations that have been achieved during the last three years—has their number increased or decreased? (If their number has increased give a high score and vice versa.) Assess and score												

TOTAL SCORE CARRIED FORWARD

Audit No 4   Personnel (*contd*)

No		1	2	3	4	5	6	7	8	9	10	SCORE B/F	
13	MOTIVATION Has the department identified new and better ways of motivating company personnel? Assess and score												
14	If incentive programmes exist assess their overall innovative quality.												
15	Does the department take creative steps to improve or maintain personnel morale? Assess and score												
16	Does the department communicate ideas about how to motivate company personnel to all other departments in a creative fashion? Assess and score												
17	Has the department made creative contributions to the whole question of employee remuneration packages? Assess and score												
18	Does the department provide a creative employee advisory and help service with the view of maintaining personnel welfare and general contentment? Assess and score												
19	PERSONNEL PRODUCTIVITY Has the department taken creative steps to improve the productivity of the department itself? Assess and score												

TOTAL SCORE CARRIED FORWARD

Audit No 4   **Personnel** (*contd*)

No		1	2	3	4	5	6	7	8	9	10	B/F	
20	Has the department made a creative contribution towards the improvement of the productivity of the personnel of other departments/ functions? Assess and score												☐
21	Has the personnel department introduced innovations in the speed with which information pertaining to company personnel flows? Assess and score												☐
22	Assess the contribution that the department has made towards enhanced productivity of the labour force.												☐
23	STAFF RECRUITMENT Has the personnel department innovated in the field of recruitment and selection procedures? Assess and score												☐
24	Have steps been taken to obtain better productivity in the cost of recruitment work? Assess and score												☐
25	Have any creative ideas been applied in communicating company information to new recruits? Assess and score												☐
26	MANAGEMENT DEVELOPMENT Have the firm's management development and training systems benefited from some creativity and innovation? Assess and score												☐

SCORE ☐

TOTAL SCORE CARRIED FORWARD   ☐

Audit No 4   Personnel (*contd*)

No		1	2	3	4	5	6	7	8	9	10	SCORE B/F	
27	What steps has the personnel department taken to motivate people to pursue self-development strategies? Assess and score												
28	Where outside training organisations are being used has the department improved its selection procedures? Assess and score												
29	Has the department improved the de-briefing procedures of course participants in a creative manner? Assess and score												
30	Assess the quality of innovation displayed in the way new recruits are being developed.												
31	INDUSTRIAL RELATIONS Has the personnel organisation demonstrated examples of a more creative approach to industrial relations? Assess and score												
32	Altogether has the relationship between management and labour improved as a result of the department's more innovative strategy? Assess and score												
33	Has the company's strike record improved as a result of new ideas implemented by the department? Assess and score												

TOTAL SCORE CARRIED FORWARD

Audit No 4   **Personnel** (*contd*)

No		1	2	3	4	5	6	7	8	9	10	B/F	SCORE
34	WORKING CONDITIONS Have any innovations taken place in the firm's working environment? Assess and score												
35	Assess the way creative ideas have helped to reduce accidents at work and/or other events that interfere with the smooth running of the firm's plants.												
36	Any innovation in the development of better leisure and recreation facilities for the firm's personnel? Assess and score												

TOTAL SCORE

Audit No 5   Research & Development

No	GENERAL	1	2	3	4	5	6	7	8	9	10	SCORE
1	Is the climate in the R & D organisation supportive of the idea-generation process? Assess and score											☐
2	Does the department's top management take an interest in the whole concept of idea-generation or does it simply expect to hear about ultimate successes? Assess and score											☐
3	Do the department's objectives include a mention of either 'creativity' or 'innovation' or both, as part of the department's climate and goals? Assess and score											☐
4	Do people in the R & D department talk about 'creativity', 'ideas', 'innovation'? Assess and score											☐
5	Can one approach top people in the R & D organisation with ideas? Assess and score											☐
6	Do people in the department know how and to whom to address their ideas? Assess and score											☐

TOTAL SCORE CARRIED FORWARD   ☐

Audit No 5 Research & Development (*contd*)

No		1	2	3	4	5	6	7	8	9	10	B/F	SCORE
7	Does the department undertake periodic 'idea-generation' exercises in order to stimulate the climate for creativity? Assess and score												
8	Does the department undertake periodic 'idea-generation' exercises in order to solve problems and/or identify opportunities? Assess and score												
9	Does a communication system exist for promoting the whole concept of creativity and innovation in the R & D functions? Assess and score												
10	Does the R & D organisation attempt to communicate and cross-fertilise ideas among the various parts of the department? Assess and score												
11	Does a system of screening and evaluating ideas exist in the R & D organisation? Assess and score												
12	Altogether, if the R & D management is able to list the successful innovations that have been achieved during the last three years—has their number increased or decreased? (If their number has increased give a high score and vice versa.) Assess and score												

TOTAL SCORE CARRIED FORWARD

Audit No 5 Research & Development (*contd*)

No		1	2	3	4	5	6	7	8	9	10	B/F	SCORE
13	PRODUCTIVITY Has the R & D organisation managed to use its facilities in a more productive way through the introduction of new and better methods? Assess and score												
14	Has the department improved its response to demands placed upon it by other departments? Assess and score												
15	Has the 'rate of exchange' between expenditure and results, in the area of R & D, improved? Assess and score												
16	To the extent that 'patents are a manifestation of creativity,' has the organisation increased the number of patents filed during the last three years? (An increased number would earn a high score and vice versa.)												
17	PRODUCT INNOVATIONS Has the R & D organisation contributed towards the development of better and/or cheaper products? Assess and score												
18	Has the department been instrumental in helping to solve quality problems? Assess and score												

TOTAL SCORE CARRIED FORWARD

Audit No 5 Research & Development (*contd*)

No		1	2	3	4	5	6	7	8	9	10	B/F	SCORE
19	Has the department helped to identify and implement a sustainable competitive advantage in the firm's product strategy? Assess and score												
20	Does the R & D organisation maintain a vigilant lookout for potential innovations among competitors, academic establishments and the world at large? Assess and score												
21	INTERFACE WITH OTHER FUNCTIONS Bearing in mind that many R & D organisations suffer from poor communication with other departments, has the department improved its interface with the marketing organisation in a creative way? Assess and score												
22	Has the department improved its interface with the production function in a creative way? Assess and score												
23	Has the department improved its interface with the personnel function in a creative way? Assess and score												
24	Has the department improved its interface with the finance department in a creative way? Assess and score												
25	Altogether has the R & D department taken steps to improve its image throughout the organisation in a creative way? Assess and score												

TOTAL SCORE CARRIED FORWARD

Audit No 5 Research & Development (*contd*)

No		1	2	3	4	5	6	7	8	9	10	SCORE B/F	
26	RECRUITING TALENT Has the R & D department taken creative steps to improve its attractiveness to would-be recruits? Assess and score												
27	Is the department able to recruit graduates more easily as a result of some innovation in its recruitment policy? Assess and score												
28	Is the number of scientists currently working for competitors, applying to join the R & D department, increasing as a result of some innovation in its image building? Assess and score												
	TOTAL SCORE												

Audit No 6   Finance/accountancy

	1	2	3	4	5	6	7	8	9	10	SCORE
No											
1 **GENERAL** Is the firm's climate supportive of the idea-generation process? Assess and score											
2 Does top management of the department take an interest in the whole concept of idea-generation or does it simply expect to hear about ultimate successes? Assess and score											
3 Do the department's objectives include a mention of either 'creativity' or 'innovation' or both, as part of the department's climate and goals? Assess and score											
4 Do people in the marketing function talk about 'creativity', 'ideas', 'innovation'? Assess and score											
5 Can one approach the top people in the finance/accountancy department with ideas? Assess and score											
6 Do department personnel know how and to whom to address their ideas? Assess and score											

TOTAL SCORE CARRIED FORWARD

Audit No 6   **Finance/accountancy** (*contd*)

No		1	2	3	4	5	6	7	8	9	10	B/F	SCORE
7	Does the department undertake idea-generation exercises to stimulate the climate for creativity? Assess and score												
8	Does the department undertake periodic 'idea-generation' exercises in order to solve problems and/or identify opportunities? Assess and score												
9	Does a communication system exist for 'marketing' the whole concept of 'Creativity and Innovation' in the finance/accountancy function? Assess and score												
10	Does cross-fertilisation of ideas take place between different areas of the department? Assess and score												
11	Does a system for screening and evaluating ideas exist in the finance/accountancy areas? Assess and score												
12	Has the number of successful innovations achieved by the department increased or decreased during the last three years? Assess and score												
13	ACCOUNTING AND CONTROL Has the department investigated and identified methods of data collection and storage which are more effective and cost beneficial? Assess and score												
	TOTAL SCORE CARRIED FORWARD												

Audit No 6   Finance/accountancy (*contd*)

No		1	2	3	4	5	6	7	8	9	10	SCORE B/F
14	Does the department respond positively to recommendations or suggestions from external sources (eg auditors) as to how accounting systems and control procedures can be improved? Assess and score											
15	Is internal audit used as a force for innovation and change within the finance/ accounting activities of the firm? Assess and score											
16	REPORTING Does the department keep itself aware of and exploit opportunities presented by changes in accounting and regulatory pronouncements so as to improve the reporting of financial information? Assess and score											
17	Does the finance function seek to influence decisions on accounting standards and reporting within the industry? Assess and score											
18	Does the department search for opportunities to improve the effectiveness of internal financial reporting? Assess and score											
19	Does the department make a creative contribution towards making better use of the firm's annual report as an aid to promoting the company's image? Assess and score											

TOTAL SCORE CARRIED FORWARD

Audit No 6   Finance/accountancy (*contd*)

No		1	2	3	4	5	6	7	8	9	10	SCORE B/F
20	TREASURY Are people in the finance function aware of modern developments in financing (eg hedging, swaps etc)? Assess and score											
21	To what extent does the department exploit innovative funding methods likely to reduce cost or risk for the company? Assess and score											
22	PROJECT APPRAISAL Are members of the finance/accounting function involved, on their own initiative, as members of multi-disciplinary project appraisal teams? Assess and score											
23	To what extent do other departments regard members of the finance/accounting team as 'score keepers' only (low score) or as creative contributors to the success of the business (high score)? Assess and score											
24	Does the department manage outside advisers effectively to produce creative schemes for improving company performance? Assess and score											

TOTAL SCORE CARRIED FORWARD

Audit No 6　Finance/accountancy (*contd*)

No		1	2	3	4	5	6	7	8	9	10	B/F	SCORE
25	PRODUCTIVITY Does the department make a creative contribution to the development of methods for improving performance through enhanced productivity (eg through more effective cost control, better inventory management etc)? Assess and score												
26	Does the department take steps to improve the productivity of its own personnel and procedures (eg less paperwork, better use of data etc)? Assess and score												
27	TAXATION Assess the department's creativity in developing schemes for mitigating the company tax charges.												
28	RECRUITMENT Has the department managed to attract talent in the field of finance/accountancy control and retain such resources? Assess and score												
	TOTAL SCORE												

Audit No 7   Central administration/services

No	PRELIMINARY POINT	1	2	3	4	5	6	7	8	9	10	SCORE
	This is an area which can cover a myriad of diverse activities and services. It would vary from company to company and will need to be adjusted accordingly. The list provided hereunder is designed to give the flavour of the audit rather than be a definitive list.											
1	GENERAL Is the climate in the various activities described as 'Central Administration/Services' supportive of the idea-generation process? Assess and score											☐
2	Do the people who are responsible for these central administration/services take an interest in the whole concept of creativity or do they simply expect to hear about ultimate results? Assess and score											☐
3	Can one approach the top people in charge of central administration/services with ideas? Assess and score											☐
4	Do members of the organisation know how and to whom to address their ideas? Assess and score											☐

TOTAL SCORE CARRIED FORWARD ☐

Audit No 7 Central administration/services (*contd*)

No		1	2	3	4	5	6	7	8	9	10	SCORE B/F	
5	Does the department undertake periodic 'idea-generation' exercises in order to stimulate the climate for creativity? Assess and score												
6	Does the department undertake 'idea-generation' exercises in order to solve problems and/or identify opportunities? Assess and score												
7	Does a communication system exist for promoting the whole concept of creativity and innovation in the central administration/services area? Assess and score												
8	Is there a communication system for cross-fertilising ideas among the various parts of the organisation? Assess and score												
9	Does a system of screening and evaluating ideas exist in the central administration/services area? Assess and score												
10	Altogether, if central administration/services can list the successful innovations that have been achieved during the last three years—has their number increased or decreased? (If their number has increased give a high score and vice versa.) Assess and score												

TOTAL SCORE CARRIED FORWARD

Audit No 7 Central administration/services (*contd*)

No		1	2	3	4	5	6	7	8	9	10	B/F	SCORE
	SPECIFIC AREAS												
11	TELEPHONE/TELEX/ FAX Are there any signs that the performance of these services have benefited from creative improvements in the last few years? Assess and score												
12	RECEPTION AREA Any evidence of innovation in the landscaping and general appearance of the reception area? Assess and score												
13	Has the quality of the welcome given to visitors to the firm at the reception area benefited from some innovation? Assess and score												
14	GATEHOUSES AND SECURITY Any signs of creative improvement in the way the gatehouse(s) manage the entry and exit to and from the company's premises? Assess and score												
15	Has the firm's security become more effective and less obtrusive as a result of the incorporation of new ideas? Assess and score												

TOTAL SCORE CARRIED FORWARD

Audit No 7 Central administration/services (*contd*)

No		1	2	3	4	5	6	7	8	9	10	B/F SCORE
16	**GENERAL ESTABLISHMENT** Any evidence of creative improvement in the way the company's premises and grounds are maintained? Assess and score											
17	Has the department benefited from some innovation in the office cleaning area? Assess and score											
18	Comment on the adequacy and quality of the car parking facilities and, in particular, comment on whether signs of creativity can be seen in this area. Assess and score											
19	Any signs of better energy conservation based on innovative strategies? Assess and score											
20	Have the quality, service and general performance of the firm's canteen improved as a result of good ideas implemented? Assess and score											
21	**SECRETARIAL/ ADMINISTRATIVE** Are secretaries/administrators encouraged to be involved in the organisation's creative processes? Assess and score											

TOTAL SCORE CARRIED FORWARD

Audit No 7 Central administration/services (*contd*)

No		1	2	3	4	5	6	7	8	9	10	SCORE B/F	
22	Have there been any improvements in the service provided by secretaries/administrators through this involvement? Assess and score												
23	Is the working partnership between managers and secretaries based on the free flow of ideas? Assess and score												
24	Has the working partnership between managers and secretaries improved since a more open style of working relationship has been in place? Assess and score												
												TOTAL SCORE	

Bibliography

Barra, Ralph

'Putting Quality Circles to Work—A Practical Strategy for Boosting Productivity & Profits', USA, 1983, McGraw-Hill Inc

Brech, Ronald

'Britain 1984: Unilever's Forecast—An Experiment in the Economic History of the Future', London, 1963, Darton, Longman & Todd

Buzan, Tony

'Use your Head', London, 1974, BBC Publications

Crocker, Olga, Charney, Cyril, Sik Leung Chiu, Johnny

'Quality Circles—A Guide to Participation & Productivity', USA, 1984, Methuen Publications

Deal, Terrence E & Kennedy, Allan A

'Corporate Cultures', Reading, Mass, USA, 1982, Addison-Wesley Publishing Co

De Bono, Edward

'Six Thinking Hats', Viking Penguin, 1985

Drucker, Peter F

'Innovation and Entrepreneurship', London, 1985, William Heinemann

Edwards, Betty

'Drawing on the Right Side of the Brain', USA, 1979, J P Tarcher Inc; UK, 1981, Souvenir Press Ltd

Foxall, Gordon R

'Corporate Innovation—Marketing & Strategy', UK, 1984, Croom Helm Ltd

Gombrich, E H — 'Art & Illusion: a Study in the Psychology of Pictorial Representation', Washington DC, USA, 1956, The Trustees of the National Gallery of Art Oxford, UK, 1977, Phaidon Press, Fifth Edition

Heller, Robert — 'The Supermanagers', New York, USA, 1984, E P Dutton Inc (Truman Talley Books)

Hickman, Craig R & Silva, Michael A — 'Creating Excellence—Managing Corporate Culture, Strategy & Change in the New Age', London, UK, 1984, George Allen & Unwin, second impression 1985

Hutchins, David — 'Quality Circles Handbook', UK, 1985, Pitman Publishing Ltd

Jantsch, Erich — 'Technological Forecasting in Perspective—a framework for technological forecasting, its techniques and organisation; a description of activities and annotated bibliography', Paris, 1967, The Organisation for Economic Co-operation and Development

Kahn, Herman & Weiner, Anthony J — 'The Year 2000', New York, 1967, Macmillan Company

Kanter, Rosabeth M — 'The Change Masters—Innovation for Productivity in the American Corporation', New York, USA, 1983, Simon & Schuster

Kepner, Charles H & Tregoe, Benjamin B — 'The Rational Manager—a Systematic Approach to Problem Solving and Decision Making', New York, USA, 1965, Macmillan Inc (The Free Press)

Majaro, Simon

'Marketing in Perspective', London, UK, 1984, George Allen & Unwin

Nayak, P Ranganath & Ketteringham, John

'Breakthroughs!', 1987, Mercury

Nierenberg, Gerard

'The Art of Creative Thinking', New York, USA, 1982, Simon & Schuster

Nystrom, Harry

'Creativity & Innovation', UK, 1979, John Wiley & Sons

Osborn, Alex F

'Applied Imagination—Principles & Procedures of Creative Problem-Solving', New York, USA, 1963, Charles Scribner's Sons, Fourth Edition

Peters, Thomas J & Waterman, Robert H Jr

'In Search of Excellence', New York, USA, 1982, Harper & Row Inc, Warner Books Inc

Pirsig, Robert M

'Zen and the Art of Motorcycle Maintenance', New York, USA, 1974, William Morrow & Co Inc, Bantam Books, 1982

Porter, Michael E

'Competitive Strategy', New York, USA, 1980, Macmillan Publishing Co Inc (The Free Press)

Raudsepp, Eugene

'How Creative are You?', New York, USA, 1981, G Putnam's Sons

Rickards, Tudor

'Problem-Solving through Creative Analysis', UK, 1974, Gower Publishing Co

Robson, Mike

'Quality Circles—A Practical Guide', UK, 1982, Gower Publishing, Reprinted 1983, 1984, 1985

Steiner, George A   'The New CEO', New York, USA, 1983, Macmillan Publishing Co Inc

University of Chicago School of Business   'The Creative Organisation', USA, 1965, The University of Chicago Press, Fourth Impression 1971

Index

337